# THE FRANCISCAN MORAL VISION:

# RESPONDING TO GOD'S LOVE

FRANCISCAN
INSTITUTE
PUBLICATIONS

# THE FRANCISCAN MORAL VISION:

# RESPONDING TO GOD'S LOVE

EDITED BY THOMAS A. NAIRN, O.F.M.

FRANCISCAN
INSTITUTE
PUBLICATIONS

Cover image is a photograph of a stained glass window
featuring Bonaventure and Thomas Aquinas
in the University Chapel of St. Bonaventure University.
Cover design by Jill Smith

ISBN 13:  978-1-57659-208-3
ISBN 10:  1-57659-208-1
eISBN 13: 978-1-57659-209-0
eISBN 10:  1-57659-209-X


Library of Congress Cataloging-in-Publication Data

The Franciscan moral vision : responding to God's love / edited
by Thomas Nairn. -- First [edition].
    pages cm
    Includes bibliographical references (pages 271-311).
ISBN 978-1-57659-208-3 (pbk.) -- ISBN 978-1-57659-209-0 (ebook)
1. Franciscans. I. Nairn, Thomas A., 1948-

    BX3602.3.F725 2013
    241'.042--dc23

                                                    2012040793


Printed and bound in the United States of America.

Franciscan Institute Publications makes every effort
to use environmentally responsible suppliers and materials
in the publishing of its books. This book is printed on acid free,
recycled paper that is FSC (Forest Stewardship Council) certified.
It is printed with soy-based ink.

**Imprimi potest:**
† JOHN O'CONNOR, O.F.M.
PROVINCIAL MINISTER
HOLY NAME PROVINCE OF THE FRIARS MINOR

# TABLE OF CONTENTS

In the *Lignum Vitae* St. Bonaventure presented a series of meditations on the mystery of Christ's role in leading humankind to God. By inviting his readers to meditate on the twelve central "fruits" in the life of Christ, Bonaventure expressed his desire to "enkindle affection," "shape understanding," and make an "imprint" on the memory of those who hoped to be a "true worshipper of God and disciple of Christ" and to know and love Christ as the "tree of life" (See *The Tree of Life*, prologue).

In the stained glass window on the cover, Bonaventure is depicted writing this spiritual text, on the right, while in conversation with his contemporary Thomas Aquinas who is holding his *Summa*, a text which presents an alternative path into the mystery of God and Christ. The window is one of a series of six telling the story of the life of St. Bonaventure, as suggested through some of the texts he wrote, in the main chapel on the campus of St. Bonaventure University.

# INTRODUCTION

In the last half century, contemporary Catholic moral theology has developed at a rapid pace. Heeding the call of the Second Vatican Council,[1] Catholic moral theologians have related their field of study more closely to biblical studies, systematic theology, spiritual theology, and sacramental theology. Emphasis on the human person rather than simply on the actions that people perform has become especially important in contemporary virtue ethics. Moral theology is no longer wedded to a neoscholastic philosophy, as contemporary writings on morality give evidence of a variety of philosophical and theological dimensions.

## I. THE FRANCISCAN MORAL TRADITION IN RECENT RESEARCH

Franciscan scholars have played a major part in this renewal of moral theology. José Antonio Merino, for example, has presented the ethical theology of Bonaventure in a contemporary way, demonstrating why the saint's personalistic approach to ethics can speak to us today.[2] The same volume explains how John Duns Scotus offers a moral theology which not only shows us how to live (*vivir*) but also how to live with others (*convivir*). José Luis Parada Navas, both in a lengthy essay on the moral theology of Bonaventure

---

[1] *Optatam totius* (Decree On Priestly Formation), par 16, in *The Documents of Vatican II*, ed. Walter M. Abbot (New York: Guild Press, 1966), 451-53.

[2] José Antonio Merino, *Historia de la Filosofía Franciscana* (Madrid: Biblioteca de Autores Cristianos, 1993).

and Scotus[3] and in a comprehensive volume on Franciscan moral theology written with Francisco Martínez Fresneda,[4] has made a further contribution to the Franciscan efforts for today's renewal in moral theology. Another Franciscan, Orlando Todisco, has addressed the economic difficulties of today's world and offers a Franciscan approach to alleviating these difficulties.[5] Olivier Boulnois uses Scotus to offer an alternative to contemporary atheistic approaches to morality.[6] Antonellus Elsässer has utilized the resources of the Franciscan intellectual tradition to reconnect moral theology to both systematic theology and to spirituality.[7] Lucan Freppert has shown the relevance of the ethics of William Ockham for today's world.[8] More recently, Johannes Freyer has forcefully united the Franciscan moral vision of the person as pilgrim to contemporary ethics.[9] Allan B. Wolter has addressed the issues of contingency and ethics and has demonstrated the major differences between Scotus's understanding of contingency and relationality and that of contemporary theories proposing relativity in ethics,[10] an argument that has been echoed by G. Pizzo.[11] Similarly, Anton Vos Jaczn and his collaborators have explained the Scotistic basis for the philosophical contingency of all moral acts and laws in a man-

---

[3] José Luis Parada Navas, *Manual de Teología Franciscana* (Madrid: Biblioteca de Autores Cristianos, 2003).

[4] José Luis Parada Navas, "Teología Moral y Política," *Manual de Teología franciscana* (Madrid: Biblioteca de Autores Cristianos, 2002).

[5] Orlando Todisco, "Ética y Economía," in *Manual de Filosofía Franciscana* (Madrid: Biblioteca de Autores Cristianos, 2004), 249-327.

[6] Olivier Boulnois, "Si Dieu n'existait pas, foudrait-il l'inventer? Situation métaphysique de l'étique scotiste," *Philosophie* 61 (1999): 50-74.

[7] Antonellus Elsässer, *Christus der Lehrer des Sittlichen: Die Chrtistologischen Grundlagen für die Erkenntnis der Sittlichen nach der Lehre Bonaventuras* (Paderborn: Schöningh, 1968).

[8] Lucan Freppert, *The Basis of Morality according to William Ockham* (Chicago: Franciscan Herald Press, 1988).

[9] Johannes Freyer, *Homo Viator: Der Mensch im Lichte der Heilsgeschichte* (Kevalaer: Butzon & Bercker, 2001), 185-257.

[10] Allan B. Wolter, *Duns Scotus on the Will and Morality* (Washington, DC: The Catholic University of America Press, 1986).

[11] G. Pizzo, "La giustizia nella dottrina della volontà di G. Duns Scoto," *Revue Philosophique Neoscolastique* 81 (1989): 3-26.

ner that does not demand the relativization of ethics.[12] They articulate an understanding of ethics and morality in a way which is mirrored in Paul Ricoeur's treatise on ethics, *Oneself as Another*.[13]

This is a long listing of the Franciscan contribution to the contemporary renewal of moral theology; a full listing would be much longer. Yet, these moral insights from the Franciscan tradition have to a great extent been overlooked by those doing moral theology in the English-speaking world since most of the works mentioned above have not been available in English. The authors of this volume of essays hope that this contribution on the Franciscan moral vision will help to broaden the conversation regarding moral theology in general and continue the work already accomplished by the many authors cited above. It is our goal to make the insights of the Franciscan moral tradition more accessible to English readers in today's Catholic Church.

## II. Retrieving the Franciscan Moral Vision

In the half century since the Second Vatican Council (1962-1965), theologians from various spiritual traditions within the Church have mined their own spiritual treasury to identify those elements that constitute their identity and their particular way of living out the Gospel call to love one another. In addition, scholars have researched the earliest sources of Christian moral teaching to recover their deep spiritual inspiration and wisdom and to present these again to our generation.

As a result of significant research and publications, a renewed vision of the Christian moral life, moral actions, and moral excellence continues to come into greater clarity. This moral vision springs from the wisdom of the tradition: from the rich spiritual vision of Christian saints and masters,

---

[12] Anton Vos Jaczn, et al., *John Duns Scotus, Contingency and Freedom. Lectura* I, d. 39 (Dordrecht: Kluwer Academic Publishers, 1994).

[13] Paul Ricoeur, *Oneself as Another* (Chicago: University of Chicago Press, 1992).

along with the Church's moral Magisterium. This vision is nourished at the wellsprings of the tradition and develops in dialogue with the Magisterium. This renewed vision offers a fuller, more spiritual and pastoral approach to moral questions than that which was prominent in the nineteenth and early twentieth centuries.

The moral theology of that time, in reaction to the advances of the Industrial Revolution and the emergence of modernity, focused on moral living primarily in terms of law. It emphasized sin and human fallenness. In an effort to train priests to hear confessions well and to give appropriate spiritual advice, this manualist tradition framed morality in terms of prohibitions rather than the striving for moral excellence. "Thou shalt not" often became the dominant moral imperative. The moral manuals perhaps too quickly centered on human sin and fallenness rather than on divine love and goodness. Granted the reality of sin, this school of morality nevertheless tended to foster a narrow vision of God as Judge rather than loving Parent and generous Creator.

In his seminal study,[14] Servais Pinckaers rightly turned attention to an earlier Christian moral vision, one centered on human excellence and fulfillment as a lifelong response to divine love. Drawing upon the wisdom of Augustine and other Church Fathers and using the moral tradition of Aristotle and Aquinas, Pinckaers's work replaced an outmoded, legalistic moral framework with one centered on human fulfillment and eudaemonism. This perspective on the good life, inspired by the ancient vision of human wisdom and developed in the Middle Ages, integrated law within a larger vision grounded in virtue, conscience, love, and Gospel values. The life of virtue and prudential judgment replaced legalism as the groundwork for moral education and development. Pinckaers's insights have offered the Dominican tradition a renewed vision for moral theology in the spirit of St. Thomas Aquinas.

---

[14] Servais Pinckaers, O.P., *The Sources of Christian Ethics* (Washington, DC: Catholic University of America Press, 1995).

How might the Franciscan tradition follow such a model, drawing upon the writings of Francis, Clare, and other Franciscan saints and scholars? How might the Franciscan spiritual vision – centered on beauty, graciousness, and generosity – frame a study of moral life, of loving action, and grace-filled decision? How might such a vision help to integrate contemporary and emerging concerns that relate to the global economic community, environmental concerns, and sustainability?

In considering these questions, we need to keep in mind that the Franciscan tradition is distinctive among those of other religious orders in that both the spirituality and intellectual tradition flow directly out of the personal religious experience of Francis, later enhanced by the spirituality of Clare. For example, the center of Bonaventure's thought is his theological articulation of the religious experience of Francis. As Gilson says so well, "What St. Francis had simply felt and lived, St. Bonaventure was to think."[15] Bonaventure took the intense mystical and ecstatic religious experience of Francis and turned it into a profound theological vision of the world and all its creatures.

In the Franciscan vision, moral living is seen as a response to divine graciousness and love. The experience and vision of Francis and Clare focus upon the human vocation to live and to act always in harmony with God's desire for the world. Such a life requires a profound spiritual basis, nourished each day by prayer and manifested in works of mercy. It is a life of Gospel witness, attentive to the poor and most vulnerable. This vision draws upon the Gospel challenge, the teaching of the Magisterium and the wisdom of the great saints of the tradition. In response to the incarnational commitment to this world as a place of beauty and grace, the Franciscan vision also draws upon the best of contemporary reflection in psychology, history, philosophy and science.

The Franciscan moral vision recalls and presents anew the vocation of the human person as image of Christ (*imago*

---

[15] Étienne Gilson, *The Philosophy of St. Bonaventure* (New York: Sheed and Ward, 1938), 60.

*Christi*), called to think, act, and live under the guidance of the Holy Spirit. Contemplating the Trinitarian life and guided by the common good, this tradition promotes the Reign of God in each action and in each moment. Taking seriously the mandate to go out to all the world and preach the Gospel, the Franciscan vision also reaches out in an ecumenical embrace and with a welcome hand to all religious and faith traditions. It embodies an optimism and energy that moves toward the future, confident in the power of the Spirit within the human heart.

As a result, the Franciscan spiritual and moral tradition brings together and highlights the continuity of the various and rich inspirations that have graced Catholicism for centuries. Moral precepts are integrated into a larger spiritual journey toward God in human wholeness and holiness. Virtues, acquired through moral training and enhanced by grace, enable the person to move continually toward inner conversion and enlightenment. True human freedom becomes the foundation and the summit of moral living, enabling the fully functioning moral agent to respond in right actions and ordered loving, in imitation of Jesus Christ, to that love that God has poured out into our hearts.[16] It remains an authentically Catholic moral vision, faithful to the Church's tradition and Magisterium.


## III. THE PURPOSE AND ORGANIZATION OF THIS VOLUME

As already mentioned, the purpose of this volume is to broaden contemporary discussions in Catholic moral theology by examining Franciscan resources that have often been overlooked in current scholarship. It is our goal to make the insights of the Franciscan moral tradition and their contemporary relevance more accessible to English readers. This volume is therefore not a general exposition of the themes and issues of Catholic moral theology. In fact, it presupposes a certain knowledge of this broader tradition. The volume is

---

[16] Rom 5:5.

not even a fully systematic rendering of the Franciscan moral tradition itself. Rather, five scholars have come together to present certain key elements of the Franciscan moral tradition, grounded in the spiritual vision of Francis and Clare and in the writings of the other great saints and scholars of the tradition.

The unity of the volume comes from the fact that the authors have worked together in a collaborative manner to develop their essays. Its unity also comes from an agreement among the authors on the important characteristics of the Franciscan moral vision. As the reader will discover in the first chapter of this work, these characteristics are rooted in the life and spirituality of Francis and Clare, especially in their profound understanding of God's love for each individual and for all of creation.

This spirituality received its theological articulation in the writings of the early Franciscan masters, including Alexander of Hales, St. Bonaventure, and Blessed John Duns Scotus, who grounded their work in a theology of the Trinity which sees God as self-diffusive goodness and insists that God's very nature is relational. This strong Trinitarian emphasis is complemented by an equally strong Christological emphasis, centering particularly in the Incarnation, which these Franciscans have described in terms of God's sharing of this diffusive goodness in that union with creation that could return this love in a supreme way.[17] These masters understand Christian morality therefore as a response to the extravagant love of God. Without denying human limitations and sin, the Franciscan tradition offers the Church an aesthetic moral vision in which humanity is called to reflect the beauty of God.

These characteristics may be articulated in the following manner:

> Characteristic One: The Franciscan moral vision affirms that on the human level there is a mirroring of the free and self-giving exchange of Father, Son, and Holy Spirit

---

[17] See John Duns Scotus, *Reportatio Parisiensis* III, d. 7, q. 4, 5 (Paris: Apud Ludovicum Vivès, Bibliopolam Editorem, 1894).

that calls people to live in free and self-giving relationships of mutuality.

Characteristic Two: The Franciscan moral vision emphasizes a dynamic realization of creative and loving freedom in response to God's love.

Characteristic Three: The Franciscan moral vision recognizes each person as an image of God. Since each person reflects the creativity of God in an individualized way, each person must be treated with profound respect.

Characteristic Four: The Franciscan moral vision is Christological in its emphasis on the Exemplarity of Christ and upon the Incarnation, Redemption, and Consummation of all things in Christ. It is thus profoundly Christian and Catholic, respectful of the Church's moral Magisterium, but at the same time it is universal and inclusive of all creation.

Characteristic Five: The Franciscan moral vision takes into account the issues of time, history, and human contingency. Human growth means development and conversion. Human solutions are not perfect but are perfectible.

Characteristic Six: At the same time, the Franciscan moral vision accepts an Augustinian vision of the person that recognizes human limitations, including the real limitations of human reason and philosophy, and the reality of sin.

Characteristic Seven: The Franciscan moral vision is a holistic vision that involves a spiritual discernment by the whole person – intellectual, affective, and volitional. It acknowledges the importance of the community in such discernment.

Characteristic Eight: The Franciscan moral vision is an aesthetic vision recognizing that the moral life is one of beauty, reflecting the beauty of God.

Characteristic Nine: The Franciscan moral vision is more properly understood as a wisdom tradition rather than a scientifically organized system of analytic thought.

Characteristic Ten: The Franciscan moral vision incorporates within it a tension that arises out of respect for both sides of several polarities – the institutional and the charismatic, the universal and the particular, the past and the future, the act and the person. It acknowledges that this tension is part of living as a pilgrim in this world.

Characteristic Eleven: The Franciscan moral vision embodies a distinct social vision that intersects the personal with the political, the individual with the communal, the singular life of virtue with the anticipation of the Reign of God for all.

We do not claim that these characteristics are unique to the Franciscan moral vision and not shared by others. We do claim, however, that these characteristics are essential to the integrity of the Franciscan vision itself. Without them the vision would cease to exist.

With these characteristics in mind, we look to the essays themselves. They are organized around three areas of inquiry, forming the three parts of the volume: (1) the spiritual and intellectual foundations of the Franciscan moral vision, (2) key expressions of the Franciscan moral vision, and (3) the Franciscan moral vision today. These characteristics are discussed in the various chapters. Particular focus on a specific characteristic is noted at the beginning of each chapter.

In Part One, Kenan Osborne analyzes the spiritual and theological foundations of the Franciscan moral vision. In Chapter One he shows how this vision is based upon the deepest spiritual experiences, insights, and inspiration of Saints Francis and Clare of Assisi. Their vision emphasizes divine graciousness and abundance, always at work in a world rich in beauty. In Chapter Two, he shows how the early Franciscan scholars, especially St. Bonaventure and Blessed John Duns Scotus, developed these spiritual insights into a theological vision. He discusses their emphasis on God as Trinity, as well as on God's gifts of creation, the Incarnation, and the sending of the Holy Spirit. Reflection upon these themes establishes the theological foundation for the Franciscan moral vision.

Part Two describes some key elements of the Franciscan moral vision. While this section is not a complete systematic study of all the elements of Franciscan moral life, it provides the reader with an overview of the Franciscan moral vision, showing its optimism based on a confidence in the presence of the Holy Spirit in the human heart. Mary Beth Ingham devotes Chapter Three to a study of beauty in the moral theology of John Duns Scotus. She suggests that in the Franciscan vision moral living might best be understood as the formation of artisans capable of bringing forth beauty in the contingent order, thus expressing their freedom and creativity in imitation of God. In Chapter Four, Thomas A. Shannon analyzes the element of generosity, explaining its origin in Bonaventure's understanding of God as "fountain fullness," drawing inspiration from Scotus's notion of God's divine liberality, and finding human expression in the transcendence of generous and transformative love. In Chapter Five Thomas Nairn describes St. Bonaventure's attention to the role of conscience in moral decision making. He shows how the moral law and the inherited wisdom of the tradition combine with human experience to guide moral decisions and inform moral judgment.

In Part Three, the authors show the contemporary relevance of the Franciscan moral vision. Thomas Nairn and Thomas A. Shannon look, in Chapter Six, to contemporary Western ethics and culture and suggest that the Franciscan moral vision, as a mediating tradition, may serve to moderate some contemporary philosophical tendencies. Finally, in Chapter Seven, Joseph Chinnici maintains that a contemporary rendering of the Franciscan moral vision can lead to the promotion of the dignity of persons, both as individuals and as members of the human community, by means of an analysis of the social, political, and economic dimensions of the Franciscan moral vision. The authors of this volume are especially indebted to the Secretariat of the English Speaking Conference of the Order of Friars Minor and its Committee for the Franciscan intellectual tradition for their encouragement and financial support. This support has enabled a level of collaboration among the authors that we hope has contributed to the coherence of this volume and the continuity among its essays.

Francis of Assisi was a man critical of his time. He raised a prophetic voice against those who abused the poor and most vulnerable and provided the basis for a vision of life that, while profoundly Catholic, also acknowledges the unity and relationality of all people, and indeed of all creation, in anticipation of the Reign of God for all. We hope that this volume will show how the Franciscan moral vision, in fidelity to its founder, continues to raise a prophetic voice in our own age. The authors realize, however, that the reality of such a vision – generosity in action – comes ultimately not from words on a page but rather from the example of those inspired by this Franciscan moral vision.

Thomas A. Nairn, O.F.M.

# PART I

# 1

## THE CENTER OF THE SPIRITUAL VISION OF FRANCIS AND CLARE: THE PROFOUND RELATIONSHIP BETWEEN GOD AND CREATION

### KENAN B. OSBORNE, O.F.M.

*The Franciscan moral vision*
*emphasizes a dynamic realization*
*of creative and loving freedom in response to God's love.*

The goal of this opening chapter can be stated in a simple way: to describe the spiritual vision of Francis and Clare. The foundation of their spiritual vision centers on three issues: the Triune God, the created world, and the profound relationship between the Triune God and creation. It was through this relational approach between God and creature that both Francis and Clare viewed the incarnation of the Logos in Jesus, the presence of the Spirit of God throughout all of creation, the blessing of the church, and the morally correct way of Christian living.

In time, the spiritual vision of Francis and Clare became the seedbed of the Franciscan intellectual tradition.[1] Their

---

[1] Johannes Freyer, *Homo Viator: Der Mensch im Lichte der Heilsgeschichte* (Kevelaer: Verlag Butzon & Bercker, 2001), 13-20; 30-38. See also Michael Blastic, "Franciscan Spirituality," *The New Dictionary of Catholic Spirituality* (Collegeville, MN: The Liturgical Press, 1993), 408-18; Wayne

spiritual insight into the relationship of created reality and the beauty of God gave rise to the Franciscan tradition, which Alexander of Hales, Bonaventure of Bagnoregio, and John Duns Scotus began to develop in a scholarly way during the thirteenth century and the beginning of the fourteenth century.

Neither Francis nor Clare had been trained in a scholarly way. Rather, their faith had been nourished in the ordinary medieval and European traditions of Christian teaching and spirituality of the late twelfth and early thirteenth centuries. Nonetheless, the eventual form of their religious life and their understanding of God occasioned a powerful spiritual movement as well as a distinctive theological approach to Christian life and thought, which has lasted down to the beginning of the third millennium.[2]

Francis's and Clare's understanding of the church and of spirituality was not rural but urban. Their leaders in Assisi were not only the clergy but also the educated and financially independent lay people. Francis and Clare were both literate and had read, at least to some degree, not only the Gospels but also other spiritual writings. In their view, a monastic or clerical vocation was no longer the only way to develop spiritual insight and spiritual life. Given all of this, one can conclude that the spiritual vision of both Francis and Clare was shaped in large measure by the theological, economic, and political changes of their age.

The vision of Francis, as mentioned above, was deeply centered on the Triune God, the created world, and the profound relationship between the triune God and creation. Let us consider each of these in detail.

---

Hellmann, "Gospel: Life or Observance: Observations on a Language Shift in the Early Documents," in *Vita Evangelica*, ed. Michael Cusato and Jean François Godet-Calogeras (St. Bonaventure, NY: Franciscan Institute Publications, 2006): 281-92.

[2] See Arnaldo Fortini, *Nova Vita di S. Francesco*, vol. I (Assisi: Porziuncula, 1959), 55-151; Giovanni Miccoli, *Francesco d'Assisi. Realità e memoria di un'esperienza Cristiana* (Turin: Enaudi, 1991), 777-78; and Thaddée Matura, "La visión teológica de San Francisco de Asís y su relación con la teología ortodoxa," *Selecciones de Francescanismo*, 25 (1996): 367-75.

## I. THE TRIUNE GOD

In almost all of his writings, Francis mentions God, often using descriptive language. The adjectives and phrases he uses to describe God help us to see the ways in which Francis understood God. For instance, in his *Exposition of the Our Father*, he writes:

> Our Father most holy: Our Creator, Redeemer, Consoler, and Savior. Who are in heaven: In the angels and the saints, enlightening them to know, for You, Lord, are light; inflaming them to love, for You, Lord, are love; dwelling in them and filling them with happiness, for You, Lord, are Supreme Good, The Eternal Good, from Whom all good comes without Whom there is no good.[3]

However, it took a lifetime for Francis himself to reach a deep understanding of God, and his life-journey had many high points and many low points. In 1204, Francis decided to join the imperial forces at war in Apulia, but on his way to Apulia he had a religious experience which began to change the goals of his life. In 1205, while praying in the chapel of San Damiano on the outskirts of Assisi, Francis again experienced the presence of God, and his goals became somewhat clearer. On this occasion, he chose to live in a manner of life which replicated the poverty of Jesus.

If we look at his writings chronologically, we can see how Francis's understanding of both God and creation developed over the years of his adult life. In 1205, Francis perceived God as the "Most High and glorious God."[4] In 1206, Francis, in front of the Bishop of Assisi and his own father, gave up his family relationship and began a life of gospel-poverty. In 1209, he wrote an exhortation for those who wanted to follow

---

[3] Francis of Assisi, "A Prayer Inspired by the Our Father," *Francis of Assisi: Early Documents*, Vol. 1 *The Saint*, ed. Regis Armstrong, Wayne Hellmann, and William Short (New York: New City Press, 1999), 158. Hereafter *FA:ED* 1, followed by the page numbers.

[4] *FA:ED* 1, 40.

him. In this exhortation, he writes about God in a familial and inclusive way.

> All those who love the Lord with their whole heart, with their whole soul and mind, with their whole strength and love their neighbor as themselves – how happy and blessed are these men and women.... They are the children of the heavenly Father whose works they do, and they are spouses, brothers and mothers of our Lord Jesus Christ.... We are spouses when the faithful soul is joined by the Holy Spirit to our lord Jesus Christ. We are brothers to him when we do the will of the Father in heaven. We are mothers when we carry him in our heart and body through a divine love and a pure and sincere conscience and give birth to him though a holy activity which must shine as an example before others.[5]

In Francis's *Rule of 1221*, we hear a series of words in which he depicts the God in whom he believed as a loving and generous parent.

> All-powerful, most holy, almighty and supreme God, holy and just Father, Lord King of heaven and earth, we thank you for yourself for through your holy will and through your only Son with the holy Spirit you have created everything spiritual and corporal and, after making us in your own image and likeness, you placed us in paradise.[6]

---

[5] *FA:ED* 1, 41-42.

[6] Francis of Assisi, *Rule of 1221*, chapter 23, in *FA:ED* 1, 81-82. There are similar passages in the *Rule of Saint Clare*. See Claire d'Assise, *Écrits,* Introduction, texte latin, traducion, notes et index (Paris: Sources Chrétiennes, 1985), ed. M.-F. Becker, J.-F. Godet, and T. Matura. For the English translation of Clare's writings see Armstrong, *Clare of Assisi: Early Documents*, I: *The Lady* (New York: New City Press, 2006).

In the *Praises of God*, written by Francis in 1224, we hear that this familial and parental God is a God of unbelievable height, depth, length, and breadth.

> You are the holy Lord who does wonderful things. You are strong. You are great. You are the most high. You are the almighty king. You holy father, king of heaven and earth. You are three and one, the Lord God of gods; You are the good, all good, the highest good, Lord God living and true.[7]

In these descriptions of God, Francis tells us that God is someone who is far above all creation. We may experience another person as mighty, but God is all-mighty. We may find someone who is holy, but God is the all-holy Lord. We may admire someone who is good, but God is all-good and the highest good. These superlative words indicate that God, for Francis, was above anything that we humans can really understand. God, in this approach, is simply "the totally Other." Francis slowly realized our human limitations: if God is above everything we know, then how can we human beings have any notion of God at all? Francis answered this question by rediscovering the reality of creation. For Francis, God's love was now seen more clearly as the *birthplace of creation*.[8]

All creation depends on God's loving will, for God freely willed to create our world. Consequently, it was in and through Francis's meditation on creation itself that he slowly began to appreciate the height and depth, the width and breadth of God's presence in creation itself, and that God's love was indeed the birth place of all creation. In the same *Praises*, Francis saw other aspects of God from which he glimpsed the deep, loving, and familial relationality of God:

> You are love, charity; You are beauty; You are our hope;
> You are justice; You are all our riches to sufficiency;

---

[7] Francis of Assisi, *Praises of God*, 1-3, in *FA:ED* 1, 109.

[8] The term, *Geburtsort*, occurs frequently in Freyer, *Homo Viator*, esp. 34-35, 120, and 163. In these passages, Freyer joins the understanding of the term, the birthplace of creation, with the foundation of Franciscan spirituality.

You are our custodian and defender; You are our hope;
You are all our sweetness.[9]

In 1225, one year before his death, Francis wrote the
*Canticle of Creatures*.[10] He could not have written this canticle earlier in his life, since the canticle evidences a deep and
mature appreciation of God and God's presence in creation.
The canticle, consequently, evidences in an implicit way an
autobiographical aspect of Francis's own journey to God.

In his phenomenological study on Francis's *Canticle of
Brother Sun*, Eloi Leclerc cites the opening words of the
poem:[11]

Most high, all-powerful, good, Lord.
Yours are the praises, the glory, and the honor,
and all blessing.
To you alone, Most High, do they belong.

Leclerc comments that Francis usually describes God in
transcendent terms, using the adjective "all." The word "all"
appears twice in the above litany of who God is.[12] However, in
the *Canticle*, Francis immediately adds an important caveat
which Leclerc describes in a sharp way:

At this point, the movement toward the Most High is
jarred by self-awareness: 'No mortal lips are worthy
to pronounce your name.' This is not a phrase intended merely for edification or tossed out in passing. It
expresses a basic attitude of innermost poverty before
the transcendent God.[13]

---

[9] Francis of Assisi, "Praises of God," nn. 4-5, *FA:ED* 1, 109.

[10] Francis of Assisi, "The Canticle of the Creatures," *FA:ED* 1, 113-14.

[11] Eloi Leclerc, *Le cantique de crèatures: Une lecture de saint François
d'Assise* (Paris: Libraire Artheme Fayard, 1970). Eng. trans. by Matthew
O'Connell, *The Canticle of Creatures: Symbols of Union* (Chicago: Franciscan Herald Press, 1977), 29.

[12] Leclerc, *The Canticle of Creatures*, 39.

[13] Leclerc, *The Canticle of Creatures*, 29.

The phrase, "no human is worthy to pronounce" God's name, included the human Francis himself. In other words, no human being, not even Francis, has a direct knowledge of God. No one has an immediate and infused knowledge of God. In Francis's approach, God is far too infinite for any man or woman to comprehend who and what God is. As a creature, Francis himself is unable to know in a direct way anything of God. Only the God who relationally creates, nourishes, and is present in our world reveals divinity to us. Accordingly, Francis places himself within creation, for it is only from that vantage point that one can ask: who and what is God? Consequently, for Francis and for all men and women, in order to know anything about God, one must contemplate creation in a deep and intensive manner. This is why Francis, in the very next line of the *Canticle of Creatures*, changes his point of view:

> Praise be to you, My Lord,
> with all your creatures.

Francis directs our thoughts, our will, and our vision to the created world, whose beauty we *can* see and whose creatures we *can* love. For Francis, God does not play a game of hide-and-seek in creation, since God is brilliantly present for those who open their eyes, their minds, and their hearts. In this brief canticle, Francis directs our attention not to God's own self, but to the created world, to Brother Sun, Sister Moon, Sister Star and Brother Wind. To the question, "Does God exist?" Francis replies, "Contemplate creation." To the question, "Can a human person know anything about God?" Francis again replies, "Contemplate creation." If God's love, power, goodness, praise, beauty, honor, and blessing are the birthplace of creation, then all of creation reflects, in a limited way, God's love, power, goodness, praise, beauty, honor, and blessing.

Francis studied creation, but he did so in a special way. Francis did not view creatures, such as the sun, moon, stars, wind, air, water, fire, and earth, simply as useful tools. Francis did not *use creation* in order that Francis himself could praise God. Francis is not saying "I, Francis, praise you, God, when I see my Brother Sun and my Sister Moon." Rather, Francis in his contemplation of creation sees that the sun, moon, stars, wind, air, water, fire, and earth *are themselves* already praising God. These creatures give praise to God simply by their own existence. In Francis's spirituality, he realized that all creatures are praising God, and in the creatures' praising of God, human beings are able to catch at least a brief glimpse of the beauty, majesty, and love which describe who God truly is.

As we shall see throughout this book, Franciscan theologians such as Anthony of Padua, Alexander of Hales, Bonaventure of Bagnoregio, Peter John Olivi, and John Duns Scotus wrote sermons, theological essays, and scholarly volumes containing statements and lengthy descriptions on Christian theology. In their writings, they *deliberately* made the spiritual vision of Francis and Clare regarding God and creatures a major and centralizing element of their scholarly syntheses.[14]

For these Franciscan scholars, knowledge of God's existence is not based on a special intuitive knowledge or on a carefully honed philosophical endeavor. Rather, it is based on the profound interconnection of God to the created world in which we live. The very presence of God can be found in each and every aspect of creation.[15] In other words, in Franciscan theology, the presentation of a creator God *shapes* and *colors* every other aspect of Franciscan theology, whether this aspect is ecclesiology or sacraments, creation or human life, the reality of sin or the theology of moral behavior.

The Franciscan theologians mentioned above stand together with a long history of early Christian writers, whose writings were clearly shaped and colored by their own theology of God. We see this God-shaping in the writings of the major Fathers of the Church such as Basil the Great, Grego-

---

[14] For a detailed listing of such passages in the individual Franciscan theologians mentioned in the text, see Freyer, *Homo Viator*, 38-67.

[15] Later in this chapter, we will see that the connection of a God created world extends far beyond the boundaries of the church.

ry of Nazianzus, Cyril of Alexandria, and Augustine of Hippo. Their respective theologies of God shaped and colored almost every other aspect of their theological themes. Similarly, the major theologians of the twelfth, thirteenth and fourteenth centuries followed this same pattern.[16] For these university scholars, their theology of God shaped and colored all other subaltern aspects of their theological writings, including their presentations on ethical life. An interrelationship of one's theology of God to all other aspects of theological thought, including ethics, is profoundly present in the Franciscan tradition. In this tradition, Franciscan moral theologians based their theology of God in large measure on the spiritual vision of God as expressed by Francis and Clare.

## II. THE THREE BOOKS OF CREATED LIFE

A deep reflection on creation is key to the spiritual vision of Francis and Clare. Nonetheless, there is a second wellspring for this spiritual vision, namely, the Holy Gospels. The Franciscan tradition has deep roots in the Bible, especially in the New Testament. In the *Rule of 1223*, Francis's opening words are "The rule and life of a Franciscan is this, namely, to observe the Holy Gospel of our Lord Jesus Christ." In a very profound way, the spirituality of all Franciscans is based on Jesus and on the gospels. Wayne Hellmann, on the basis of the writings of Francis and on Thomas of Celano's *Life of St. Francis*, concludes:

> The Gospel shaped the project, the *propositum*, of his [Francis] life and so therefore his life's work was to live, do, and proclaim the Gospel. The Gospel was his mission. It was there Francis could find "the teaching of Our Lord Jesus Christ" and "retrace his footsteps."[17]

---

[16] These theologians include among others Anselm of Canterbury, Peter Lombard, Albert the Great, Thomas Aquinas, Alexander of Hales, Bonaventure and John Duns Scotus.

[17] Hellmann, "Gospel: Life or Observance...," 285. See especially 287 and 289.

Both the book of creation and the book of the Gospels are necessary components of the spiritual vision of Francis and Clare. By reading these two books, Francis was gradually enabled to describe his spiritual vision concerning who and what God is, and this spiritual vision provided the base for all subsequent Franciscan theology. Without an understanding of the spiritual vision of Francis based on the book of creation and on the Book of the Gospels, the development of Franciscan theology makes no sense whatsoever. These two books, therefore, are a major foundation for an understanding of Franciscan moral teaching.

There is yet a third book which is also necessary, namely, the book of each individual's internal life. This book is written by the Holy Spirit in the heart of each person. Both Francis and Clare refer again and again to this interior book in which they discover God's plan for their lives.[18] The book of one's internal life is clearly expressed when Francis on many occasions states "the Lord led me" ... "the Lord gave me" ... "the Lord called me." In Clare's writings, this same reliance on the book of one's internal life finds a clear presentation when she speaks about the intimacy she has with her lover, Jesus. In the book of one's internal life, both Francis and Clare realized the closeness of God in determining what they should do and how they should ethically lead their lives. However, the book of one's internal life cannot be seen alone. It has to be seen in the trilogy of books: the book of creation, the book of the Gospels, and the book of one's internal life. Through creation and through the gospels, the Holy Spirit speaks directly to Francis and Clare. There is no in-

---

[18] Franciscan spirituality and Franciscan theology are inseparably united. The Dominican intellectual tradition is strongly bound to Albert the Great and Thomas Aquinas. Both of these men were attracted to the Dominican Order, but in their respective writings, the spiritual vision of the founder, St. Dominic, does not play the same kind of role which the spiritual vision of Francis and Clare plays in the theologians of the Franciscan Order. In the Augustinian tradition, the followers of this tradition spend most of their energy on the intellectual and theological issues of Augustine. Augustine's spirituality is not a central part in the Augustinian tradition in the same way in which Francis and Clare's spirituality is a major factor for the Franciscan intellectual tradition.

nate understanding of God, nor is there a special and mystical revelation made to a few chosen individuals. Rather, God speaks to all of us internally when we contemplate the book of creation, the book of Holy Scripture, and the book of one's internal life.

From the above description of the spiritual vision of Francis and Clare, we can derive two major characteristics of the Franciscan tradition in its intellectual and moral aspects. Both are strongly based on Francis's understanding of creatures and their relationship to God.

## A. Franciscan Spirituality and Franciscan Theology are Relational and Familial

All creation is bonded together in a brother-sister relationship. In Franciscan philosophy, this familial trait is echoed through the over-arching presence of "relationality" which one finds abundantly in the works of Alexander of Hales, Bonaventure, Peter John Olivi, and John Duns Scotus. To understand the meaning of "relationality" as presented by these Franciscan theologians, one must first study the familial relationship of all creation which undergirds the spiritual vision of Francis. In one of the previous citations from Francis, we heard that God was the heavenly Father, and all of us were brothers, sisters, spouses, and mothers. Gender seems to disappear in this familial approach for the family ties are more important than the gender ties.

When Francis was composing the *Canticle of Creatures*, he wrote these words which honor the moon:

Praised be You, my Lord, through Sister Moon and the stars,
In heaven you formed them clear and precious and beautiful.[19]

---

[19] The Italian text from Cajetan Esser, *Opuscula Sancti Patris Francisci Assiensis* (Grottaferrata: Collegii S. Bonaventurae Ad Claras Aquas, 1978), 84, reads: "Laudato si, mi signore, per sora luna e le stelle, in celu l'ài formate clarite et pretiose et belle."

When Francis wrote that the moon and the stars were "clear," he used the Italian word, *clarite*, a word similar to the name Clare. At this juncture, Leclerc offers a lengthy section on the masculine-feminine approach found in *Brother* Sun and *Sister* Moon. In these first two stanzas, he writes,

> Brother Sun symbolizes and gives expression to the entire interior dynamism of the soul; its vital energies, its creative powers, its power to expand, influence and conquer. Brother Sun represents the power of daylight and of the enterprising and conquering mind.[20]

Francis, however, does not imprison himself:

> The praise of the moon gives voice to a spirit that is open to the depths, the nocturnal part of our being. But this very openness already represents a transformation of the soul, the kind of transfiguration that can here find expression in a great feminine symbol of the cosmic universe.[21]

Leclerc does not say that there is a reference to Clare in the Canticle. Leclerc carefully writes:

> We only ask the following question: may not the values attached to 'Sister Moon and Stars' unconsciously symbolize certain interior values with which the name and life of Clare are not unconnected.[22]

In every sense of the word, she is Sister "Clare" or "Bright." Leclerc, in this section of his book, stresses the fact that from Clare's entry into his life, a woman was always a part of his life, and Francis was always a part of Clare's life. There is something extremely important for a familial context of spir-

---

[20] Leclerc, *The Canticle of the Creatures*, 85-86.
[21] Leclerc, *The Canticle of the Creatures*, 87.
[22] Leclerc, *The Canticle of the Creatures*, 82.

ituality, namely, the interactive presence of the feminine and the masculine. In Franciscan spirituality, we can say that Francis and Clare loved and respected each other deeply, and in their approach to others, to creatures and to God, their respective spiritualities contained both femininity and masculinity. A genuine spirituality needs both.

## B. The Entire Created Universe with No Exceptions Forms the Family of God

In the Franciscan view of the universe, no creature is left out of this familial relationship. In the thirteenth century, the European understanding of the created world was completely different from the globalized world we know today. For medieval Europeans, the world was basically Europe, and Europe was basically Christian. The term "creation," for the Europeans of that period of time, meant by and large the Christian Europe which they personally experienced on a day-to-day basis.

At that same time, there were, of course, other dimensions of the world which were not Christian. For example, during the eleventh, twelfth, and thirteenth centuries, there was a growing Islamic presence within the European worldview. The crusades made the presence of a non-Christian dimension very clear to the Christian people of Western Europe.[23] In the field of trade, Arabic people controlled all of North Africa, parts of Spain, and much of the mid-Eastern world. On a day-to-day basis, Christian traders in these areas met with and did business with non-Christian, Arabic-speaking people. In the areas of North Africa, Spain, and southern Italy, there were Arabic scholars who were in contact with Chris-

---

[23] In 1095, Pope Urban II summoned the leaders of the west to provide an answer to the Byzantine emperors' request for help to fight against the Seljuk Turks. The major goal of the crusades was to liberate Jerusalem and the Holy Land from Islamic rule. The first crusade (1096-1099) was a success. These crusades made Europe very conscious of the Islamic religion. The strength of its adherents in present day Turkey and Palestine, as well as the Mediterranean coast from Egypt to Morocco and southern Spain makes our current world extremely conscious of our brother and sister Muslims.

tian scholars and a crossover of ideas began to flourish. To a much smaller degree, there were also Jewish groups, and at times Christian scholars and Jewish scholars had some contact with each other in Spain, in the Kingdom of Naples, and in a few parts of southern France.[24]

For Francis of Assisi, the phrase "all creation" included these non-Christian areas and the people within them.[25] Creation also included the physical or natural areas of human life: sun, moon, stars, etc. God's love was the birthplace for the totality of creation, whether Christian or not, whether human or non-human. The universality of creation is a central part of Francis's spiritual vision of God, and through this spiritual vision the *universality of creation* became a major component of the Franciscan intellectual tradition, both philosophically and theologically. Universality, however, contains the idea of inclusivity. Francis's spiritual vision was and remains today an inclusive vision not an exclusive vision. God, for Francis, is universally inclusive. One must first experience the "good" in each and every creature before one even begins to see the "limitations" or even the "bad" in a creature. For Francis, this is true since every creature has been initially made in the image and likeness of God.[26]

---

[24] See Idit Dobbs Weinstein, "Jewish Philosophy," *The Cambridge Companion to Medieval Philosophy*, ed. A. S. McGrade (Cambridge: Cambridge Univeristy Press, 2003), 121-46. In this article, she highlights four scholars: Saadiah Gaon, Ibn Gabriol, Moses Maimonides, and Gersonides. She also mentions a few other minor figures. In some ways, she tends to overstress the Jewish influence on medieval thought.

[25] See Imam Mohammad Bashar Arafat, "Islam and Christianity: Two Faiths and One God," and Fareed Munir, "Islam and Franciscanism: Prophet Mohammad of Arabia in the Spirituality of Mission," *Islam and Franciscanism: A Dialogue* (St. Bonaventure, NY: The Franciscan Institute, 2000), 17-42. Both of these authors are of the Muslim faith. See also Giulio Basetti Sani, *L'Islam nel piano della salvezza* (San Domenico di Fiesole: Edizioni Cultura della Pace, 1992); Jean Gwenolé Jeusset, *Dieu est Courtoisie: François d'Assise, son Ordre et la'Islam* (Nantes: Atelier Ste Claire, 1985); Paul Moses, *The Saint and the Sultan* (New York: Doubleday, 2009).

[26] At times, non-Christians and non-Christian religions have been summarily dismissed by Catholic writers. Too often, these authors have portrayed the limitations and imperfections of non-Christians without first noting their positive characteristics.

These two basic dimensions of the Franciscan approach, the relational/familial character of all creation and the inclusive universality of creation, have major implications for today's renewal of moral theology. For Francis, the terms of brother and sister do not include only beautiful things, such as Brother Sun and Sister Moon, Brother Fire and Sister Water. Included in creation are Brother Leper and Brother Robber. The terms brother and sister include creatures that are struggling and imperfect. Brother Tree praises God when in the spring it blooms with flowers, but Brother Tree also praises God when in late autumn the leaves wither and fall, leaving an ungainly sight of bare limbs. Little babies praise God just by their existence; young men and women praise God by their exuberance; old men and women, who are haggard, weak, and near death, praise God even in the last gasps of life-giving breath. No creature is so ungainly or so sinful that he or she is no longer our brother and sister.

When this familial characteristic is applied to the community called church, we see that for Francis the church itself includes the good and the perfect as well as the sinner and the imperfect. A familial church has good members and weak members, but all members must be treated as brothers and sisters. Francis's understanding of God shaped and colored this aspect of his understanding of the church. The church is a *familial church*, and all members in the church are brothers and sisters to one another.

The universality of God's creation moves beyond church boundaries. This was true for Francis of Assisi and remains true throughout the Franciscan intellectual tradition. Today, there is an emphasis on the union of all Christians – not just Catholics – for we are all brothers and sisters to one another. It is God who has created these "other" Christians. If today's ecumenical movement could absorb more of this familial and inclusive approach, a renewed theology of church would become far more credible.

When we move beyond the Christian dimension, the Franciscan familial approach to spirituality and theology takes on a deeper inclusiveness. A familial and inclusively universal approach to creation moves the contemporary ecumenical movement of Christian Churches into dialogue with other religions and into a spiritual dimension of prayer and good works not motivated by Christian principles. The dialogue with other religions cannot be simply interpreted as an intellectual dimension of endless discussions. Living together and praying together are also major aspects in these inter-religious encounters.

Francis found in Brother Sun and Sister Moon the same God whom he had found in Brother Leper and Sister Prostitute. This all-encompassing and creature-centered spiritual vision of a loving God, which slowly developed throughout the ups and downs of Francis's life, shaped the way in which Francis understood the relationship between church and non-church. Both the church and the non-church are included in his familial love of God.

For Francis, brothers and sisters exist beyond church walls. However, it is one thing to speak of the sun, moon, water, and fire as brother and sister. It is another thing to speak of non-Christians as brothers and sisters. The sun, moon, water, and fire are usually not described either as Christian or much less as Catholic. The denominational terms, Christian and Catholic, do not apply to the physical world. The sun can be "Brother Sun," but Brother Sun is not a baptized Christian.

When one's focus includes the entire human world, then the terms, Christian and non-Christian or Catholic and non-Catholic, apply with greater intensity, for in this approach, the familial and all-inclusive characteristics of Francis's spiritual vision moved to a deeper level of relationship. Brother Sun and Sister Moon include the physical world, but Brother Presbyterian and Sister Lutheran involve the denominational world. Brother Hindu and Sister Buddhist involve the multi-varied religious world. If in today's globalized, multicultural, and inter-religious world, the familial and all-inclusive characteristics of God's creative and loving action are applied to the contemporary world at large, then a Christian must acknowledge a loving presence of God in

Brother Buddhist and Sister Hindu, in Brother Daoist and Sister Islamist.[27]

On June 24, 1219, Francis set sail from either Bari or Brindisi and eventually reached the Christian troops which had almost surrounded the Muslim city of Damietta at the mouth of the Nile, just north of Cairo. The crusaders had successfully laid a siege to the city of Damietta, disallowing any food, water, etc., to be given to the many Muslims in the city. The crusaders encamped around the upper Nile, and the Islamic forces were camped at Al-Adilia, near Lake Manzala. A no-man's land divided the Christian and Islamic forces.

Francis wanted to go into the Muslim-held territory in an effort to convert some of the Arabs to Christianity. The leaders of the Christian army and the Bishop at Acre, Jacques de Vitry, were against such an undertaking. In the end, Francis simply stated that he and another brother, Illuminato, were ready to go. Jacques de Vitry wrote a letter for posterity, stating that he had not authorized the trip. Through this letter, it is clear that Jacques de Vitry did not want to be blamed for Francis's death, for he knew first-hand that Francis was already considered a saintly man throughout much of Italy.[28] When the two Franciscans crossed the no-man's land be-

---

[27] In contemporary theology, scholars struggle to relate the Christian religion to non-Christian religions. A growing number of theologians turn to the distinction between the kingdom of God and the church. These theologians indicate that the kingdom of God is more extensive than the Christian Church. In their view, both kingdom and church have their own distinctive centers of unity and unicity. Other theologians move to the distinction between the role of the Incarnate Jesus for the Christians and the role of the Holy Spirit at work beyond the Christian sphere. John Paul II, in *Redemptoris missio* (13-20) itemizes the major differences between the kingdom of God and the church. He states that the church is not an end unto herself (19); that the church is at the service of the kingdom (20); that the church is ordered towards the kingdom of God (18); and that the church is distinct from both Christ and the kingdom of God (18). Paul VI, in *Evangelii nuntiandi*, writes in a similar way (8-10). In n. 53, Paul VI indicates that non-Christian religions themselves are holy and provide holiness to their followers. This is a major step, since the ordinary position of the Catholic Church was a focus on individual non-Christians who might be holy; Paul VI moves from the individual to the non-Christian religion itself.

[28] See the material on Jacques de Vitry in *FA:ED*, I, 578-89.

tween the Christian forces and the Muslim forces, they were immediately captured by Muslim soldiers. The only Arab words Francis knew were the name of the sultan of Egypt, Malik-al-Kamil. He kept repeating this name, and the Muslim soldiers thought that he was perhaps an emissary from the Christians to the Sultan, so they took him to Al Marsurra just south of Damietta where Malik-al-Kamil resided. At first the sultan and the court discounted any peaceful efforts, but little by little the sultan began to realize that Francis was truly a man of God and the two began to talk with each other about God. Francis, for his part, saw that the sultan was a man of deep prayer and love of God. In the end, after lengthy discussions, the sultan had a few of his soldiers escort Francis and his companion back to the Christians at Damietta. Both the sultan and Francis honored and respected the spiritual depth of each other. Brother Francis had met Brother Malik-al-Kamil.

A major point of this event is its highlighting of the familial and inclusive approach to the Franciscan spiritual vision. Francis ended the time with the sultan, recognizing him as a holy man. Without expressing the following in a direct way, Francis recognized him as a creature of God who was trying to love God in a strong and deep way.

Francis's experience did not end in Damietta. In 1224, Pope Honorius III called for a new crusade and the crusaders wanted to kill Sultan al-Kamil. Undoubtedly, Francis was perplexed over this threat to a person whom he had met personally and whom Francis considered a holy individual.[29] His forty-day retreat on Mount La Verna was centered on the meaning of the feast of the Holy Cross. Why was Jesus who was a holy man killed? But on Francis's mind there was another: Why was the sultan, a holy man, threatened with death? Francis did not make Jesus and the sultan equal, but, in his meditations during the forty days of his retreat, the killing of holy people certainly was part of his reflections on

---

[29] See Moses, *The Saint and the Sultan*, 180-81, in which he cites Michael Cusato, a Franciscan who has researched this crusade and its impact on Francis.

the meaning of the cross. At the end of this retreat, Francis had a deep religious experience in which the cross took on a profound meaning. He is also said to have received the stigmata, an experience which has received much study and evaluation. More important than the stigmata, however, was his religious experience of the meaning of the death of Jesus on the cross. In a secondary way, the threat to the life of Brother Sultan placed Francis's view of Jesus' crucifixion on a larger scale than the scale of Jesus' death with a Christian theological framework. Francis's view of creation was broadened by his religious experience on Mount La Verna. The entire world is relationally united in a familial way because God's internal love, in the Franciscan tradition, is the *birthplace of all creation*. For Francis, the crucifixion of Jesus was a moment of love, calling us to love in return a holy God who loves each one of us unto the end, as the Gospel of John describes.

Let us now turn to St. Clare and her approach to God and creation.[30] Although Clare was deeply influenced by Francis of Assisi, she also developed her own characteristics for a spiritual vision of God. Clare was the first woman ever to write a rule for religious women, and her rule is clearly feminine in its expression. Regis Armstrong writes:

> There has always been a temptation to interpret Clare's *Form of Life* in light of that of Francis from which it borrows. However, it is a unique document articulating that demanding expression of religious life that she perceived was her calling and, at the same time, a startling sense of individual freedom that was based on Clare's experience of the maturity of her sisters. Clare's insistence on its recognition and acceptance by the Church not simply as a privilege

---

[30] For the writings of Clare, see *Chiara d'Assisi: Scritti: Introduzione, Testo latino, Traduction, Notes e Index*, ed. Marie-France Becker, Jean-François Godet, and Thaddée Matura (Paris: Les Éditions du Cerf, 1985); also *Clare of Assisi: Early Documents, The Lady*, ed. and trans. Regis Armstrong (New York: New City Press, 2006); hereafter *CA:ED* followed by page numbers.

but as a right forged a new understanding of the role of charism in the unfolding of the Church's life.[31]

This *Form of Life* was confirmed by Innocent IV in 1253, the very same year in which Clare died.

In the spiritual vision of Clare, how did she understand God? Was her understanding of God similar to that of Francis or is there something special in the way Clare envisioned God? The Sisters of the Monastery of St. Clare, at Nantes, France, published a four-volume work entitled *Towards the Discovery of Clare of Assisi*.[32] The second volume is entitled *Clare Discovers the Love of God in the Church*.[33] The Poor Clares at Nantes begin their volume by asking: "Who God is for Clare and her Sisters."[34] The answer is: "The knowledge of God of Clare and her Sisters is experiential; it is the fruit of their relationship and their contemplation."[35] The authors then list eight themes which describe the experiential fruit of their relationship and contemplation:

God is a God who loves.

God is the source of all grace and of many favors.

The many names that Clare gives God are different aspects of his countenance.

The titles and attributes which she gives to God are different discoveries of His being and His action.

God is Trinitarian.

God is Father.

---

[31] Armstrong, *CA:ED*, 27.

[32] The original work was produced by the Sisters of Nantes, *À la Découverte de Claire d'Assise* (1988); the English translation was done under the guidance of the general editor, Mary Francis Hone, *Towards the Discovery of Claire of Assisi* (St. Bonaventure, NY: The Franciscan Institute, 1992 onward).

[33] Hone, *Towards the Discovery of Clare of Assisi*, Volume II, *Clare Discovers the Love of God in the Church*, ed. Regis Armstrong and Pacelli Millane, O.S.C. (St. Bonaventure, NY: The Franciscan Institute, 1992).

[34] Hone, 1.

[35] Hone. 1.

Clare and her Sisters have a personal relationship with the Holy Spirit.
They are particularly attentive to divine inspiration.[36]

These eight characteristics are not direct citations from the writings of Clare. Rather, they are the summary statements of the nuns who compiled these four volumes. These eight phrases are only "key words" which unite a series of citations from the writings of Clare.

In the sections which follow this introductory page, each theme is presented with a detailed listing of verbatim statements taken from diverse documents, such as Clare's letters, her *Form of Life*, her *Testament*, her *Blessing*, the documents from the process of canonization, and citations from the *Legend of St. Clare*.

Let us consider the first theme: "*It is a God who loves.*" In the *First Letter* to Agnes, Clare writes that the Lord Jesus who is God incarnate will take care of Agnes:

Whom in loving, you are chaste; in touching, you become more pure; in embracing you are a virgin; whose strength is more robust; ... whose love is more courteous; ... whose embrace already holds you.[37]

Clare has no problem using phrases descriptive of marital love for one's love of God. In this use of human love, Clare, in her own way, stresses the familial and intimate nature of the Franciscan vision.

---

[36] Hone. 1. One could ask why this listing of characteristics has credibility, for the list itself is the work of scholars and not a list made by Clare herself. This is true, but the scholars who worked on this list were some of the best scholars on the life and work of Clare. See the detailed explanation of this scholarship in Armstrong, *CA:ED*, 28-34; also Hone, *Clare Discovers the Love of God in the Church*, viii-xii. Moreover, each title in the listing is followed in Hone's volume with sections which provide citations from Clare's writings which substantiate the individual characteristic in the list. Thus, one should read the titles of the small list, and then move to these same titles in the book itself and check the references made to the writings of Clare.

[37] Clare of Assisi, "The First Letter to Agnes of Prague," *CA:ED*, 44; Hone, 3.

In Clare's *Fourth Letter* to Agnes, she writes in a similar way:

Draw me after you, let us run in the fragrance of your perfumes, O heavenly Spouse! I will run and not tire, until You bring me into the wine-cellar, until your left hand is under my head and your right hand will embrace me happily, You will kiss me the happiest kiss of your mouth.[38]

Clare's symbolic use of human love to describe divine love evidences the intensity of God's love, which for Clare surpasses any and every form of human love. In Christian theology from the time of Paul onward, the love of wife and husband has been used to present the depth and height, the length and breadth of God's love for the men and women in the church of Christ (Eph 5:21-33). Clare's use of human love between husband and wife indicates that she, as well as Francis, had a familial vision of spirituality. She, too, understood that God's love is the *birth place of creation.*[39]

There is another vital aspect to Clare's spiritual vision. Francis refers to this aspect when he writes that the Lord led him, or the Lord gave him brothers, or the Lord appeared to him in the chapel of the Portiuncula and on the heights of Mount La Verna. In all of these references, Francis speaks about the third Franciscan book, the book of one's inner life, in which God speaks to us in a quiet but loving way. In her *Form of Life*, Clare states: "If anyone [a woman who wants to join the Ladies of Assisi] comes to us by divine inspiration ..."[40] In this passage, notice the emphasis on divine inspiration in the heart of this newcomer. Clare goes on to state that

---

[38] Clare of Assisi, "The Fourth Letter to Agnes of Prague," (hereafter 4LAg), *CA:ED*, 57; Hone, 3.

[39] Clare was deeply impressed by the spirituality of Francis. He was, in many ways, her spiritual director. The relationship between Francis and Clare is described here and there throughout the early Franciscan documents. See, for example, the "Assisi Compilation," *Francis of Assisi: Early Documents*, Vol. II *The Founder* (New York: New City Press, 2001): 128-29; 188-89.

[40] *Form of Life*, II, 1, *CA:ED*, 110.

the new member should take care of her possessions "as the Lord may inspire her."[41] Again Clare writes: "The Lord frequently reveals what is best to the least [among us]."[42] Again: "The Most High Heavenly Father saw fit by his grace to enlighten my heart to do penance according to the example and teaching of our most blessed Father Saint Francis."[43] Again: "By divine inspiration you have made yourselves daughters and servants of the Most High King."[44]

These and many other citations from the writings of Clare could be cited. They all indicate that Clare remained constant in her belief that, throughout her life, the Lord had revealed to her inmost heart a way of life for which she asked for papal approval again and again. She was sure that God had spoken to her in the book of the inner life, and this form of life corresponded to the Gospels. Both books, therefore, confirmed her position. She was determined to convince the pope that this was God's will. She urged her Sisters to do the same:

> By divine inspiration you have made yourselves daughters and handmaids of the Most High, Most Exalted King, the Heavenly Father, and have taken the Holy Spirit as your spouse, choosing to live according to the perfection of the holy Gospel.[45]

We speak, today, of "women's intuition." Clare attests to this quality, but she indicates that it is actually God who works deep with a human person, and that the "woman's intuition" in these instances is part of the book of the inner life. Clare's intuition about the spiritual life was not at first accepted by either church authority or aristocratic authority. This was also the case with Agnes of Prague. Nonetheless, these women held to their deep conviction that a higher authority had called them to this way of life, and that their

---

[41] *Form of Life*, II, 9, *CA:ED*, 110.
[42] *Form of Life*, IV, 18, *CA:ED*, 115.
[43] *Form of Life*, VI, 1, *CA:ED*, 117.
[44] *Form of Life*, VI, 3, *CA:ED*, 118.
[45] *Form of Life*, VI, 3, *CA:ED*, 118.

way of life reflected the Gospel of Jesus himself. In the end, both the church and the aristocratic authority removed their resistance.

After the death of Francis, there were decades when the Friars and the Poor Ladies had to defend their way of life. The Franciscan spiritual vision was, in itself, not a new vision, but it was not the ordinary spiritual vision which had developed in medieval tradition through the insights of Benedict and subsequent monastic authors.


## III. THE PROFOUND RELATIONSHIP
### BETWEEN THE TRIUNE GOD AND CREATION

The Franciscan spiritual vision was rooted in the New Testament, but it was also rooted in the book of creation and the book of the inner life. Francis and Clare gradually developed their spiritual vision, and in retrospect we can see that their insights eventually produced a major spiritual and theological movement in the Catholic Church. It is this spiritual and theological movement which has become extremely popular in the Christian world today, not only among Catholics, but also among Protestant and secular authors. The amount of recent books and articles on Francis, Clare, as well as on the Franciscan theologians mentioned above has risen exponentially.[46]

On the basis of this vision of God, both Francis and Clare then began to understand the meaning of the Incarnation,

---

[46] The exponential rise in writings on Franciscan spirituality, philosophy, and theology can be seen in the lengthy bibliography in Freyer's volume, 390-432. Much of this bibliographical material represents the European interest in Franciscan studies. A bibliography focused on Clare can be found in Margaret Carney, *The First Franciscan Woman* (Quincy, IL: Franciscan Press, 1993). See also, Joan Mueller, *Clare's Letters to Agnes: Text and Sources* (St. Bonaventure, NY: The Franciscan Institute, 2001), 16-23. See also *Manual de Teología franciscana*, ed. José Antonio Merino and Francisco Fresneda (Madrid: Biblioteca de Autores Christianos, 2003). Each contributor provides a lengthy bibliography relevant to his theme: See Francisco Martinez Fresneda, "Textos y contextos de la Teología franciscana," 3; Luis Iammarrone, "La Trinidad," 57; Juan Iammarrone, "Cristología," 149.

the presence of the Holy Spirit throughout all of creation, the beauty of the church, and the moral way in which Christian life should be led.

The relational God-Creation which centers the spiritual vision of Francis and Clare overflows into their understanding of the Incarnation of the Logos in the human nature of Jesus. The birthplace of the human and created aspects of the incarnation, namely Jesus' human nature, was also God's love. It was not Adam's sin that brought about the Incarnation; rather, God's love is the womb in which Jesus' humanity was first desired and conceived. For Francis, Jesus was the gift of God that most clearly mirrored who and what God is. However, what captivated Francis in a special way was the humility of the Incarnation, for God did not enter into creation as a mighty Lord and King. Rather, God came to us in a quiet, humble, and almost unnoticed way. Jesus became our humble brother. Just as the familial world for Francis included the least and the poorest, so too did God's love for the poor find its place in the womb of a poor woman, Mary, and in the makeshift manger at his birth in Bethlehem. When Francis wanted to portray the meaning of the Incarnation to the people of Greccio, the celebration took place on a dirt road with ordinary people dressed as Mary and Joseph, and as angels and shepherds. The animals, which were also a part of the Greccio scene, grazed for food and gave little attention to the baby in Mary's arms. At Greccio, we have a visual presentation of how God, in a very humble way, so loved the world that he sent us his only Son so that we might have eternal life. The motive of the Incarnation, to use theological language, was God's love for men and women which finds its reflection in the humility of the Logos-made-flesh.

Clare, in so many of her writings, portrays Jesus as the one who loves. In the *Third Letter* to Agnes, Clare writes:

May you totally love him who gave himself totally for your love, at whose beauty the sun and the moon marvel, whose reward and their uniqueness and grandeur have no limits; I am speaking of him, the Son of the Most High, whom the Virgin brought to birth.[47]

In the fourth letter to Agnes, Clare speaks of human love for Jesus, mirroring divine love. For Clare to love Jesus and to have Jesus be the lover of either Clare or Agnes is described in words of human love which give a small echo of divine love. She writes:

> Happy, indeed, is she to whom it is given to drink at this sacred banquet so that she might cling with her whole heart to Him whose beauty all the blessed hosts of heaven unceasingly admire, whose tenderness touches, whose contemplation refreshes, whose kindness overflows, whose delight overwhelms, whose remembrance delightfully dawns.... Gaze upon that mirror each day, O Queen and Spouse of Jesus Christ, and continually study your face in it that you may adorn yourself completely, within and without.[48]

Jesus mirrors the love of God, or as Clare expresses it: "Look, say at the border of this mirror, that is, the poverty of him who was placed in a manger and wrapped in swaddling clothes. O marvelous humility! O astonishing poverty! The King of angels, the Lord of heaven and earth, is laid in a manger!"[49] Clare, similar to Francis, celebrates the humility of the Incarnation.

Francis and Clare treasured the presence of the Holy Spirit who spoke to them in the depths of their soul. They both honored a divine inspiration deep within them as the presence of the Holy Spirit.[50] During their lifetimes, each of them continually read three books: the book of creation, the book of Scripture, and the book of the inner life. In their day-to-day contact with these three books, God spoke to them. The spiritual vision of Francis and Clare begins with the ac-

---

[47] *Third Letter to Agnes* (hereafter 3LAg), *CA:ED*, 51.
[48] 4LAg, *CA:ED*, 55.
[49] 4LAg, *CA:ED*, 56.
[50] See Hone, 22-25 for direct citations in the writings of Clare.

tion of God in their lives through their meditations in and through creation, in and through the Word of God, and in and through the deep experiences in their soul. God's presence to them through all of these areas is primary. Their response was secondary.

In God's self-revelation to them, they began to understand God in a very special way. The world which came from God's womb of love was a world of immense beauty. Through the world, Francis and Clare encountered a God of profound love, for it was God's profound love that became the birthplace of creation.

Confronted by such love and beauty, the response of Francis and Clare was one of amazement and humility. The humility of the Incarnation is seen in the Logos who became one of us in the individual human nature of God. That Jesus suffered and died on the cross also became a major theme of his meditations, but his considerations did not focus on a redemptive or salvific aspect of his death. Rather, Francis saw in the crucified Jesus a love that was not loved in return. Clare's meditations on Jesus centered on the love of God which one finds in all that Jesus does, and she uses the sexual love between a woman and a man to describe the height and depth, the length and breadth of God's love.

They also cherished the presence of the Spirit of God in the three books which they contemplated each day. In creation, the Spirit of a loving God was reflected in Brother Sun and Sister Moon, in Brother and Sister Leper, and in each individual creature. The Spirit of God, for Francis, was present even in Brother Sultan.

Only on the basis of God's primary action in the lives of Francis and Clare, and on the basis of their reaction to this God of love, beauty, familial presence, and all-inclusive care did they choose to live in poverty and humility. For Francis and Clare, the poverty and humility of their lives make no sense unless one considers the special way in which they responded to the presence of God who is love and beauty and who is familial and all-inclusive. The deepest focus of their spiritual life was on their relation to a God who is love and beauty and who is familial and all-inclusive. Moral living for these two holy people was a response to a God of beauty, love, justice, and peace.

## IV. Conclusion

In the succeeding chapters, we will see that the key words: love, goodness, beauty, familial, and all-inclusive, keep appearing in the theological works of later major Franciscan scholars. The theological endeavors of the thirteenth- and fourteenth-century Franciscan scholars were profoundly based on the Scriptures, especially the Gospels. Their philosophical and theological writings were also richly nourished by the major Patristic writers, by Augustine in the western dimension of the Christian thought, and by John Damascene and Dionysius the Areopagite in the eastern dimension of the Christian thought. They were deeply conversant with the Latin translations of both Plato and Aristotle. In their inclusion of all these sources, the early Franciscan scholars remained solidly based on the spiritual vision of Francis and Clare.

The same Franciscan approach, based on spirituality, philosophy, and theology, unites the essays of this volume on moral theology. We will see how all three of these dimensions, spirituality, philosophy, and theology, interact with each other as the various authors formulate their ethical insights on specific moral issues. In a more fundamental way, we will also see how the Franciscan vision of God remains the basic spiritual and theological dimension which colors and shapes all other aspects of the Franciscan tradition, and in a special way the dimension of moral theology.

In Chapter Two, we will consider how this spiritual vision of Francis and Clare gave birth to a theological tradition which bears the name "Franciscan."

# 2

# THE DEVELOPMENT OF THE SPIRITUAL VISION OF FRANCIS AND CLARE INTO A MAJOR SPIRITUAL AND THEOLOGICAL TRADITION

## KENAN B. OSBORNE, O.F.M.

*The Franciscan moral vision affirms*
*that on a human level there is a mirroring*
*of the free and self-giving exchange*
*of Father, Son, and Holy Spirit*
*that calls people to life*
*in free and self-giving relationships of mutuality.*

The previous chapter focused on Francis and Clare and their approach to God. This chapter focuses on the way in which Franciscans, from the last years of Francis's life down to the early years of the fourteenth century, developed a uniquely Franciscan theological tradition based on Franciscan spirituality.[1] During these years, Franciscan spiritual-

---

[1] In 1224, Francis of Assisi wrote a brief note to Anthony of Padua, blessing his work as a theological teacher of the younger Franciscans. One might say that this date, 1224, marks the official beginning of the interconnection of the spirituality of Francis with theology. 1308 marks the death of John Duns Scotus, one of the most outstanding Franciscan theologians of the late thirteenth and early fourteenth centuries. During these eighty-four years, at least three hundred Franciscans became theological scholars either in the European universities or in regional Franciscan institutes of theological studies.

ity and Franciscan theology not only grew in importance; they mutually shaped each other in an intense way. From its beginning, Franciscan spirituality and Franciscan theology have codetermined each other. Franciscan theology has never been simply a science (*scientia*). It has always been both a science and spiritual wisdom (*scientia et sapientia spiritualis*). At times, the history of this codependence has not been peaceful, but even the moments of difficult interaction helped clarify both the spirituality and the theology involved.[2]

This chapter is divided into three parts: the importance of Trinitarian theology in the writings of the early Franciscan scholars; the centrality of creation, Incarnation, and the sending of the Holy Spirit in the writings of the early Franciscan scholars; and its implications for Franciscan moral theology.

Through his research on these early Franciscan theologians, Johannes Freyer has put together a detailed study in which he indicates how the Trinitarian God as understood by Francis and Clare forms the spiritual center of all Franciscan theological thought. In his opening chapter, Freyer writes:

> Franciscan theology remains from its point of departure onward a true follower of the spirituality of the founder of the Franciscan Order.... The inner-trinitarian love-dynamic of God's communication and sharing is at one and the same time the birthplace of creation and of men and women, because the Triune God shares its own self in love to all reality outside the Godhead, and from this loving sharing God wants to be part of all that God has created.[3]

---

[2] See Grado Giovanni Merlo, *Nell Nome di San Francesco* (Padua: Detrick Francescane, 2003). For an English translation see Merlo, *In the Name of Saint Francis: A History of the Friars Minor and Franciscanism until the Early Sixteenth Century*, trans. by Raphael Bonnano and Robert J. Karris (St. Bonaventure, NY: Franciscan Institute Publications, 2009). I am deeply indebted to his insights for the material in the first part of this chapter.

[3] Johannes Freyer, *Homo Viator: Der Mensch im Lichte der Heilsgeschichte* (Kevelaer: Butzon & Bercker, 2001), 120.

Freyer's description of the Trinitarian God emphasizes relationality, an important Franciscan value noted in earlier chapters. In God's inner life, there is a dynamic interrelationship of love flowing through God's triune nature. In God's external actions of creation, Incarnation, and sending the Spirit, God is again described as relational, since God shares God's own goodness and love with every creature. In Franciscan theology, God is not simply the first cause of all created beings or the first principle of existence. God does something far more than cause creation. God *loves* creation into existence. God's love is both the core of life within God, and it is also the dynamism which loves us into existence.[4]

## I. THE IMPORTANCE OF TRINITARIAN THEOLOGY IN THE WRITINGS OF THE EARLY FRANCISCAN SCHOLARS

In response to the two dominant approaches to Trinitarian theology of his time (Augustine and Richard of St. Victor), Bonaventure forged a third western approach, in which he utilized the writings of John Damascene (c. 675-749) and Dionysius the Areopagite (fifth – sixth century). Both of these authors were Greek, but some of their works had been translated into Latin. Alexander of Hales, one of the main teachers of Bonaventure, frequently cited these two Greek scholars, and a phrase used by these Greek writers, namely, "goodness is diffusive of itself" (*bonum est diffusivum sui*) became the centering of Bonaventure's theology of the Trinity. Hugh of St. Victor, another theologian who influenced both Alexander and Bonaventure, also quotes Dionysius several times in *The Celestial Hierarchy*.[5] The phrase, "goodness is diffusive of itself," is reminiscent of Francis's view of God's love as the birthplace of creation.

The spiritual vision of Francis and Clare, the writings of the New Testament, and the works of John Damascene and

---

[4] Freyer, *Homo Viator*, 67-96.

[5] See Paul Rorem, *Hugh of Saint Victor* (Oxford: Oxford University Press, 2009), 167-76.

Dionysius provided Bonaventure with a unique understanding of God, and his understanding of the Triune God colored and shaped his entire theological vision. If one does not understand Bonaventure's theology of the Triune God, one cannot appropriately understand his positions on creation, Incarnation, the sending of the Holy Spirit, the sacramental life of the church, and the moral dimensions of human life.[6]

The first theological form of Trinitarian theology which had a lasting impact in the west was that of Augustine. His theology centered on the intellectual or psychological analogy of human thinking and its reflection of a Triune God. Augustine's volume on the Trinity, *De Trinitate*, has been read and reread from its appearance somewhere between 400 and 420 down to the present day. Augustine also wrote other works in which the Trinity was theologically explained. For instance, in one of his sermons, Augustine wrote:

> I say that the Father is memory, the Son understanding, and the Holy Ghost is will.... I do not say that these things are to be equated even by analogy with the Holy Trinity, that is to say are to be arranged according to some exact rule of comparison. This I do not say. But what do I say? See, I have discovered in you [his listeners] three things which we see as exhibited separately but whose operation is inseparable.[7]

In his book on the Trinity, *De Trinitate*, Augustine presented more than twenty triadic groups for exploration, such as memory-knowledge-love, memory-understanding-love, and memory-understanding-love of self. He finally settled on

---

[6] Bonaventure's theology of Trinity is deeply indebted to the Trinitarian theology of his mentor, Alexander of Hales. See Luis Iammarrone, "La Trinidad," *Manual de Teología Franciscana*, ed. Antonio Merino y Francisco M. Fresneda (Madrid: Biblioteca de Autores Christianos, 2003), 75-118. Iammarrone's opening paragraph connects the spirituality of Francis with Franciscan theologians: "En esto ha permanecido siempre fiel a la experiencia mística de Dios que guió y penetró toda la vida espiritual de Francisco de Asís," 57. See also *Summa Alexandrina Halensis*, I (Quaracchi: Collegium S. Bonaventurae,1924-1928), 465-66.

[7] Augustine, Sermon 52, 10-23.

the one mentioned in his *Sermon* cited above: the memory of God, the understanding of God, and the love in God. Augustine simply sees that in the unity found in human memory, understanding, and love, there is an analogical basis for appreciating to some degree what the unity of a Trinitarian God means.

Thomas Aquinas accepted Augustine's triad as his own theological base, and through his use of Aristotelian categories, he provided a more detailed presentation of Trinitarian theology.[8] Generally, the Augustinian-Thomistic theological approach to the Trinity was presented in the theological textbooks written during the century before the Second Vatican Council.

A second form of western Trinitarian theology, equally authentic to the Christian tradition, was developed by Richard of St. Victor (d. 1173), who selected as his major analogy for Trinitarian theology one of Augustine's other analogies, namely the analogy of interpersonal love. This triune approach focuses on the lover—the beloved—and the bond of love between them. Mutual love also involves not simply the love of the lover and the beloved. It also includes a mutual love as seen in their love for a third beloved, namely a child born of the man and woman. These three, Richard states, are coequally in love. A man deeply loves a woman, and a woman deeply loves a man. When a child is born, they both continue to love each other and without lessening their mutual love, they enter into a love relationship with their child. Richard of St. Victor was struck by the openness of marital love to a third person without losing the mutual love of husband and wife. This coequality provided Richard's Trinitarian teaching its distinctive analogical character.[9]

---

[8] See Anne Hunt, *Trinity: Nexus of the Mysteries of Christian Faith* (Maryknoll, NY: Orbis Books, 2006), 17-23. See also Anselm Min, *Paths to the Triune God* (Notre Dame, IN: University of Notre Dame Press, 2005).

[9] See Richard of St. Victor, *Richard of St Victor: Selections*, Eng. trans. Grover Zinn, Classics of Western Spirituality (NY: Paulist Press, 1979), 388. See also Michael Schmaus, "Trinität bis zum Ausgang der Scholastik," *Handbuch der Dogmengeschichte*, II/Ib (Freiburg im B.: Herder, 1985); and Richard of St. Victor, *The Twelve Patriarchs, The Mystical Ark, Book Three of Trinity*, Eng. trans. Grover Zinn (NY: Paulist Press, 1979). For a rejection

Bonaventure, following the insights of Alexander of Hales, focused his theology of God on three terms: *being, love,* and *diffusive goodness.* In doing this, Bonaventure established a third western theological approach to the Trinity.[10] John Duns Scotus also focused his theology of God on three words: *being, love,* and *freedom.* To the realities of *being, love,* and *diffusive goodness* in Bonaventure and to the realities of *being, love,* and *freedom* in Scotus, both men added the important aspect of *infinite,* and the addition of infinite to these realities presents us with a relational God of incredible dimensions. Naturally, these theologians described God with many other words and phrases as well, but in their respective theologies of God, these particular words became central. We can diagram how these key terms need to be understood in the following way.

| BEING<br>GOODNESS<br>LOVE<br>FREEDOM | IN GOD<br>ALL OF THESE<br>ARE INFINITE | INFINITE BEING<br>INFINITE GOODNESS<br>INFINITE LOVE<br>INFINITE FREEDOM |
|---|---|---|

Diagrams can be helpful, but at the same time they have limitations. The above diagram helps us to consider the theologies of God as found in Bonaventure and Scotus in an orderly way. When we focus on the middle step in the above diagram and refer to God as *infinite being,* as *infinite love,* as *infinite diffusive goodness,* and as *infinite freedom,* we are simultaneously making a major coalescence in the reality of divine life. Each of these terms is *infinitely interrelated,* which means that one cannot consider a single dimension without concomitantly including all other infinite dimensions. Infinity unites these dimensions in a unitive manner. The diagram does not clearly indicate this infinite "co-extentionality" and "coextensive relationality."

---

of Richard's view of the Trinity, see Anselm Min, *Paths to the Triune God* (Notre Dame, IN: University of Notre Dame Press, 2005), 171 and 369, n. 4.

[10] See Olegario González, *Misterio Trinitario y Existencia Humana: Estudio Histórico Teológico en Torno a San Buenaventura* (Madrid: Ediciones Rialp: 1965). In great detail, González explicates the bases for Bonaventure's third form of Trinity in the West.

Iammarrone explains one of these dimensional interrelationships, namely being and love in Bonaventure. What he says has repercussions for the other dimensions as well. He writes:

> New Testament revelation affirms that "God is love" (1 John 4:8, 16). The profound richness of such a definition, for Bonaventure, becomes actual in the intimate life of God, who is a most perfect communion of three persons centered in their reciprocal love. For Bonaventure, goodness [in God] is the life of being insofar as it is love.[11]

Iammarone continues this line of thinking when he writes:

> The Christian concept of God is agápe, that is, the love of giving. In no way does this contradict, according to Bonaventure, the concept of God insofar as God is Ipsum Esse or Being in its essence. Even more, this position places in complete evidence that being agápe is the same as essential being insofar as God, in virtue of God's fullness or infinite richness communicates his very being.[12]

Bonaventure is saying that in God, being is love, and therefore, in God love is being. On this basis, one can further argue that if God is diffusively good, infinite, and free, then being in God is likewise diffusively good, infinite, and free. The *infinite* dimension of God's being, goodness, love, and freedom can only be understood as infinitely coextensive with each other. In human life, diffusive good, love, and freedom are not coterminous with being. We are still "being" when we are not good, when we do not love, and when we are not free.

---

[11] Iammarrone, "La Trinidad," 75-76.
[12] Iammarrone, "La Trinidad," 76.

In order to clarify this divine coalescence of being, good-ness, love, and freedom, let us briefly consider the meaning of each of these four terms, as they have been interpreted in Christian theology. In the presentation of each category, the goal is to provide a sharper understanding of both Bonaven-ture's and Scotus's Trinitarian theology.[13]

## A. Being

In the western world, the term *being* has acquired a pro-found meaning due to Greek philosophers.[14] *Being* has be-come a technical word in metaphysics. In the European phil-osophical world, *being* is the *ultimate basis of what all things are*. To describe this ultimate basis one has to employ other terms such as essence, nature, substance, reality, existence, etc. The precise meaning of these words was also part of the Greek philosophical heritage. One speaks of substantial be-ing as opposed to accidental being. Actual realities have "ac-tual being," and possible realities, which do not exist, have only "possible being." Most western people feel at home with this kind of being-language.[15]

A complicating factor entered the philosophical world when Christian philosophers referred to the *Being of God* in contrast to the *being of all creatures*. Since Divine Being is totally different from created being, Arabic/Persian and Christian writers have attempted again and again to distin-guish how Divine Being is distinct from created being and at

---

[13] For a more detailed explanation of this interrelationship, Osborne, *A Theology of the Church for the Third Millennium: A Franciscan Approach* (Leiden: Brill, 2009), 209-48.

[14] The western world is indebted to Parmenides for the term, 'be-ing.' See Enrico Berti, "Parmenides," *A Guide To Greek Thought* (London: Belknap Press, 2000), 138-49.

[15] In postmodern philosophy, however, the term being and existence has been clearly redefined for western scholars. One finds this in the works of Husserl, Heidegger, and Tillich. In Husserl, the separation of the object from the subject is removed; in Heidegger the term being (Sein) has no divine counterpart since Heidegger clearly states that Sein is intelligible only within a finite world; in Tillich, existence ends with death, since be-yond the grave the human person no longer exists. Rather, the human person is essentialized.

the same time they wanted to indicate how both divine and human beings are, at least to some degree, alike. All western Christian theologians, whether Augustinian, Dominican, or Franciscan, believe that God's being and created being are different, but they describe this difference in ways which are both philosophically and theologically distinct.[16]

Medieval Christian scholars, when they appropriated Aristotle's understanding of being into the theological world, modified Aristotle's view of being in two basic ways. First, these Christian scholars presented the Christian God as the Supreme Being or as Being-in-itself. Secondly, the Christian God as Supreme Being was presented as the creator of all finite beings. Aristotle did not present Being-in-itself in terms of the "Christian God." Aristotle's Unmoved Mover in no way corresponds to the Christian God. Thirdly, Aristotle did not present God as the creator of all finite beings.[17] In the scholastic period, Aristotle's philosophy, through these major adaptations, was made more harmonious with Christian thought.[18] Nonetheless, the Aristotelian term "being" was transformed by scholastic theology by "relating being" to other key philosophical words. In the Franciscan tradi-

---

[16] Too often, scholars state that for Thomas Aquinas the relationship of being to God and creatures is analogical, and for Scotus the same relationship of being to God and creatures is univocal. Today, this analogical-univocal label for Thomistic-Franciscan thought has been more carefully studied and presented by Franciscan scholars. See Osborne, *A Theology of the Church*, 137-65.

[17] For a carefully worded analysis of Aristotle's presentation of God, see Pierre Pellegrin, "Aristotle," *A Guide to Greek Thought*, 32-53.

[18] The western philosophical position is far more complicated and nuanced than I am able to present here. It should be noted, however, that in almost all of the Asian languages there is no word which corresponds to the western term, 'being.' Naturally, Asian authors have used a word in their own languages to translate the western term 'being' and its cognates. However, these co-opted Asian words merely serve the needs of translation for western philosophical volumes. The same is true of the Native Americans from the northern parts of Canada to the southern tip of South America. Native Americans do not think in a 'being' way. The same is true for the many languages in Africa and on the islands off the East African shoreline. All of these non-western linguistic groups are based on a relational form of episteme and do not have a native word corresponding to the western term, 'being.'

tion, these other key words are *goodness, love, freedom*, and *infinity*.

In his *Commentary on the Four Books of Sentences*, Bonaventure answers the first question, "Does God exist?"[19] very briefly. A similar question appears in his *Disputed Questions on the Trinity*.[20] In both instances, Bonaventure is not asking a reality-question: "Does God actually exist or not?" Bonaventure had no doubt that God exists, and in his writings he makes it clear that all men and women should acknowledge the existence of God. In his questions, Bonaventure is focused on our intellectual ability to reasonably acknowledge that God exists.[21]

In the second question of the *Sentences*, however, Bonaventure goes into greater detail about God. Here he speaks of a relational, Trinitarian God. The question reads: Whether a plurality of persons can be attributed to God? (*Utrum in Deo ponenda sit personarum pluralitas?*)[22] Bonaventure answers his second question in the affirmative, and he provides four reasons why a plurality of persons – and therefore relationality – should be predicated of God. He describes these four aspects as follows:

1. **Simplicity (*Simplicitas*)**: In virtue of simplicity (*simplicitas*), the divine essence is communicable and can exist in multiplicity (*communicabilis et potens esse in pluribus*).

2. **Primacy (*Primitas*)**: In virtue of firstness (*primitas*), a person is born to produce another from one's self (*persona nata est ex se aliam producere*). This

---

[19] Bonaventure, I Sent., d. 8, q. 1, a. 1, q. 2, *Opera Omnia* (Quaracchi: Collegium S. Bonaventurae, 1882-1902).

[20] Bonaventure, *Disputed Questions on the Trinity*, q. 1, a. 1, WSB III, introduction and translation by Zachary Hayes (St. Bonaventure, NY: Franciscan Institute, 2000).

[21] "The basic question, for Bonaventure, is never about the existence or non-existence of God, but only about the impossibility of reasonably thinking of God as non-existing.... There can be no rational doubt about God's existence." See Zachary Hayes, "Bonaventure: Mystery of the Triune God," *The History of Franciscan Theology*, ed. Kenan B. Osborne (St. Bonaventure, NY: Franciscan Institute, 2007), 53.

[22] Bonaventure, I Sent., d. 2, a. 1, q. 2.

firstness he calls "non-born-ableness" (*innascibilitas*) and fontal fullness (*fontalis plenitudo*).

3. **Perfection (*Perfectio*)**: In virtue of perfection (*perfectio*), plurality is both apt and at hand (*apta et prompta*).

4. **Blessedness and Love (*Beatitudo et Caritas*)**: In virtue of blessedness and love (*beatitudo et caritas*), plurality is voluntary (*voluntaria*).[23]

All four of these realities, simplicity, primacy, perfection, and blessedness-love, are based on the very nature of God. All four form the basis for a plurality of persons in God. *Only because* the very being of God is itself simplicity, primacy, perfection, and blessedness-love can Christians speak of a plurality of persons.[24] In the case of simplicity or *simplicitas* he writes: "In virtue of simplicity, essence is communicable and able to be in plurality." In the case of primacy or *primitas* he writes: "To produce another." In the case of perfection or *perfectio*, he describes it as *apta et prompta*, which indicates that perfection is apt (*apta*) and at hand (*prompta*). The terms apt and at hand are clearly relational since one is apt or at hand *for something or someone*. In the case of blessedness and love (*beatitudo et caritas*), Bonaventure describes them

---

[23] Bonaventure, I Sent., d. 2, a. 1, q. 2.

[24] The reader will find that throughout this chapter I use a parallel to Bonaventure's approach. Bonaventure's argument is this: only because the very being of God is itself *simplicitas, primitas, perfectio* and *beatitudo et caritas*, can Christians speak of a plurality of persons. I use a different format: stressing the fact that since God's very being (*esse* and *ens*) is relational, we are able to speak of a plurality in God. That we refer to this relationality as Father, Son, and Spirit is metaphorical. In actuality, God is not a father if by this we use a "univocal" understanding of father. Nor is God a "son" if we use son in a univocal way. Nor is God a "spirit" if we use spirit in a univocal way. The three names, father, son and spirit, have clear meanings in our human languages. When applied to God they are only analogical or equivocal. But analogy is metaphorical if one begins with a secondary meaning. If we apply the term "Father" to God and God is the basic analog itself, then human paternity can be only metaphorical; if we apply the term father to humans as the basic analog, then divine paternity can only be metaphorical. The Trinity is not based on metaphors. The Trinity is based on divine *esse* and *ens* and these are relational in themselves.

as voluntary (*voluntaria*).[25] Since these attributes, blessed-ness and love, are voluntary, they arise from God's infinitely free will. This implies that there is a loving relationship.

Each of the basic realities of God has, in Bonaventure's explanation, a profound relational characteristic. If these four words provide Bonaventure with an understanding of God, then for Bonaventure God is indeed ultimately relation-al. On the basis of this ultimate relationality, we can speak of God – but only secondarily – as specifically triune, using the metaphorical terms: Father, Son, and Spirit. One might state the situation as follows: God is first and basically "relation-able." Only on this basis of "relationability" can one speak of God as triune.

By now it is becoming clear why González and other Franciscan scholars can say that Bonaventure has formu-lated a third western theology of the Trinity, very different from that of Augustine, or Richard of St. Victor, or Thomas Aquinas. The Trinitarian theology of Bonaventure is based in some measure on the early Eastern Fathers of the church and in this respect it is part of the tradition of the Christian Church. It is unique in the same way that Augustine's, Rich-ard's and Thomas's Trinitarian theologies are unique.

## B. Good

The relationship of two realities, namely God and good-ness, is especially central for Bonaventure's understanding of God. For Bonaventure, God is goodness. Bonaventure came to this insight in many ways because of the spirituality of Francis and Clare, and the diffusive goodness of God became a major position in Bonaventure's theological understanding of the Trinitarian God.

In his *Nicomachean Ethics,* Aristotle raised the ques-tion: what is morally good and what is morally evil?[26] In this context, Aristotle was interested in the ethical dimension of goodness. In metaphysical contexts, Aristotle and other

---

[25] Bonaventure, I Sent., d. 2, a. 1, q. 2.

[26] Aristotle, "Nicomachean Ethics," *The Basic Works of Aristotle,* ed. Richard McKeon (New York, NY: Modern Library, 1941), I, 2-13, 935-52.

philosophers have connected "being" with "good" in an onto-logical way, and even in a transcendentally ontological way. These philosophers taught that every being is in itself good (*omne ens est bonum*). In the history of western philosophy, "good" denotes an ontological quality of being as well as a transcendental quality. Metaphysically, all beings are good at the very basis of their essence, nature, and existence. If being is good at such a profound depth, then all reality is likewise good in its transcendental dimension.

However, if all reality is good, then how do we account for the presence of evil in our day-to-day world? Based upon the primacy of being over non-being, Western philosophers generally reply that evil is basically an absence, a negative. Evil itself has no actual being. Evil is always the "lack" of something good or the "privation" of something good, just as the term "blindness" refers to the absence of sight. Unavoid-ably, a "pseudo-form of being or actuality" appears linguistically when one speaks of evil. Some "thing" has to "be" before it can "be evil." Some thing not only must first "be" but also must first "be good" before one can speak of something as evil. When one speaks of evil, the "pseudo-form of being" be-comes evident in such statements as: "it *is* evil to do x." Or to say: "that action *is* evil." If evil is the lack of being, how can we say, in these cases, that "evil *is*" or "that an action *is* evil." Unfortunately, this is the result of the way language is used: when we *speak* about evil, we have no choice except to use the term *is* in a "pseudo-form" as if evil *is*.

God is good, and goodness in Bonaventure's approach is a divine dimension which he defines in a very special way. He uses the term "diffusive" or even more sharply "self-diffusive" to describe God's goodness. Because goodness is diffusive of its very self, it is a radically relational term. Diffusion of goodness entails both diffusion "from" and diffusion "to." This clarification indicates that one must employ relational lan-guage, namely, diffusive goodness has a relation to its source and it also has a relation to its object or goal.

It is not too difficult to think of God's diffusive goodness in regard to creation. The goodness found in all of creation comes *from* God as a gift *to* all of creation. Created goodness comes from the divine nature. Everything that God does is done well. The world is the recipient of God's goodness. This God-creation approach has its own validity, but it rests on a presupposition, namely, that God – who has gifted all creation and each creature – is not merely good but intrinsically or essentially good. This way of considering creation and God moves from the goodness of creation to the intrinsic goodness of the divine Creator.

Bonaventure's position on divine goodness takes a slightly different tack. In this way, he moves to a different and more profound level. To understand his approach we must set the goodness of creation aside for a moment. In doing this, we raise a different question: "If there were no created worlds at all, is God still diffusively good?" In this second consideration, we are not viewing God relationally as a creator of a distinct world. Rather, we are looking at God relationally from within God's own self. We face a new and radically different question: "Is God in God's own self – just as God – diffusively (and therefore relationally) good?" In this inner-God context, the term diffusive raises the same two issues: diffusive *from what* and diffusive *toward what*? In God, can there be intrinsically a "from" and a "toward"?

If someone is good, the person usually wants to share this goodness with others. The goodness within a human person is a goodness which, more often than not, needs to be shared with others. For Bonaventure, God is being and God is also good. Therefore, in God's own being there is the reality of God diffusing God's own self. Through the word *being*, Bonaventure states that God is and exists. Through the word *good*, Bonaventure tells us *how* God exists. God exists by giving. God's inner goodness is relational and a gift. But since there is as yet no creation, *to whom* does God give? Bonaventure answers: to God's own self. Within the very nature of God, this diffusive and relational, dynamic "good-being" provides the basis for what Christians call Trinity.

Time and again, Bonaventure describes God in a relational way. Only because God in God's own self is *sui diffusi-*

*vum*, can there be a diffusion of God's goodness to something which is not God. For Christians, this other-than-God reality is evident in creation, in the Incarnation, and in the sending of the Spirit. God's actions are both internal (*ad intra*) and external (*ad extra*). The dynamism of God is an internal sharing of goodness. Externally, the dynamism of God is a sharing of goodness with a creature. Creation is not simply an action of God as first cause. Creation is a diffusive action of God's own being and goodness to those who are not God. Too often a "first cause" tends to be mechanistic. For Bonaventure, and for Scotus, goodness and love as well as the giving of goodness and the sharing of love surpass a mechanistic approach. In a theological way, this moving beyond a "first cause" echoes the words of Francis of Assisi cited above: "Lord God, you are good, all good, supreme good."

Keeping in mind this approach of Bonaventure to God's internal goodness and love, let us inquire how Scotus understands God's own infinite goodness and love. In the writings of Scotus, God's love and goodness permeate his theology of God, but he emphasizes perhaps more than Bonaventure the infinity and freedom of God. No creature has "infinite goodness" and no creature is "infinitely free." God, in God's own self, is infinitely and freely loving and good. Nothing outside of God is the basis why God is infinite, loving, and free. Allan Wolter states Scotus's position as follows:

> What he [Scotus] is trying to rule out is the suggestion that this natural goodness [namely the natural goodness of creation itself] somehow moves God's creative will in the way his own infinite goodness does, for no creature has a claim to actual existence simply in virtue of the sort of thing it happens to be.[27]

Wolter is stressing that for Scotus, God's own goodness is *self-moving*. God is not ultimately moved because of the "goodness" seen in a creature. If God is self-moving – and

---

[27] Allan Wolter, *Duns Scotus on the Will and Morality* (Washington, DC: The Catholic University of America Press, 1986), 17.

this does not mean a move outward to creation – how is God *internally self-moving*? What does moving one's self involve?

In the same way that diffusive love requires some sort of relational dimension, so too does self-moving require some sort of relational dimension. Theoretically, God is first of all a relational being; only secondarily can God be called Trinitarian. Before one arrives at the number three there is a need not only for a base of "one," but a base for a "relational one." All of this is conceptual, since, in actuality, God is both being and simultaneously diffusive goodness and infinitely free love. The conjunction of being with diffusive goodness, love, freedom, and infinity indicates that the very nature of God is relational. Only on the basis that God's very nature is relational can we arrive at Father, Son, and Holy Spirit. God does not need a creature in order to be diffusively good, to be loving, to be free, and to be infinite.

It is one thing to say that God is or God exists. It is another thing to say that God is diffusively good, loving, free, and infinite. The western term, "being," denotes a form of immutability. One person either exists or does not exist. An individual thing either is or is not. To be, in the western understanding of being, does not connote or denote relationality. One is or is not. One exists or does not exist. Being tends to be monolithic and non-relational.

Goodness, however, denotes relationality, and relationality often denotes some form of degree. For instance, one person evidences goodness more than another person does. One person is more loving than another person. One person is more free than another individual. No human person is infinitely good, loving, and free, which means that each person can always exhibit more goodness, love, and freedom.

How do the Franciscan scholars unite immutable being with relational goodness? They do this by viewing God as a relational God in God's own being. Being itself is relational. Nowhere in the writings of Bonaventure and Scotus do we find this last sentence: being itself is relational. However, given the additional terms which are coextensive with being, namely goodness, love, freedom, and infinity, the understanding of "being" cannot help but be relational. The conclusion that being itself is relational seems to be unavoidable. The term *infinity* is key to this conclusion. When the term *infinity* is applied to the terms being, love, self-moving, self-diffusive goodness, and freedom, then all these terms become co-extensive and, therefore, interrelational. In this approach, *being* is not more infinite than the other terms, love, self-diffusive goodness, self-moving, and freedom.

## C. Love

In John's Gospel, we read: "God is love" (1 John 4:16). For John, God is intrinsically love. God's very being is love. Scotus took these words seriously. Scotus unites being and love in a way similar to Bonaventure who united being and goodness together. God's being is "being in love."[28] If God is Being Itself, Scotus argues, then God is Love Itself. The "being" of God cannot be understood unless it is simultaneously seen as the "love" of God. A conclusion cannot help but be drawn: namely, being, when predicated of God who is also love, is dynamic and relational, not static and immutable. For Scotus, God's dynamism is love-being, and God's love-being is relational.[29]

When we say that God is love, we mean something much deeper than mere preference or enjoyment. In Scotus, God's very being is intrinsically and infinitely love, just as in Bonaventure God's very being is intrinsically diffusive goodness. The words from the Gospel of John are a powerful witness to this combination of God as love and being. In John's Gospel, from chapter thirteen to chapter twenty-one, the term love

---

[28] See Freyer, 59: "Two biblical principles guide Scotus in his search for God: 'I am who am,' [Exodus 3:14] and 'God is love' [1 John 4:16]. The two biblical passages form the basic point of departure for Scotus' further thinking on God." In this section, Freyer describes how Scotus interrelates, in an intrinsic way, being and infinite love. In Scotus, the two terms express one and the same reality: God.

[29] Scotus, Ord. I, d. 3, p. 1, q. 2, n. 59; Ord. I, d. 2, p. 4, q. unica, n. 2; also Ord. I, d. 2, p. 1, q. 2 n. 89, in *Opera Omnia*, Civitas Vaticana, vv. 5 to 9.

dominates the message of the author.[30] Love helps us understand the washing of the apostles' feet by Jesus. Love helps us understand Gethsemane. Love is expressed in the arrest, suffering, and death of Jesus. Love helps us understand Jesus' words to his mother, "Woman, behold your son!" and the words to the disciple whom he loved: "Behold your mother." In John's Gospel, love is the reason why God did not accept the people's rejection of Jesus when they crucified him. Out of love, God would not take our "no" as the answer to his gift of Jesus. "God so loved the world that he gave his only son" (John 3:16). In love, God gave new life to the crucified Jesus through the resurrection. In love, God, through the risen Jesus, has given us everlasting life. God's gift of the resurrection is a major sign of God's compassionate and forgiving love. In spite of our own rejection of Jesus, whenever we sin, God continues to say "I still love you."

When Scotus says that God is intrinsically love and intrinsically being, he is saying – at least indirectly – that both being and love are relationally interconnected. Scotus continually stresses that God's being and God's love are one and the same. This union of being and love is a central part of the Franciscan theology of a Trinitarian God.

Scotus, throughout his career, continually posed the question: can the human intellect come to any knowledge whatsoever about God? From a theological standpoint, he also posed a continual question: can the human intellect have some understanding of a Trinitarian God? Ingham offers an overview of Scotus's early position on the Trinity and also his subtle changes in a later position.[31] Ingham stresses that mutual-

---

[30] Up to the thirteenth chapter of John's Gospel, the term which is used most frequently is "life." From chapter twelve on, it is the word "love" which dominates the fourth Gospel.

[31] Mary Elizabeth Ingham, "John Duns Scotus: An Integrated Vision," *The History of Franciscan Theology*, ed. Kenan Osborne (St. Bonaventure, NY: The Franciscan Institute, 1993), 185-230. She concludes the section on the divine essence as Trinity with this statement, 218: "The Trinity is a communion of persons which exemplifies the goal of all human activity: that union with another or others out of live lies at the heart of reality, and that this union is generative and life-giving. In its fullness, the human experience and mutuality is the image of divine life."

ity, which includes love, pervades Scotus's entire presentation on the one God and on the Triune God. After a lengthy section on Scotus's approach to individuality (*haecceitas* or "thisness"), Ingham states:

> Close examination of Scotist texts reveals another, deeper concern to unify all aspects of reality both human and divine. This deeper concern I call mutuality, which I understand to mean a dynamic state of relatedness existing between two or among three or more individuals.... Although Scotus does not use the word itself, I identify his discussion of essential order in the *De Primo Principio* as offering a type of mutuality.[32]

Ingham goes on to state that "[t]he centrality of relatedness and mutuality appear in an exemplary manner in Scotus's discussion of the Trinity."[33] Ingham moves on to show that Scotus's earlier writings on the Trinity emphasized the traditional approach, namely, that relationality was the primary basis for the three persons in the Trinity. In a later writing, the *Lectura*, Scotus advances a different position, namely that each Trinitarian person is understood in an "absolute" way, and only then is there a "relational interplay" among the three persons.[34] To express the depth of the Trinitarian discussion, one can place relationality itself at the very core of divine life, which is being, love, goodness, freedom, and infinity. From this foundational relationality, one arrives at the distinction of the three persons in the Trinity.

## D. Freedom

In the theological world of the thirteenth century, it was Scotus who championed the absolute freedom of God in a most powerful way,[35] but God's freedom was also a part of the

---

[32] Ingham, "John Duns Scotus: An Integrated Vision," 210-11.
[33] Ingham, "John Duns Scotus: An Integrated Vision," 212.
[34] Ingham, "John Duns Scotus: An Integrated Vision," 212-18.
[35] Giorgio Pini, *Categories and Logic in Duns Scotus: An Interpretation of Aristotle's Categories in the Late Thirteenth Century* (Leiden: Brill, 2002)

spiritual vision of Francis. For Francis, all creation is a free gift of God. In the first rule, Francis writes:

> All powerful, most holy, almighty and supreme God, holy and just Father, Lord, King of heaven and earth, we thank you for yourself, for *through your holy will* and through your only Son with the Holy Spirit, you have created everything spiritual and corporal, and after making us in your image and likeness, you placed us in paradise.[36]

Francis sees that all creation comes to us as a gift of God when he writes *through your holy will*. In his comments on this section of the rule, Freyer notes that Francis is considering the inner-dynamic of the Trinity, which is a freely given love, to be the foundation of all created beings, even the ultimate foundation of all creation.[37] Creation exists because God freely loved creation into existence.

Freedom is a term which is used at many levels. Two-year-old children are inquisitive and want to run around *freely*. Teenagers are looking forward to more and more *freedom* from parental control. In the United States, *freedom* has become a politically over-arching term, as we find in such phrases as: freedom of the press, freedom of expression, freedom to vote, etc.

In a recent book by Mary Beth Ingham and Mechthild Dreyer, *The Philosophical Vision of Duns Scotus*, the issue of the rational will and freedom is analyzed at great length.[38]

---

writes, 200-01: "Scotus, like (Radulphus) Brito, maintains that relations are real things, really distinguished from the other categories. Actually, in his questions on the Metaphysics and in his Sentences commentary, he pays much attention to this issue, and he can be regarded as one of the fiercest champions of the reality of relations."

[36] Francis of Assisi, *Regula non bullata*, 23:1 (italics added), in *FA:ED* 1, 81-82.

[37] Freyer, *Homo Viator*, 34.

[38] Mary Beth Ingham and Mechthild Dreyer, *The Philosophical Vision of John Duns Scotus* (Washington, DC: The Catholic University of America Press, 2004), especially chapter four, "The Rational Will and Freedom," 146-72.

There is a major interplay between the intellect and the will, and by the time of Scotus's *Reportatio*, his position on this interplay reaches its maturity. Scotus does not attempt to liberate freedom from reason; rather, he integrates the two in a way which maintains the basic freedom of the will and yet the will itself, prior to any willing, non-willing, or refraining from willing/non-willing (*velle/nolle/non velle*), exists in a nature that clearly has its own nature-for-the-good. The will operates on the basis of its pre-operational "rational nature." In this sense, the will for Scotus is rational not irrational.[39]

Throughout the thirteenth century, Aristotle's axiom that everything which is moved must be moved by something else was widely discussed by almost all the scholastic philosophers and theologians. These scholars interpreted Aristotle's axiom in various ways. This discussion often focused on the relationship of the human will and the human intellect. Thomas Aquinas adhered to this axiom in a strong way, and his adherence to Aristotle shaped the way that he related the will's activity to the intellect's activity and vice versa. Scotus's approach to freedom of the will did not depend so strongly on Aristotle's axiom.[40]

Scotus, however, sees in the free will of a human being the highest image of God. God is absolutely free. Even though humans are limited in their freedom, one's finite free will images the very center of God at least in a limited way. Every human person has free will, and any constraint of one's free will needs to be morally and philosophically justified in a way which does not negate the freedom of one's will.

Human freedom, though essential for moral living, is not absolute. Again and again, we find ourselves limited in what we can and cannot do. Civil laws often limit our freedom. For instance, we may want to travel in our car at a speed of

---

[39] Ingham/Dreyer, *The Philosophical Vision of John Duns Scotus*, 168-72. This issue will be taken up in Chapter Three by Mary Beth Ingham herself.

[40] For a thorough discussion of Thomas Aquinas's view, see John F. Wippel, *The Metaphysical Thought of Thomas Aquinas* (Washington, DC: The Catholic University of America Press, 2000), 444-59. In his discussion, Wippel presents the view of Thomas Aquinas in a thorough way.

eighty miles per hour, but we are in a twenty-five mile-per-hour speed zone, and the flashing red light of the police car indicates that we will pay for our "misuse" of freedom.

For Scotus, the absolute freedom of God is highly emphasized, and his emphasis on God's freedom can be found rooted in the spirituality of Francis and Clare.[41] Francis often says: "The Lord gave me brothers." "The Lord led me to the lepers." "The Lord told me to rebuild the church." Francis surrendered his free will to the wishes of God. Francis *let* God love him in and through his surrendering of himself to God. God gave Francis, along with all other human beings, a free will. In this gifting, God *lets* men and women be free. God's *letting* is a freely given gift. Human *letting* is also a freely given gift, for human love is freely given and freely received.

In the Franciscan theological approach to God, God is infinitely relational: infinitely diffusive goodness and infinitely loving freedom. Francis and Clare caught a glimpse of God's diffusive goodness and loving freedom as they contemplated the world around them (the book of creation). God's diffusive goodness and loving freedom allowed Francis to see a brother and sister in all creation. When Francis and Clare read about Jesus (the book of the Scriptures) they saw in the human Jesus God's diffusive love and God's loving freedom. When they turned into the depths of their own being (the book of the interior life) they listened to the same God who is diffusive love and loving freedom. What Bonaventure and Scotus presented in a theological way was based on the spiritual vision of Francis and Clare. Their presentation of a relational God is the foundation for the entire Franciscan intellectual tradition. The theological presentation of a relational God shapes and colors all other subaltern aspects of theology.

---

[41] Cf. Fryer, *Homo Viator*, 32, where he notes that Scotus's "voluntarism" or an emphasis on the will plays a major role in Franciscan theology.

## II. THE CENTRALITY OF CREATION,
## INCARNATION AND THE SENDING OF THE HOLY SPIRIT
## IN THE WRITINGS OF THE EARLY FRANCISCAN SCHOLARS

In the twelfth and thirteenth centuries, theologians focused on the Triune God in three different ways, as we have seen above. These theologies of God centered on the life of God *ad intra*, in God's own self. With this theology of God *ad intra*, theologians then turned to the actions of God *ad extra*, or to a God who is a creator-God. In our Christian faith, there are three actions of God *ad extra* which are central. The first is creation itself. The second is the sending of the Logos into the humanity of Jesus (the Incarnation). The third is the sending of the Holy Spirit. How do these three actions of God *ad extra* interrelate with one another? In the history of Christian theology, various theological positions have taken place.

When the medieval theologians attempted to provide a resolution to their efforts to unite creation, Incarnation, and the sending of the Spirit, they confronted a major problem, namely the issue of evil or, more pointedly expressed, the issue of human sin. How can we join together creation, redemption, and Incarnation? Did the Incarnation take place in order to redeem sinful humanity, or was the Incarnation an original part of the creative action of God?

For some theologians, the Incarnation was not part of God's original plan of creation. Only when Adam and Eve had sinned did God decide to send Jesus as our redeemer. Other theologians, in the tradition of the Christian Church, preferred the position that God, from the very first moment of creation onward, included in his act of creation the sending of both the Logos-made-flesh (Jesus) and the sending of the Holy Spirit.

Both theological positions have deep roots in the New Testament, in the writings of the early Fathers of the Church, and in the Christian tradition generally. Since the Reformation in the sixteenth century, almost all of the western Christian Churches have presented the first view: when God created the world, there was a time of grace and goodness. The sin of Adam and Eve, however, rejected this grace and goodness and when this happened, God provided a second chance for holiness and redemption. This second chance was the sending of Jesus who died for our sins.

Franciscan theology, however, did not accept this theological view of the redemption. Rather, the Franciscan theologians retained the Eastern Church approach that from the very beginning of creation, a major part of God's plan was to send his Son into our world. For the Franciscans, creation and incarnation are of one piece.

The dividing issue for these two approaches centers on the meaning and role of redemption. Why did Jesus die? Did the death of Jesus bring about the salvation of all men and women, or was there a different message in the death of Jesus itself? In his book, *Jesus: An Experiment in Christology*, Eduard Schillebeeckx combed the views of biblical scholars and arrived at the following conclusion.[42] In the New Testament there are three different interpretations for the death of Jesus.

1. The death of Jesus was interpreted as that of a prophet-martyr. This view has some basis in the Old Testament passages, for there were indeed some prophets who were martyred because their teaching was not acceptable.
2. The death of Jesus was interpreted as a key part of the divine plan of salvation. In this view, Jesus' death, in the same way as his life, was part and parcel of God's plan from creation onward.
3. The death of Jesus was interpreted in terms of redemption or an atonement death, and therefore salvation of sinful men and women depended on the death of Jesus.

Schillebeeckx treats each of these interpretations in detail, citing passages from the New and Old Testaments for

---

[42] Eduard Schillebeeckx, *Jesus: An Experiment in Christology* (New York: Crossroad, 1981), 272-94.

each respective position. At the end, he offers the following summation.

> All that we have established so far is that in early Christianity there were three complexes of tradition, existing side by side, in which Jesus' death is variously interpreted, three blocks of tradition all of which appear to be *very* old, but with no very cogent grounds for assigning any chronological order to them.[43]

In the New Testament itself, there are several attempts to provide a "theology" for the ignominious death of Jesus. No one view dominates the New Testament writings. Rather, in these three approaches to the meaning of the death of Jesus, we can see how the early Jesus-communities struggled to find a theological understanding of Jesus' death in relationship to Jesus' role as messiah or *Christos*.

The same struggle can be seen in the Christian communities which developed during the second and third centuries. In this period of time, baptismal creeds were formulated. In these creeds, the wording simply reads: we believe that Jesus died for our sins. No explanation of his death and its relation to sin is stated. The judgment of J. N. D. Kelly regarding a theology of redemption in the first few centuries of Christian history remains valid. He writes:

> The development of the Church's ideas about the saving effects of the incarnation was a slow, long drawn-out process. Indeed, while the conviction of redemption through Christ has always been the motive force of Christian faith, no final and universally accepted definition of the manner of its achievement has been formulated to this day. Thus it is useless to look for any systematic treatment of the doctrine in the popular Christianity of [the sub-apostolic age].[44]

---

[43] Schillebeeckx, *Jesus: An Experiment in Christology,* 294.

[44] J. N. D. Kelly, *Early Christian Doctrines*, 5th ed. (London: Continuum, 2004), 163.

The redemption did not become a major battleground for rival theological schools until the twelfth century, when Anselm wrote his famous book, *Cur Deus homo* (c. 1097). In the Christian writings prior to Anselm, a student has to pick his or her way through a variety of theories on redemption, all of which appeared here and there during the first ten centuries. These early statements on redemption are often unrelated to each other and some are even mutually incompatible. In some early theological writings, a few authors simply placed incompatible positions on redemption side by side.[45]

In the theological history of redemption, three different positions appeared: Jesus was presented as a *Victor*, or Jesus was presented as a *Victim*, or Jesus was presented as a *Revealer*.[46] In other words, in the crucifixion of Jesus, Christians can see Jesus as a victor over death, sin and the devil. Or, Christians can see in the crucifixion of Jesus that Jesus repaid the debt which the sin of Adam and Eve required. Or, Christians can see in the crucifixion of Jesus how much God loves us. The death of Jesus is an expression of God's love.

In recent times, theologians have reformulated the standard three theologies of the redemption.[47] Whether any of these new views will ever become common in the Christian community remains an open question. However, the theological view of Jesus as Victim has tended to dominate – even today – the Anglican, Protestant, Roman Catholic, Pentecos-

---

[45] Kelly, *Early Christian Doctrines*, 375. In the history of soteriology, three different theological positions have been proposed: Jesus as Victor, Jesus as Victim, and Jesus as Revealer. For an excellent study of these three forms of soteriology see Gustav Aulén, *Christus Victor*, Eng. trans. A. G. Hebert (New York: Macmillan, 1969).

[46] For a clear presentation of the three standard soteriologies, see Gustav Aulén, *Christus Victor*.

[47] See F. W. Dillistone, *The Christian Understanding of Atonement* (London: Westminster, 1968); Dieter Wiederkehr, *Belief in Redemption: Explorations in Doctrine from the New Testament to Today* (Louisville: Westminster/John Knox, 1979); and Neil Ormerod, *Creation, Grace and Redemption*; René Girard, *I See Satan Fall Like Lightning* (Maryknoll, NY: Orbis, 2007); Raymund Schwager, *Jesus in the Drama of Salvation: Toward a Biblical Doctrine of Redemption* (New York: Crossroad, 1999); Anthony W. Bartlett, *Cross Purposes: The Violent Grammar of Christian Atonement* (Harrisburg, PA: Trinity Press International, 2001).

tal and Free Church understanding of Jesus' death. That Jesus died for our sins is echoed in the many hymns of these churches. Jesus as Victim is the ordinary or standard view of the death of Jesus. Let us consider this standard situation in some detail, for there are some serious problems in this theological approach to the death of Jesus.

## A. The Standard Christian Approach to Redemption

At creation, God produced a world which we call Paradise, the Garden of Eden, or a place of perfect bliss and delight. Such a Paradise required no redeemer, since there was no sin. If there was no need for a redeemer, there was also no need for the Incarnation, since the Logos became flesh in order to save humankind from its sinful state. In this theological format, there is a disjunct between creation on the one hand and Incarnation on the other hand. Adam and Eve were in the state of grace in the time after they were created. Being in the state of grace means that the Holy Spirit was with them. Only when they sinned did they lose sanctifying grace and the presence of the Holy Spirit in their life. At this juncture of serious sin, Adam and Eve needed salvation. It was at this same juncture that God promised to send Jesus to be the savior of the world. Only through some form of redemption could they once again be filled with the Holy Spirit. In this approach, there is also a disjunct between creation and the sending of the Holy Spirit. A resending of the Holy Spirit became necessary so that Adam and Eve, and also all further human offspring, might once again attain the grace of God and eternal salvation.

In many ways, this approach to the relationship of creation, Incarnation, and the sending of the Spirit remains a standard part of contemporary theology, whether Anglican, Protestant, Evangelical, Free Church, or Roman Catholic. In all of these churches, the hymns and the liturgical prayers continue to speak of creation as an initial act of God. Because of original sin, the Incarnation of Jesus and the sending of the Spirit became God's way of saving men and women through their belief in Jesus. This theological view has had a long history in the Christian community. However, it is only a theological tradition. It is not a defined doctrinal tradition.

## B. The Franciscan Approach to Redemption

The Franciscan approach to redemption is different, but it is a position which is based on the New Testament and on the early Fathers of the Church. This approach to redemption was, therefore, not a theological view only since the time of Francis, Clare, Bonaventure and Scotus. Rather, Franciscan medieval theologians emphasized an approach to redemption which was a very strong position in many of the early Fathers of the Church.

In his essay, "Était-il nécessaire que le Christ mourût sur la croix?" (Was it necessary that Christ die on the cross?), Luc Mathieu summarizes the Franciscan position in a clear and concise way.[48] He states that Scotus carefully explains Anselm's approach, wanting to honor Anselm as best he can.[49] However, Scotus's basic issue with Anselm centers on Anselm's position that the death of Jesus was necessary. Scotus begins his own presentation on the basis of God's absolute gratuity for all actions *ad extra*. He unites creation, the sending of the Logos, and the sending of the Holy Spirit. All three actions *ad extra* arise from an infinitely free and loving God, and all three actions *ad extra* are willed by God in union with each other. Matthieu interprets Scotus's foundation as follows:

> The benevolent will of God prompts God to offer the sinner a possibility of salvation, thereby associating him/her to the glory of his Christ who is the crowning point of created reality. God's pardon is an act of pure gratuity, of pure benevolence, which is connected to the act of creation, but which, from our point of view,

---

[48] Luc Mathieu, "Était-il nécessaire que le Christ mourût sur la croix? Duns Scot À Paris" (Turnhout, Belgium: Brepols, 2004), 581-91.

[49] See John Duns Scotus, *Opus. Oxoniense* (Civitas Vaticana: 1982 ff.), ed. E. Balić, III, d. 20, q. 1.

is formally a secondary reference to the primary vision [or creation]: to create all things and to establish them in Christ. There is no other necessity than the divine free will, and God's gratuitous love and omnipotence.[50]

The Tridentine *Decree on Justification* corroborates Scotus's position. In the official text, we read: "The beginning of justification in adults must be based on the prevenient grace of God through Jesus Christ, by which they are called through no existing merits of their own."[51] The human nature of Jesus in its essence and in its actions is a created human nature, and therefore the human actions of Jesus, including his human suffering and his human dying, cannot be seen as an "infinite satisfaction." Rather, his suffering and dying are meritorious because they reflect the grace or gift of God. Forgiveness of sin is a gift of God.

Freyer emphasizes that the Franciscan theologians of the thirteenth century maintained a form of soteriology which was based on the gift of God's forgiving grace.

First of all, it must be stated that in the Franciscan theology, there is no special teaching on justification. This [a theology of justification] is subordinate to the Franciscan teaching on grace.[52]

Actually, one might make this more precise: Franciscan soteriology is based on the Trinitarian God who is *bonum sui diffusivum* (Bonaventure) and on the infinite free and loving will of a Trinitarian God (Scotus). Such a foundation precludes any possibility of a creature, including the human nature of Jesus, necessitating God in any way at all. It also indicates the radical contingency of all creatures, whether this creature is Satan who has no ability whatsoever to ne-

---

[50] Matthieu, "Duns Scot À Paris," 588.

[51] Henricus Denziger, *Enchiridion Symbolorum: Definitionum et Declarationum de Rebus Fidei et Morum* (Fribourg: Herder & Co., 1937) Conc. Tridentium 1525, Sessio VI, 797, 286.

[52] Freyer, *Homo Viator*, 244.

cessitate how a Trinitarian God acts, or whether this creature is the human nature of Jesus, who again has no ability in and through his human nature to necessitate how a Trinitarian God acts. Matthieu states this situation in a Franciscan way.

> Furthermore, was it necessary that humanity be restored and that Christ had to suffer? It is important not to forget that creation is a divinely gratuitous act, as is every divine action *ad extra.* The predestination of humanity for both existence and for glory which is supernatural purpose [of human life] is itself contingent and totally gratuitous. This predestination finds its only raison d'être in the free will of God.[53]

The two citations from Matthieu which I have cited above sum up in a very clear way the position of Scotus on salvation. Indeed, God's creative act, God's salvific act, and God's action of risen life for men and women are all presented as gratuitous acts of a loving and compassionate God. Scotus's point of departure is consistently based on the absolute freedom and love of God's will. Many Franciscan theologians today have expressed the same understanding of redemption which Matthieu has presented.[54]

The cosmic view of Bonaventure in which everything is a vestige, image, and a similitude helps us today to see God's love and compassion in a globalized and multi-cultural world. To all of this should be added the need to unite creation, the mission and manifestation of the Logos, and the mission and manifestation of the Spirit. This interconnection is a central part of the Franciscan tradition and is a major foundation of Franciscan moral theology.

Hayes expresses the central approach of Bonaventure as follows:

---

[53] Matthieu, "Duns Scot À Paris," 584.
[54] See the writings of Johannes Freyer, Juan Iammarrone, Bernardino de Armellada, Leon Seiler, Déodat de Basly, Zachary Hayes, Ambrose Van Si Nguyen, and José Antonio Merino.

This understanding of the revelatory character of creation and of history is held together by the affirmation of the identity of the divine Word as *increatum*, *incarnatum*, and *inspiratum*. As *increatum*, the eternal Word lies at the very center of the mystery of the triune God. As *incarnatum*, the same Word lies at the center of creation, both in a metaphysical sense and in an historical sense. As *inspiratum*, the same Word resides at the center of the spiritual life by the power of the divine Spirit through whom the Word became the *verbum inspiratum* in the human heart. It is, however, through the history of Jesus of Nazareth as the incarnate Word that the mystery of the Eternal Word comes to most explicit consciousness.[55]

Bonaventure sees the incarnate Jesus as the exegesis in time of the eternal mystery in which all created reality is grounded. He unites creation itself to the Incarnation, for God, from the very beginning, included in the creative act the Incarnation of the Logos in the human nature of Jesus, and God also included in the creative act the sending of the Spirit.[56]

Scotus is even more insistent on this interconnection of creation-incarnation-sending of the Spirit. In Scotus, we have the predestination of the incarnate Logos. In the *Reportatio* he writes:

Therefore, I state the issue in the following way: first of all God loves God's own self; secondly, he loves himself in others and this is a chaste love; thirdly, he wants to be loved by another who can love him in a supreme way, and here I am speaking of a love of someone outside of God; and fourthly, God foresaw the union of

---

[55] Hayes, "Bonaventure: Mystery of the Triune God," 84.

[56] Bonaventure in the *Collations on the Seven Gifts of the Holy Spirit* makes a strong reference to the "standard approach" for the meaning of the death of Jesus. See Collation I, 6. In many other works, however, Bonaventure presents what is referred to in the text above as the "Franciscan Approach."

that nature, which would love God in a supreme way, even though no human person had sinned.[57]

In this paragraph, Scotus makes his position very clear. That "God loves himself" is the first and most fundamental aspect of God, for God is infinite love. Secondly, this love is *ad intra* when he says "he loves himself in others," and this is the Trinitarian love. Thirdly, God's love moves outward and God, considering all possible creation, centers on a created human nature (Jesus) who will love God in return and in a supreme way. Fourthly, this love of the human Jesus, united to the Logos, has precedence over the sinful fall of other humans.

## III. IMPLICATIONS FOR FRANCISCAN MORAL THEOLOGY

What Francis, Clare, and the other Franciscans came to see is this: the most high, relational God has related all creatures in a wondrous, beautiful, overarching way. From the very beginning of time, human beings in a special way have been loved into existence by our relational God. The more deeply the Franciscans studied the length and depth, the height and breadth of the created world, the more over-awed they became. For them, moral behavior was a "re-action" to God's relational *ad extra* magnificence. For them, a moral attitude was first and foremost a reaction of wonder and thanksgiving. In their reaction to the infinite, loving, self-giving, and absolutely free God, the Franciscans acknowledged the beauty of God. Even more, they acknowledged that they wanted to love God above all else – the first commandment, which is the basis of all morality.

The Franciscan theology of God, in its depths of relationality and freedom, has shaped every aspect of Franciscan theology, including moral theology. Unless one understands this vision of a relational, loving, infinite, absolutely free and

---

[57] Scotus, *Reportatio Parisiensis* III, d. 7, q. 4, 5, *Opera Omnia*, t. 23 (Paris: Apud Ludovicum Vivès, Bibliopolam Editorem, 1894).

diffusively good God, one will never quite comprehend what Franciscan moral tradition is about.

With this Franciscan approach as the foundation for theology, let us turn our attention to the ways in which such a theology of God, creation, Incarnation, and the sending of the Spirit affects and colors a Franciscan understanding of moral theology. How does one respond to the free and gracious God who has loved us into existence? How does one respond to a created world whose birthplace is the love of God? For Franciscans, moral theology is a response to God, but to which God?

The relational Trinitarian God is not only a relation of Father and Son, but a relation of Father, Son, and Holy Spirit. Bonaventure carefully presents this triadic interrelationship. Creation, he writes, occurs only because God, the Supreme Being, is fundamentally a relational Supreme Being. Freyer states Bonaventure's position in this way:

> Since Bonaventure describes God, The One Who Is [Der Seiende], as the personal being in relationship, who is self-sharing and from whose sharing creation comes, must the relationship and sharing of the highest being not be present even prior to creation?[58]

Consequently, when one wishes to understand Bonaventure's view of creation in its spiritual depth, one must study what Bonaventure has written about the Triune God. The Holy Spirit, in Bonaventure, is presented as the love of the Father for the Son and the love of the Son for the Father.[59] Even more, Bonaventure writes that the Spirit is not only the unifying love between Father and Son, the Spirit is also the goodness (*bonitas*) of both Father and Son. This goodness, in Bonaventure, is diffusive goodness (*bonitas sui diffusiva*).

---

[58] Freyer, *Homo Viator*, 48.

[59] Bonaventure, *Commentary*, I, d. 32, a. 1, q. 1, conclusion: "The Father and the Son love each other, that is the Father loves the Son and the Son loves the Father. Therefore, the [following] statement is true: the [interpersonal] love which is the Holy Spirit is the love binding the Father to the Son and the Son to the Father."

Creation takes place because the Triune God is a diffusive reality, not only *ad intra* but also *ad extra*.

Bonaventure clearly speaks of creation as an *ad extra* gifting of the Triune God. In this gifting, the Holy Spirit is a gift and a goodness given to all creation. In the *Breviloquium*, he writes that "a creature is the effect of a creative Trinity."[60] He also states that "every just and holy spirit possesses the Holy Spirit as an infused gift."[61] The *Breviloquium* contains a summation of Bonaventure's understanding of creation in the following way:

> From all we have said, we may gather that the created world is a kind of book reflecting, representing, and describing its Maker, the Trinity, at three different levels of expression: as a vestige, as an image, and as a likeness.[62]

The entire created world is a book in which the relational God – Father, Son, and Holy Spirit – is present and readable. We do not *read into* creation the presence of God; rather, God's own self *reads out* of creation. It is our task to listen and to understand God's voice in all of creation. In creation, the Son – the Word of God – speaks most clearly in and through the human nature of Jesus. The Holy Spirit speaks most clearly in and through the entirety of creation.

In 1268, only six years before he died, Bonaventure delivered his *Collations on the Seven Gifts of the Holy Spirit*.[63] These lectures were held at the University of Paris, and the audience included young Franciscan students, Franciscan professors, and any other student or professor at the university who wished to attend. There were nine conferences. Beginning on February 25, 1268, the first Sunday of Lent,

---

[60] Bonaventure, *Breviloquium*, part II, chapter 1, *WSB* IX (St. Bonaventure, NY: Franciscan Institute Publications, 2005), 60-61.

[61] Bonaventure, *Breviloquium,* part II, chapter 12, *WSB* IX, 97.

[62] Bonaventure, *Breviloquium*, part II, chapter 12 *WSB* IX, 96.

[63] Bonaventure, *Collationes de Donis Spiritus Sancti*, *Opera Omnia*, vol. 5, 457; Eng. trans. by Zachary Hayes, *Collations on the Seven Gifts of the Holy Spirit* (St. Bonaventure, NY: Franciscan Institute Publications, 2008).

a conference was given weekly throughout Lent. However, three of the conferences – the fifth, sixth, and seventh – were held during the celebration of the Annunciation. The fifth conference was presented on the vigil of the Annunciation; the sixth and seventh conferences were presented on the morning and on the afternoon of the feast itself. These collations or conferences represent a maturity of Bonaventure's position on the Holy Spirit.

Bonaventure's *Collationes* are bluntly ethical. He tells his audience that each person should treasure, both in thinking and acting, the seven gifts of the Holy Spirit. He is deeply concerned about the ethical response of his listeners to the gifts which the Holy Spirit, through Jesus, has offered to each person. Bonaventure's goal is to inspire the moral life of student and professor alike, and he does this by extolling each of the seven gifts of the Spirit. Without opening our minds and hearts to the presence (or gift) of the Spirit, one will never be gifted by these seven qualities of moral behavior.

What are the implications of Bonaventure's many discussions on the Holy Spirit? How do these implications affect our life at the beginning of the third millennium? The implications which follow cannot be directly attributed to Bonaventure himself. Nonetheless, the implications for our day and age are based on his writings and are of importance even though they move beyond the vision of Bonaventure himself.

For contemporary moral theology, the first implication is this: today, based on Bonaventure's writings, we can learn something of God who is present in all creation as vestige, image, and similitude. Consequently, we can find the presence of God in the moral expression developed by cultures other than the Euro-American culture.

Secondly, based on Bonaventure's writings, we can learn something of God and the ethical life in religions other than the Roman Catholic religion. Consequently, we can find the presence of God in the moral and sanctifying realities of Hinduism, Islam, Buddhism, Judaism, etc.

Thirdly, when Bonaventure's theology of the Holy Spirit is brought into the globalized third millennium, the understanding of moral life is not merely globalized, but our understanding of the presence of the Holy Spirit is likewise globalized. Bonaventure writes: "The creative Trinity, (*Trinitas fabicatrix*) shines through (*relucet*), re-presents itself (*repraesentatur*), and is reading itself out (*legitur*) in every created reality."[64] The goodness we see diffused throughout all of creation is, in a special way for Bonaventure, the diffusive goodness of the Holy Spirit, for in the relational Trinitarian life itself, the Spirit is the goodness given by the Father to the Son and the Son to the Father.

Scotus's approach to the sending of the Trinity complements what Bonaventure has offered. When he speaks of the sending of the Holy Spirit into the world, Scotus says again and again that this is a free act of a loving God. Creation is not necessary. The Incarnation – the sending of the Logos into the human nature of Jesus – is not necessary. The sending of the Holy Spirit into the world is likewise not necessary. All three actions of God *ad extra* are co-terminus and all three actions *ad extra* are unnecessary.

The actual world we live in is totally contingent, for its origin and birthplace is the love of God. In no way is the Incarnation or the sending of the Holy Spirit dependent on the sin of Adam and Eve. All creation, including Adam and Eve, comes from the divine love which at one and the same time willed to send the gifts of both Logos and Spirit together with the gift of creation. Human beings are meant and helped by God to realize that their entire life and surroundings are gifts of God, and, in a humanly free way, they are called to a response of gratitude and love. It is this conjunction of the free sending of the incarnate Logos and the Holy Spirit into creation from its initial coextensive moment of creation that makes Adam, Eve and every human being a moral or ethical person. Adam and Eve, as well as every other human being, is faced with this overwhelming gift of God – creation itself, the sending of the Logos into the human nature of Jesus, and the sending of the Holy Spirit into the entirety of creation. Faced with such profound gifting, persons are meant

---

[64] Bonaventure, *Breviloquium*, part II, chapter 12, *WSB* IX, 96.

to respond to the giver. This response to God the Giver is the foundation of Franciscan ethics. Each person has been given these three gifts. The very giving of these three gifts, together with the human response to the God-giving of these gifts, is the ultimate basis of Franciscan moral theology. The gospel message, in the Franciscan approach, is a message of love calling for a response of love.

The sending of the Spirit in the works of Scotus entails another very important issue. Scotus maintains that each person has been gifted with free will, and that each is called on to love God with his or her own human free will. The human soul is not simply a space in which the Holy Spirit loves God. The human soul, through its free will, also loves God and does so freely.[65]

Franciscan scholars present the center for moral theology, namely, human free will, which itself is a gift. This human free will in and through its own freedom responds to the gifting of God. God, in such a rich way, has gifted human life, and human beings respond to this gifting by a return of love and thanksgiving. We do so freely. It is on this basis that Franciscans build their vision of moral theology.

The basis of Franciscan ethics is not natural law; nor is it found in the Ten Commandments; nor is it utilitarian ethics; nor is it rational ethics. The basis of Franciscan ethics is God's gracious gifting of creation itself, together with the gifting of the Incarnation and the gifting of the mission of the Holy Spirit. Franciscan theology teaches that each human being is gifted with freedom and that every human being is called on to respond morally to the overwhelming generosity of God, and to do so in a free and personal way.

---

[65] See Kenan Osborne, "A Scotistic Foundation for Christian Spirituality," *Franciscan Studies*, Vol. 66 (2006): 363-406.

PART II

# 3

# MORAL GOODNESS AND BEAUTY

## MARY BETH INGHAM, C.S.J.

*The Franciscan moral vision is an aesthetic vision,*
*recognizing that the moral life is one of beauty,*
*reflecting the beauty of God.*

The moral vision of the Franciscan tradition flows from its spiritual intuitions, traced out in the previous chapters. In this chapter, we focus on a particularly Franciscan way of envisioning moral living: as a life surrounded by and devoted to beauty. The chapter serves both a foundational and an integrating function. First, our analysis of beauty both as a moral experience and as a rational, moral goal integrates traditional elements such as moral law and virtue around the *praxis* of the fully mature moral agent. Second, the analysis lays the groundwork for discussions in subsequent chapters, particularly those that highlight freedom as generosity and conscience as the dynamic activity of rational moral presence to concrete circumstances. As we pursue this discussion, we bring together four of the eleven characteristics of the Franciscan moral vision for a more sustained consideration. While our primary focus will be the centrality of beauty and its moral implications, this chapter also highlights decision making as holistic spiritual discernment, the dynamic of creative loving, and the primacy of interpersonal relationships in imitation of Trinitarian love.

In her 1998 Tanner lectures, Elaine Scarry, Cabot Professor of Aesthetics at Harvard University, calls for the recovery of an authentic intellectual appropriation of beauty. In her talks, published under the title, *On Beauty and Being Just*,[1] Scarry argues both for the centrality of beauty and for the recovery of an authentic sense of the beautiful. Such a recovery is essential, she states, for any genuine model of human living.[2] Indeed, beauty is the central human experience capable of informing our society and our world today, needed today, by our society and our world.

Three elements of Professor Scarry's argument about the need for an authentic recovery of beauty connect with Franciscan moral thinking: conversion, creativity, and generosity. First, the experience of beauty opens to a moment of *personal conversion*, transforming the individual and her perception of the world. The experience of beauty stops us short; we sense the need to look again, to pay closer attention to what is happening. Looking again, we question our initial attitudes, we are invited to revise our opinions, ready to admit we may have made a mistake.[3]

Second, the authentic experience of beauty calls forth and inspires both *creativity* and *generativity*.[4] The work of art, it-

---

[1] Elaine Scarry, *On Beauty and Being Just,* The Tanner Lectures, Yale University, 1998. Later published by Princeton University Press, 1999.

[2] "But the claim throughout these pages that beauty and truth are allied is not a claim that the two are identical.... It is instead the case that our very aspiration for truth is its [beauty's] legacy." *On Beauty and Being Just,* 52. And again, "It is the argument of this chapter that beauty, far from contributing to social injustice in either of the two ways it stands accused, or even remaining neutral to injustice as an innocent bystander, actually assists us in the work of addressing injustice...," *On Beauty and Being Just,* 62.

[3] Citing Simone Weil's *Waiting for God*, Scarry writes: "At the moment we see something beautiful, we undergo a radical decentering. Beauty, according to Weil, requires us 'to give up our imaginary position as the center.... A transformation then takes place at the roots of our sensibility, in our immediate reception of sense impressions and psychological impressions.'" Scarry, *On Beauty and Being Just,* 111.

[4] "This phenomenon of unceasing begetting sponsors in people like Plato, Aquinas, Dante the idea of eternity, the perpetual duplicating of a

self inspired by the experience of beauty, reveals the dynamic creativity of the artist. Admiring the work, we long to be artists too, we are inspired to imitate what we see. Creativity gives birth to creativity, generativity births generativity.

Finally, the authentic experience of beauty opens us to *generosity*: the extension of our attention beyond the beautiful object to other objects worthy of notice. We recognize objects we may have overlooked in the past.[5] We recognize relationships where we did not see them before. At once we see ourselves differently, we value creation differently and we become even more inclusive in our acts of love and justice.[6] We are ready to expand our moral universe to include more persons and more forms of life, to broaden our moral categories toward deeper and richer acts of justice.

Scarry's argument should come as no surprise to those living and working in the Franciscan tradition. Here is a contemporary call for the return to something that Franciscans know well: the *via pulchritudinis,* or the way of life centered on beauty,[7] where creativity and relationship, solidarity, mutuality, and generosity are the central virtues of moral living.

---

moment that never stops. But it also sponsors the idea of terrestrial plenitude and distribution, the will to make 'more and more' so that there will eventually be 'enough'." Scarry, *On Beauty and Being Just,* 5.

[5] Scarry deems this the "error of undercrediting, on the side of a failed generosity." *On Beauty and Being Just,* 14.

[6] Scarry speaks of the experience of beauty as sponsor to an experience of radical de-centering that results in the generous broadening of our moral categories. Such ability to extend and broaden our moral reflection is key, she argues, to concrete acts of distributive justice and environmental stewardship. See *On Beauty,* 95-112.

[7] Benedict XVI recently highlighted the *via pulchritudinis* as a singular pathway to transcendence: "A work of art is the fruit of the creative capacity of the human person who stands in wonder before the visible reality, who seeks to discover the depths of its meaning and to communicate it through the language of forms, colors and sounds. Art is capable of expressing, and of making visible, man's need to go beyond what he sees; it reveals his thirst and his search for the infinite. Indeed, it is like a door opened to the infinite, [opened] to a beauty and a truth beyond the every day. And a work of art can open the eyes of the mind and heart, urging us upward." Conference given at Castel Gandalfo, Italy, August 31, 2011. (For English text, see http://www.zenit.org/article -33326?l=english).

The Franciscan moral tradition has great resources in its own *via pulchritudinis*: its unique path of beauty.[8]

Our discussion in this chapter relies upon the teaching of one particular Franciscan, John Duns Scotus. From his teaching we draw out some of the implications that flow from his vision of moral beauty. We begin with a consideration of the nature of moral goodness understood through the lens of the beautiful. Following this, we look more closely at the role of the moral artist in moral situations. Finally, we consider the implications of this vision for moral *discernment*, or the particular way of prudential judgments as they appear in a concrete situation for our consideration. At the close, we will draw out several implications of the Franciscan vision of moral decision making for today.

## I. THE EXPERIENCE OF BEAUTY AND ITS LINK TO HARMONY

As we saw in earlier chapters, the Franciscan vision is primarily an Augustinian vision, centered upon the journey of human longing for God. Augustine's reflection on his own spiritual journey focused often on his experience of beauty in creation and how this deeply personal experience opened the door to his transformative encounter with the divine. In his *Confessions*, he writes, "Do we ever love anything save what is beautiful? What then is beautiful? And what is beauty? What draws us and delights us in the things we love? Unless there were grace and beauty in them they could not possibly draw us to them."[9] Following in this vein, Bonaventure also highlights the importance of delight as our response to the beauty of creation in the earliest stages of our spiritual journey. For Bonaventure, as for all Franciscans, creation represents the primary mode of invitation, a gift from the hand

---

[8] For a fuller development, see M.B. Ingham, *Rejoicing in the Works of the Lord: Beauty in the Franciscan Tradition* (St. Bonaventure, NY: Franciscan Institute Publications, 2009).

[9] *Confessions* IV, 13, trans. F.J. Sheed (Indianapolis: Hackett, 1993), 61.

of the Divine Artist. Such a gift sparks human desire and longing and delights the human heart.[10] Joy and desire are identified as essential guides along the way.

The identification of beauty with delight serves as a central element in reflections upon the experience of beauty as integral to human fulfillment. Closer consideration of the experience of delight expands the notion of beauty beyond the visual to the auditory: beauty is also experienced as harmony. From earliest times, several important elements have been identified with beauty and these, too, can be extended to harmony: patterns, symmetry and repetition. These elements express the ordered relationship of parts that belongs to our concepts of beauty as well as harmony. In a painting, for example, we notice patterns that recur; or that are placed in symmetrical or balanced relationship with other colors or other forms. In music, the repetition of a musical phrase or harmonic blend can evoke a response of delight.

Proper proportion is another important aspect of beauty: here everything fits in its place, there is not too much of one thing. The relationship of balance is pleasing to the eye and ear. Harmonic chords and tonal passages also express this idea of proportion.[11] Because of the important role of desire in the spiritual journey, Bonaventure notes, contemplation (the activity of the highest form of wisdom) has both cognitive and affective dimensions. We are to be those "lovers of divine wisdom and inflamed with a desire for it" wishing to give ourselves "to glorifying, admiring, and even savoring God."[12] The saint adds the aspect of luminosity as central to our experience of beauty. Luminosity suggests that beauty

---

[10] "After the beginning of contemplation, progress in it follows. This requires two things: great joy in regard to the gift that has been given and a strong desire to continue in the pursuit of it." Bonaventure, *Commentary on the Gospel of St. Luke*, 9, 33, n. 60, ed. and trans. Robert J. Karris, O.F.M. (St. Bonaventure, NY: Franciscan Institute Publications, 2003), VIII part 2, 235.

[11] Musical harmony depends upon mathematical relationships. Harmonic tones are, therefore, highly precise in their numerical ordering.

[12] St. Bonaventure, *Itinerarium Mentis in Deum,* ed. Philotheus Boehner, O.F.M. and Zachary Hayes, O.F.M., Prologue, 4, *WSB* II (St. Bonaventure, NY: Franciscan Institute Publications, 2002), 41.

can enter our lives as a type of *theophony*: a divine revelation.[13] Many spiritual traditions emphasize how the experience of harmony, particularly inner harmony, signals a moment of divine presence.

Such a discussion of harmony and beauty as central elements of moral living has deep historical antecedents in Patristic spiritual writings. Ambrose's *De Officiis*[14] is a notable example. In this work, Ambrose presents seemliness (*decorum*) as a characteristic of moral action that reveals the internal spiritual dynamic of moral ascent. Seemliness, or decorum, he points out, is a property of all virtuous acts and reveals their twofold harmony. First, relative to the whole and grounded in consistency, the moral action expresses rational harmony with a fuller, cosmic order. Second, the relationship of part to whole reveals the harmonic integrity of the moral action as it expresses personal character throughout a lifetime. Ambrose states, for example, that it is seemly to live in accordance with nature, which "endows us with the character and appearance which we ought to maintain. If only we could preserve our innocence as well, and not corrupt, by our wickedness, the gift given to us!"[15] Moral decisions should reflect the created beauty of the world (general seemliness) and of each of its parts, as at the moment of its creation: "So, the seemliness which shone in each of the parts of the world individually was quite dazzling when they were joined together into a complete whole. Wisdom proves this, when she says: 'I was the one he applauded ... when he rejoiced at the completion of the world.'" (Prov 8: 30-31).[16]

For Ambrose, cosmic harmony reveals the relationship of goodness, wisdom and divine reason. To follow this divine-cosmic model constitutes wisdom: "If a person maintains a consistent character in his life as a whole, and due measure

---

[13] An excellent study of Bonaventure's discussion of beauty and its relationship to luminosity can be found in E.J. Spargo, *The Category of the Aesthetic in the Philosophy of Saint Bonaventure* (St. Bonaventure, NY: The Franciscan Institute, 1953).

[14] Ambrose, *De Officiis*, edited with an introduction, translation and commentary by Ivor J. Davidson (Oxford: Oxford University Press, 2001).

[15] Ambrose, *De Officiis* I, 46. 223, 247.

[16] Ambrose, *De officiis* I, 46. 224, 247-49.

in all his individual actions, with good order besides, and if he preserves a constancy in the words he uses and a moderation in the works he does, then seemliness will be the most striking quality about his life: it will shine like the reflection in a mirror."[17] The confluence of moral wisdom, faith, contempt of the world, and grace bring together into one person the model of the "truly happy *(beatus)*."[18]

Beauty and harmony, joy and delight, belong to our spiritual lives as rational beings. Most spiritual traditions draw an overt link between the beauty and harmony of the present, created world as a way of understanding the beauty and harmony of the divine, the source of all that is and of the beauty of all that exists. The recognition and enjoyment of beauty never rests with the particular work of art or piece of music. Rather, this recognition and enjoyment always point beyond themselves to a greater, richer reality upon which the particular work depends. As spiritual beings engaged in this world, seeking to promote goodness, beauty, and harmony around, we do well to visit often the source of our own rootedness: to stay in touch with beauty and, through beauty, to stay in touch with the divine.

## II. THE CONTOURS OF SCOTUS'S ETHICAL VISION

The centrality and importance of beauty in Scotus's moral vision have received little attention from scholars.[19] Too often, he is identified wrongly as a thinker who advanced a variation of the Divine Command Theory because he emphasized God's will and the contingency of the natural and moral domains. This error of interpretation originated in a general scholarly failure to notice or even appreciate Scotus's own spiritual tradition. Without such an appreciation, scholars have missed how important Franciscan intuitions can and

---

[17] Ambrose, *De Officiis* I, 47. 225, 249.

[18] Ambrose, *De Officiis* I, 49. 242, 257.

[19] A good listing of the few studies on this topic can be found in Trent Pomplun's recent "Notes on Scotist Aesthetics in light of Gilbert Narcisse's *Les Raisons de Dieu," Franciscan Studies* 66 (2008), 247-68.

do frame a spiritually informed, aesthetic vision of moral life. They have not noticed how this vision informs his understanding of the centrality of divine love, of the human person, of the dignity of creation, and, most important, of the precise nature and fragility of moral relationships and moral living.

Scotus views moral goodness as part of a larger frame of beauty and harmony at the heart of reality. At the highest level, he identifies the first practical principle: *God is to be loved*. This principle is metaphysically foundational; it is a self-evident truth.[20] Scotus affirms, "If God exists, then God is to be loved."[21] In other words, just as it is rational to love what is good, so too it is rational to love the highest good in the highest manner. This first principle is naturally known to all rational agents. In this way, it serves as the foundation for moral living, and especially, for the believer, it calls for relational living in imitation of the Trinity.

All moral propositions flow from this central moral truth of love. Subordinate moral truths demonstrate a harmony with the first principle. Indeed, the harmonic relationships that ground all reality offer the objective basis for our moral judgments. The first practical principle, *God is to be loved*, is found in our rational moral center, or as the biblical tradition states, it is "written on the human heart."[22] Its truth is known naturally to all rational agents. This means that moral living is not restricted to believers, for all rational agents have access to moral truth at its highest and most foundational level. Because Scotus defends this first principle as one of love, and because it is self-evident by virtue of the meaning of its terms, he cannot be a "Divine Command Theorist." Divine Command morality must always justify how it is not guilty

---

[20] A self-evident truth, also known as an analytic proposition, is one whose truth is immediately known on the basis of its terms.

[21] John Duns Scotus, *Ordinatio* III, d. 37, unica, n. 5. English from Allan B. Wolter, *Duns Scotus on the Will and Morality* (Washington, DC: CUA Press, 1997), 202. All references will be to this later edition, ed. William Frank.

[22] Rom 2:15. Allan Wolter identifies the influence of Hugh of St. Victor on the Franciscans in this regard. Hugh writes, "Was it not like giving a precept to infuse into the heart of man discrimination and an understanding of what he should do?" See *Will and Morality*, 25.

of 'begging the question.'[23] When he identifies the first principle, *God is to be loved*, as an *analytic* truth, Scotus provides a certain and sure grounding for his moral vision, one that is founded upon the rational recognition of a primary truth. All other truths may now flow from this, including those commands given in the Decalogue.

Following from this first principle are others that Scotus identifies with *moral science*: these principles highlight the importance of honesty, justice, respect for life, and civil society. They are to be found in every culture and coincide with what medievals understood as *natural law*. For Scotus, such principles lie in a harmonic relationship with the first principle of love. As foundational moral principles, they are both taught in a theoretical manner and, more importantly, are the result of reflection upon experience. From these secondary principles various cultures have derived other practices that belong to customs of civil society. Respect for the welfare of others (a second tier principle) manifests itself in common practices: cultural behavior, customs, codes of conduct, and civil laws, etc. The harmonic relationships of lower to higher principles and to the first principle reveal how all moral principles form a harmonic scale, flowing from God's nature as love to human reality.

At the most basic and particular level of concrete situations, we come to individual moral judgments. Here we find our own particular way of acting, how we care for others, how we control our anger or other emotions, what we do in our personal life. These judgments and actions, too, are meant to be related harmonically to higher principles. With the various levels of moral fabric, from highest level of love for God to the lowest level of love for the neighbor, we recognize the power and the richness of harmony in our life and in our societies. In Scotist thought, this harmonic moral vision arises

---

[23] That is, it does not presume its answer in the question. For example, if morality is based on divine command, then how can the first principle to love God be anything other than a divine command? It does not solve the problem to say "I must love God because God commands it and God commands it because I must love God." There must be another, more foundational ground for divine command.

out of a sustained consideration of divine graciousness and the abundant beauty of the natural order.

Scotus re-frames moral living within the experience of beauty. He elaborates a theory of moral decision making that is more akin to artistic practice. In this way, Scotist thought cuts across some of the contemporary moral and ethical divisions, making it difficult to categorize him. For example, while he affirms the primacy of a first practical principle, his moral vision does not fall neatly with a Kantian rule or law based moral approach.[24] He emphasizes the role of God's will, yet Scotus is not a divine command moralist. While the mature moral agent is attentive to the particular contours of a moral situation, moral decision making is not a type of utilitarian calculus, where good actions are identified within a pragmatic assessment of "what works." Scotus's moral vision focuses on the agent, and to some degree resembles an Aristotelian virtue-based model, yet, here again, the Franciscan nuances an Aristotelian naturalist teleology.[25]

With his focus on the human person as moral subject and key to any moral vision, Scotus's moral perspective may be more fruitfully identified as a Franciscan *personalist* vision of moral living. He does not frame moral living around a narrow set of cases or moral dilemmas. Moral development is better understood as a lifelong journey of ongoing conversion toward beauty: a way of seeing and living in the world. This journey is centered on the human capacity to respond freely and generously to the good. Within this vision, the moral person appears as artisan whose vocation is to be creative of beauty in the world.

Moral wisdom, or prudence, appears within this vision as an activity of discernment. The moral agent "sees" or better still, "hears" something in the present situation that calls forth her creative response. Scotus's approach to moral decision making as artisan-like activity and to the moral agent

---

[24] "God is to be loved" is not a Scotist Categorical Imperative, nor is his moral vision based on duty.

[25] Scotus criticized Aristotle's ethical vision as overly *deterministic*. He did not think the approach adequately protects the type of freedom that moral choice requires.

as trained craftsperson may offer a significant contribution to contemporary moral discussion. His Franciscan approach may be just what Scarry is calling for: a renewed moral foundation based on love and beauty, a dynamic model of moral reasoning and judgment as a prudential discernment of goodness and beauty, and a vision of moral action as that which gives birth to beauty, in the person and in the world.

Before going any further, however, we must make one important point. In her lectures, Scarry takes care to distinguish her approach from contemporary aesthetical theories that reduce the experience of beauty to subjective categories of personal taste. She criticizes post-Kantian philosophy insofar as it underestimates the experience of beauty. By contrast, in her work she seeks to reintroduce beauty in all of its classic and objective splendor.

Scotus, as well as all classical and medieval thinkers, would agree. For them, as for Scarry, the rational judgment about beauty does *not* belong to the eye of the beholder. Beauty is *not* primarily a subjective experience of personal preference, nor is it merely an affective response to the world around us. We do have an affective response to concrete situations, but this is the result of a rational perception of beauty mediated by our sense awareness, and honed by years of moral training. Reflecting upon our experience of the world around us, we recognize the way that all reality reveals beauty in its deepest constitution.

As we have seen, the experience of beauty belongs to a larger spiritual journey, reaching back to Patristic authors and reinforced within the Franciscan journey begun with Francis and Clare.[26] For all these spiritual authors, created beauty participates in divine beauty beyond time and change. Like light, true beauty is diffusive of itself, it is God's glory manifest in creation. None of this is merely subjective, for authentic beauty depends upon the right ordering of elements, just as right loving depends upon the deeper rational order of divine love.

---

[26] See above, Chapter Two, 47-83.

## A. The Lens of Beauty and Moral Goodness

Duns Scotus uses beauty to explain moral goodness as a visual experience. Goodness, like beauty, is a formal perfection of being: the proper integration of all that is fitting for an act to be whole or complete. Such integration involves careful attention to time, place, manner and to the harmonizing of all elements with the agent's intention. Moral goodness makes an act beautiful because it "includes a combination of due proportion to all to which it [the act] should be proportioned (such as potency, object, end, time, place, and manner), and this especially as right reason dictates ..."[27]

Without the integration of everything needed, our moral sensibilities are not satisfied: something is missing. This notion of integration and harmony, as it applies to moral goodness, touches an aspect of our own affective reaction to moral beauty. Recall, for example, an experience when you entered a room or a situation and felt uneasy about what was going on. Perhaps you felt uneasy or anxious about what was *not* going on. In either case, something was missing. Some aspect that was necessary for harmony was not present. This example illustrates how we do have a rational moral sensitivity that often expresses itself in our affective response to the world around us. It does not mean that our moral judgments are "funny inner feelings." It means, rather, that attention to our affective response to a situation opens the way for deeper reflection upon fundamental moral principles, acquired moral knowledge, and the particular needs of a given, concrete situation. Here, the tradition identifies the important role of "right reasoning": the intellectual and rational task of moral analysis, decision, and choice.

Scotus explains that authentic moral goodness admits of a two-fold excellence: both internal harmony and external beauty. The morally good act is both suitable (fitting or seemly) for an individual to perform. It possesses its own internal coherence or suitability, something another person

---

[27] John Duns Scotus, *Ordinatio* I, d. 17, n. 62 (Civitas Vaticana: Typis Polyglottis Vaticanis, 1950), V: 163-64.

would recognize and admire. This suitability involves three foundational elements: who the person is, what the person is doing, and the power by which the agent does what she does.

### 1. Core Moral Questions

In a moral analysis, these elements could be framed as core questions. The first question, "who am I?" takes into account my own personal identity as well as integrity of character and my role in this situation. This is important because, while truth may need to be told, I may not be the appropriate person to speak the truth. The second question, "what am I doing?" looks at the action insofar as it expresses the excellence of my own identity, or (in the case of a vicious act) betrays who I am. Scotus argues that this type of self-knowledge is a given: everyone knows who they are and what they are doing.[28] These two questions act as the moral foundation for any situation. A third question involves the choice itself: do I myself choose to act freely? Am I under any undue pressure or coercion? We know, for example, that a forced act, or an act performed out of fear, is not completely voluntary, and therefore involves diminished responsibility. All moral living depends upon such personal and foundational self-awareness, awareness of the particular circumstances, and genuine freedom of choice.

These three elements constitute the *natural* dimension of goodness. This dimension is also likened to beauty by Scotus:

> I say that natural goodness is like beauty of body, which results from a combination of all that is internally harmonious and is becoming to the body, such as size, color, and figure (as Augustine wants to say of a good face in Book VIII of *The Trinity*: 'Good is the face of a man with regular features, a cheerful expression, and a glowing color'). And this natural goodness is not

---

[28] Reflection on our own experience may cause us to question this assertion. However, we do note that police officers ask this question of drivers who exceed the speed limit, i.e., "do you know how fast you are driving?"

that which is coextensive with being,[29] but that which is opposed to evil and is a second perfection of a thing, in which we find united all that is becoming to it and is internally harmonious.[30]

A good act is "becoming" or "fitting" to a person. It is internally harmonious and pleasing to the observer. We have here, however, only the *first* level of goodness. *Natural* beauty serves as the foundation upon which *moral* beauty depends. An act which has no natural beauty cannot have moral beauty. If an act of deception is unbecoming or incoherent, then no "little white" lie can be morally justified. In other words, Scotus would argue that no amount of sincerity or good intention, no beneficial outcome or consequence can transform an unbecoming act into a beautiful one: there must be some level of internal goodness, beauty, or harmony in the act itself, and this at the most basic level.

### 2. Additional Moral Elements

Scotus's moral analysis builds levels of beauty upon levels of beauty, beginning with the most foundational natural harmony that the initial act possesses. Additional moral dimensions can be added to enhance the beauty of any action. These aspects involve the end or reason (the intention) for which the act is performed, the manner in which one performs the act, the timing of the act and its place. To be perfectly and completely good, "an act must be faultless on all counts."[31] In such a case, all aspects of the situation are pres-

---

[29] Scotus refers here to *metaphysical* goodness as distinct from *moral* goodness. As explained earlier metaphysical goodness is the goodness of reality, of all that exists. Nothing created is evil. Moral goodness refers to the relationship of all that exists to God and the moral intentionality of ordered loving and right action. Evil as a moral category can be understood as an absence or a profound disorder in loving.

[30] John Duns Scotus, *Ordinatio* II, d. 40, in *Will and Morality,* 176.

[31] *Quodlibetal Question* 18, n. 18.16. English from *God and Creatures: the Quodlibetal Questions,* Alluntis and Wolter, eds. (Princeton, NJ: Princeton University Press, 1975), 404.

ent and appropriately so. The harmony is full and complete. The beauty is stunning.

While he sets a high standard (almost divinely high) for moral perfection, Scotus does not espouse an "all or nothing" moral approach. The moral standard is one at which we aim: not necessarily one which we fully achieve. An act does not have to be perfectly good in order to be morally good. True to the Franciscan spiritual and intellectual tradition, Scotus understands moral progress to be a type of pedagogy into wisdom, not looking primarily to the law or to absolute principle to determine the best way to act. However, neither is this purely subjective or situation-based moral theory. As a moral teacher, Scotus integrates and balances all elements: fundamental and derived moral principles, right reasoning, ordered loving, concrete moral situations. The moral agent is like the dancer, like the artist or craftsman, like the actor, like the juggler or tightrope walker: the moment for decision and choice brings forth all moral elements in a dynamic, unified moment of *praxis*. Such an act requires concentration, training, practice and mindfulness.

One advantage of an approach centered on beauty is the way in which it helps us identify nuances within moral living. We can distinguish between actions which lack full perfection, but which nonetheless, reveal some dimension of moral goodness. For example, I might tell the truth in a given situation (a naturally good act), but at the wrong time. Or, in a more complex moral setting, the truth may not be mine to tell. For example, I might be aware of a marital infidelity on the part of a friend. I might take it upon myself to break the news to her husband, all in the name of honesty and integrity. Furthermore, my intentions might be very sincere, since both of them are my friends. I might even succeed in revealing the truth with the appropriate level of tact. And yet, I have overstepped the bounds of friendship. I have entered into a relationship more deeply than I should. The painful truth of such an act is really hers to tell. A more appropriate response on my part would be first to support her in her own self-revelation to her husband. Second, to support him and their marriage, as they live with the truth and into the future.

In this example, I may have been too quick to see the first moral action ("tell the truth"). Had I reflected at greater depth, I might have discovered a broader and richer, more morally appropriate way to promote a deeper truth that mattered: the truth of their love for one another and the integrity of their family life. My action was not vicious: it was not fully virtuous however. Moral goodness admits of a spectrum that includes degrees of greater and greater integration and harmony.

A different sort of action in this situation could easily be vicious. For example, I might tell the truth to her husband in order to hurt him, or to hurt their marriage. I might even take delight in giving the bad news. Clearly, the disorder here has to do with my intention to cause pain to another. This action is in some sense ugly and vicious. Indeed, more reflection shows how, with my evil intent, there would be no further or deeper act that I could have performed. I wanted to cause harm, and I did. I could cause no greater harm here; I could do nothing worse.

But in the morally good act and person, there is always the possibility of more good, of a more perfect way to achieve my moral aim. In the first example, my aim was to be a person of integrity, and I thought that telling the truth was the most appropriate way to live that integrity. I was mistaken. There was another way I could have acted to live with integrity. In the second example, my aim was to hurt my friend, her husband, and the marriage. And I did just that. While both actions caused pain, and (from a utilitarian point of view) could have had identical consequences (the rupture of our friendship), the second is clearly different and more serious.

## B. Moral Principles and Harmony

Moral goodness admits of degrees of richness and deeper perfection: it gives way to life. Moral evil is flat and stillborn. One interesting aspect of Scotus's overall discussion of moral goodness is that he does not emphasize the disordered acts. He concentrates on human goodness and how we can always act more harmoniously, and more beautifully. The better the act is, the more levels of beauty it possesses. Like a musical chord, higher levels of goodness enhance and enrich the moral beauty of a situation.

Musical imagery appears regularly in Scotus's discussions. He presents the image of chords on a harp to capture the relationship of internal order with delight in the listener. The strings of a harp are plucked in a certain order, he states, and this order can admit of harmony or dissonance. When such an order is harmonic, either because a certain string is plucked after another or because the two (or more) strings are struck simultaneously, the sound produces pleasure and delight in those present. This delight is not a function of the individual notes themselves, taken separately, but rather of their ordered relation with one another.[32]

Scotus uses this musical image to describe as well the relationship of human moral action to God's response. The divine ear *hears* the morally good act informed by love and, pleased with its harmony, rewards the act. The presence of charity within the ordered act resembles harmony within music.[33]

Scotus also uses musical imagery in his discussion of natural law and the relationship of moral law to fundamental moral principles. The fundamental principle, *God is to be loved*, functions in the same way that a tuning fork produces a pure tone, one that might be used by the piano tuner to set all other tones of the keyboard. This first *tone* represents the highest standard for action. This first is that against which all other moral principles are measured.[34]

---

[32] John Duns Scotus, *Lectura* I, 17, pars 1 unica, n. 95 (ed. Vat. XVII: 211).

[33] John Duns Scotus, *Ordinatio* I, 17, n. 152 (ed. Vat. V, 212).

[34] For a fuller discussion of the way in which moral judgments are presented as a recognition of harmonic relationships, see Mary Beth Ingham, "Duns Scotus: Moral Reasoning and the Artistic Paradigm," *Via Scoti: Methodologica ad mentem Joannis Duns Scoti* (Roma: Edizioni Antonianum, 1995), 825-37.

The commands of the second table of the Decalogue (those involving the neighbor) are said to be in tonal harmony (*consona*) with this first principle of all moral living.

The other way in which things belong to the law of nature is because they are exceedingly in harmony (*consona*) with that law, even though they do not follow necessarily from those first practical principles known from their terms, principles which are necessarily grasped by any intellect understanding those terms.[35] Now, it is certain that all the precepts of the second table also belong to the natural law in this way, since their rightness is very much in harmony (*valde consona*) with the first practical principles that are known of necessity.[36]

For Scotus, truth telling and respect for property do not possess the type of absolute moral status that belongs to the command to love God above all things. Scotus notes that even one's respect for parental authority could admit of exception. His point in all of this is twofold: first, moral living is primarily centered on love and on ordered loving. Second, there is a difference between legality and morality: not every legal act can be morally justified.[37] Additionally, the law (which functions on the basis of general practice) does not necessarily fit with every concrete situation. As we know, the complex fabric of human life admits of exceptional situations that do not always fit general principles and broader legal categories. Here is where prudential judgment and good decision making are essential. Here is where the training of the moral individual is paramount.

The important point in all of this is clear: every moral person strives to follow the fundamental law of love for God and neighbor within every particular set of circumstances. In this way, every action can work to promote the harmonic in-

---

[35] Here is an example of how Scotus understands the first practical principle, *God is to be loved*, as a primary and self-evident proposition.

[36] Scotus, *Ordinatio* III, suppl. dist. 37, Codex A, in *Will and Morality*, 203.

[37] Abortion, torture or any inhumane treatment are examples here of actions that might be legal but not moral. The legality of any action does not make it morally good.

tegrity and coherence of moral principle with concrete daily living.

Just as the fullest beauty rings out where all notes are in harmony, so too the harmony of moral integrity possesses all levels of goodness present and all dimensions complete. But, to recall what we said above, this is not to suggest that partial harmony does not constitute goodness. One might give to the poor or help a neighbor grudgingly. The gift of money or time to one in need is itself a morally good act. Giving such a gift half-heartedly or grudgingly is simply not the morally *best* act I might do. However, I would rather do a morally good act half-heartedly than not at all. Moral goodness, like beauty, admits of levels and degrees of harmony and perfection. A lesser moral act is no less morally good, merely because it is not perfect.

In like manner, moral education in the Franciscan tradition is centered on an ongoing moral pedagogy and conversion. Through the moral community and moral mentoring, the young person learns by imitating the best actions of others: not blind imitation and repetition, but trained emulation. Stories and examples of wise and generous actions have a powerful impact on the learner. Like Jesus, we learn to serve others, not always by washing their feet, but by humbling ourselves in generous acts of love.

## C. The Moral Person as Performing Artist

If the morally good act is like a work of art or beautiful piece of musical harmony, and moral judgment involves having a well-trained moral "ear," then the moral person can be likened to a performing artist or musician. Here we might also think of a dancer whose dance requires inner harmony as well as outer beauty of movement. Scotus describes moral artistry in terms of the balance of our two inner moral dispositions: our natural disposition to love the self and our free and rational disposition to love the good for itself alone. Let us consider these two important aspects of the moral agent.

Scotus inherited two important aspects of moral living from Anselm, the great Benedictine master. In his discussion of rational willing,[38] Anselm had identified two metaphysical orientations within the will that constitute human rational freedom. The first is the natural *affectio commodi,* the deep desire for happiness and security within every living being. The second, more proper to rational beings, is the *affectio justitiae,* or the affection for justice. Here is the free and rational desire we possess. It is the affection for justice that draws us toward integrity and honor. It inspires us to search for goods of lasting value. This higher moral affection enables us to control our other desires and, where needed, offer a counter-weight to the affection for happiness. Alexander of Hales, writing at the beginning of the thirteenth century, had identified goods of intrinsic value as possessing "intelligible beauty."[39] Goods of this type are the proper object of the affection for justice. Bonaventure, in his *Hexaemeron* identified justice as that which "beautifies" creation: the deformed it makes beautiful; the beautiful it makes more beautiful; the more beautiful it makes most beautiful. In this way we see how, even earlier within the Franciscan tradition, the human metaphysical desire for justice is identified with the desire for beauty.[40]

The affection for justice is not simply a desire for intelligible beauty. Scotus calls it the seat of our freedom, the "checkrein" on the affection for happiness. And, more important, this higher affection is not lost as a result of original sin.[41]

Therefore, this affection for justice, which is the first checkrein on the affection for the beneficial, inasmuch as we need not actually seek that towards which the

---

[38] In the *De casu diaboli,* ch. 12-14. Scotus makes use of Anselm's discussion in *Ordinatio* II, d. 6.

[39] Alexander of Hales, *Summa Theologica* I, 3, 3, n. 103 (Quarrachi: Ad Claras Aquas, 1924), I: 162.

[40] Bonaventure of Bagnoregio, *Collationes in Hexaemeron* 1:34 (V, 335). See José de Vinck, *The Works of Bonaventure,* Volume V, *Collations on the Six Days* (Paterson, NJ: St. Anthony Guild Press, 1970), 17-18.

[41] Indeed, nothing of the dignity of creation is lost through original sin!

latter affection inclines us, nor must we seek it above all else (namely, to the extent to which we are inclined by this affection for the advantageous) – this affection for what is just, I say, is the liberty innate to the will, since it represents the first checkrein on this affection for the advantageous.[42]

This higher affection is rational and free; it constitutes the moral domain and distinguishes us from the animal kingdom. According to Scotus, moral action would be impossible without both affections. Moral perfection requires that the two be balanced in an internal harmony of our rational desire. The dynamic interaction of these two affections offers the metaphysical constitution of freedom as self-mastery: the ability of the person to wait before acting. Their interaction can be likened to the poise of the dancer, who holds herself with an internal check, and moves to the cadence and timing of the music. Their interaction can be likened to the chorus member, whose timing and breathing are essential to the harmonic performance.

## D. Moral Judgments and Harmony

How does the mind make judgments according to such a harmonic model? By comparing one thing or several things to a standard, in the way instruments in an orchestra are tuned to the concert master before a performance, or in the way singers harmonize with one another by attentive listening and adjusting their voices. This act of comparison, when fruitfully harmonious, results in delight and affirming assent: this is right; this is beautiful; this is fitting. We are on key.

Traditional studies of Scotus speak of this act of judgment as belonging to the intellect, known as right reason or prudence. The intellect issues a moral command (a moral standard) and the will is supposed to obey.[43] Scotus presents

---

[42] Scotus, *Ordinatio* II, d. 6., in *Will and Morality*, 298-99.

[43] Language of 'intellect' and 'will,' so common to medieval discussions, should not confuse us into understanding the human person as a divided

texts where this is indeed the model used. In another text, however, he places the rational will at the center of his moral vision. He refers to the will as the only rational potency. This claim seems odd, for how can the will, normally understood as a rational *appetite*,[44] be capable of the rationality required for moral judgment?

In the textual discussion where he makes use of Anselm's two moral affections,[45] Scotus explains that the will, like the intellect, is a *vis collativa*. This type of power (*vis*) brings things together. The will, like the intellect, is a comparative faculty capable of placing one thing alongside another and becoming aware of how the two relate to one another. Here we find an enhanced description of the activity of rational love, one that meets our musical analogy above. The will, as the seat of human rational desire, does not only follow the direction of the intellect; it also compares simple notions or even actions with propositions. Like the ear, the will listens for moral resonance. By means of this comparative listening, the rational will is aware of harmony between principles and actions, between one principle and another, between one type of action and another.

Scotus describes this innovative recasting of the will's recognition of moral truth in the following way:

> But if you object: "which kind of understanding reveals this, one that is erroneous or one that is correct?" I answer: not an erroneous judgment, but a *simple grasp* [italics mine], to which it does not belong to be mistaken or to say the truth (for these are states of the composing and dividing intellect). Nor is it necessary that the intellect [previously] grasp something

---

self, between knowing and choosing. Rather, these two terms refer to 'faculties' or 'powers' of the human rational soul. They express the particular functioning of rationality that involves both desire (=will) and judgment (=intellect). Although the faculties are twofold, they are united in the one person. Scotus himself emphasizes that they are only *formally* (i.e., conceptually) distinct in the unified person. Ockham will also insist upon this important point.

[44] A designation of the will that Scotus rejects.

[45] *Ordinatio* II, d. 6.

as attributed to another, or something as not attributed to another, but it is rather sufficient that the
will connects this with that, because the will is like
the intellect a "power that relates things among each
other" (*vis collativa*). Consequently, the will can relate
whatever simple notions that are shown to it, just like
the intellect.[46]

Scotus calls such a judgment a "simple grasp." Such moral
insight is not propositional in nature (that is, not the result
of the intellect "composing and dividing"). The will "connects"
one thing with another, relating the two and judging the harmony or consonance present. Like the intellect, the rational
will brings items together and perceives their relationship.
Like the intellect, the rational will grasps (or "hears") something about the concrete situation, linking principles to actions, joining theoretical knowledge to particular situations.
This produces a type of "moral judgment" in the will – a judgment of moral resonance understood as a "simple grasp" or
immediate awareness. This assemblage of different simple
items or notions could be as primitive or as sophisticated as
one would wish.

Let us now bring together all the elements of moral beauty we have seen thus far: principles, desires, intentions, judgments, and actions. We can appreciate Scotus's analysis by
taking a very simple moral situation whose aspects are clear-
cut and straightforward: principles, knowledge and action.
An example here might be:

Basic principle: I always try to act out of love for God.
Moral principle: Giving to the poor expresses love for God.
Situation: Here is a poor person and I am in a position to
  give something.
Action: I give something to the person.

---

[46] Scotus, *Ordinatio* II, d. 6, q. 1, n. 19 (ed. Vat. VIII: 32-33).

The moral harmony in this example is not difficult to hear at all. Like a four-note chord, all aspects from principle to action line up nicely.

There can be other, more intricate moral situations whose numerous aspects challenge the trained moral ear to hear the potential harmony and to act to bring it out.

Consider, for example:

Basic principle: I always try to act out of love for God.

Moral principle 1: Giving to the poor expresses love for God.

Moral principle 2: Supporting someone's drug addiction does not.

Situation: Here is a poor person who looks like an addict.

Action: Shall I give a few dollars or not?

In this second case, something is present that offers a false note, a dissonant sound that stops my moral ear. How do I reconcile all aspects? How do I act out of my basic moral principle in this case? How do I achieve my moral goal?

In each of these rather simple cases, the "moral ear" belongs to the rational will: our capacity to relate principles, knowledge, circumstances and action into a single moment of choice. In the first case, I can act quickly. In the second, I may need to engage in some creative thinking in order to come to a better moral action than the immediate gift of a few dollars. There might be something more life-sustaining that I could do in this situation: provide food rather than money, help the person to a shelter.

Scotus's identification of the rational will as a *vis collativa* can be enhanced with other textual references to the manner by which we make moral judgments. He emphasizes, for example, the *immediacy* of the act of prudential judgment. The moral expert possesses an immediate grasp or inner awareness of what should be done. Full moral maturity integrates moral principles with the demands of a concrete and particular state of affairs, perhaps in the same way that a musical performance does not replace musical theory: rather, it depends upon it and integrates theory with the demands of a particular performance.

Hence prudence is simply a habit that is more immediately directed toward practice, so that a prudent person knows immediately the means to use and does not have to reason backward from principles to other prior principles. A science, like moral philosophy, by contrast, is only mediately practical,[47] because it teaches how one should behave in regard to actions through a process of reasoning.[48]

Prudential judgment, the excellence of moral reasoning, belongs to one who knows what to do, not merely because he knows the theoretical rules and deduces from them, but on the basis of years of training and experience (rehearsals) informed by rational reflection. Moral rehearsals, like musical rehearsals, involve ongoing and continual practice. They assume a certain amount of creativity as well as some trial and error. More important, moral proficiency, like musical proficiency, takes a great deal of time and patience. The goal is to be like the person of moral wisdom who exercises moral judgment immediately, just as a trained artist acts immediately and with a high degree of excellence.

Scotus actually likens the morally mature person to the trained artist or artisan, one who knows what to do immediately because of a lifetime of rehearsal, practice and training. Such knowledge is not merely theoretical; it is the result of years of reflection and action.

> Hence, just as an artist with a [theoretical] knowledge of his art in mind is more remotely practical than one who knows [how to do or make something] simply from experience and not deductively from any art he possesses, so too one who knows the science of

---

[47] To speak here of mediated reasoning means there are intermediate propositional steps along the way, as reasoning is guided, slowly but surely toward the correct conclusion. For example, deductive reasoning is mediated reasoning, rather than immediate. Scotus's point here seems to be that the morally mature agent is capable of swift action, due to an equally swift recognition of what should be done.

[48] Scotus, *Lectura* prologue, Pars 4, q. 1-2, in *Will and Morality*, 134.

morals is more remotely practical than one who possesses prudence.[49]

Moral wisdom, then, is not abstract nor theoretical in nature. It is that practical wisdom which develops through learned moral habit just as the artisan or musician learns by actual performance. Moral conclusions are not merely the result of deductive, syllogistic reasoning. In his discussion of prudence (moral wisdom), Scotus combines both the expertise of learned experience (the result of many long hours of rehearsal) with the attention to a specific and concrete set of circumstances. Such a delicate interaction of principles with contingent reality might best be clarified by developing the musical analogy for a moment.

Like musical training, moral education and judgment involve both inductive and deductive domains of reasoning. There is both a science of moral reasoning as well as a craft for moral decisions, just as music has both theoretical and practical dimensions. In fact, one cannot learn music theory without practice. We must go beyond the mechanical reproduction of notes to the capturing of the emotion and depth of the notes. So also in the moral life we must go beyond the mechanical application of principles to capturing the depths of the moral reality.

Likewise, the moral realm is defined not only by general principles and norms, but also by rational action and decision within a concrete and particular situation. Moral wisdom (prudence) is a human craft, learned from experiences, but ultimately rational in its general intent. Principles are helpful but incomplete; universal norms are imperfect because they are far too general. The moral person develops rationally within a community of other moral artists where right appetite is fostered and supported by laws and customs. Perfect and complete moral reasoning can only occur in the concrete particular act of moral decision making.

What can we extrapolate from all this in regards to the person as moral artist? First, like the artist, the morally

---

[49] Scotus, *Lectura* Prologue, Pars 4, q. 1-2, in *Will and Morality,* 134-35.

mature person is self-aware: she is conscious of her desires and her moral attractions; she knows who she is and what she is doing. In addition, she balances her self-related needs against the needs of others. She has appropriate restraint in her own decisions and actions. She knows when she can hold back her own desires in favor of the needs of others or in favor of the needs of integrity in a given situation.

Second, this person is attentive to the present demands of the situation at hand. She knows what to look for in the moral equation, she can tell the difference between morally significant and morally insignificant aspects, between details that are irrelevant and those that make the moral situation what it is. She can balance, compare, and harmonize what she sees with the domain of moral principles. She can see how to use principles in concrete situations to bring forth the most beauty possible, to strengthen relationships and introduce justice.

Third, she is also attentive to persons within the situation. She is alert to the good. She listens for harmonic tones that reveal what could be done in a given setting, especially in a situation where the raw material for beauty is not all she would hope for. She is nimble and graceful in action. She brings together principles, acquired skill, the deepest rational desires, and the specific aspects of the particular situation at hand. Here we see an excellent example of dynamic moral "listening" and harmonic attunement. Like any performing artist, the moral agent works with the material at hand. To the moral situation before her, she must bring all the skill of a lifetime of training (moral science) and all the attention to the particular demands to whatever imperfect conditions are before her.

Our deepest natural desire to love the good for its own sake reveals the extent to which the human heart (that is, the center of our rational moral being) echoes the divine heart (the ground for all that exists). The resonance between our heart and God's heart, between our moral center and God's Trinitarian moral center is mediated by beauty. This central focus on Trinitarian love and beauty enables Scotus to draw out the implications of a moral vision centered on beauty, yet one that never loses the metaphysical and moral foundations needed to avoid subjectivism or relativism. God's loving nature, rational, creative and free, grounds all moral decisions because God's love constitutes beings as they exist.

This *ordo amoris* is not simply an order of human loving, but an order of God's triune love and communion. If it were not, moral decisions would fall into the realm of human preference. In other words, for the Franciscan tradition, excellent moral agency seeks to imitate divine Trinitarian life. The moral goal is to act as would the divine Artist, aligning oneself and all aspects of the moral moment with the divine love for beauty. In affirming the first moral principle as love for God, Scotus confirms the scientific character of charity. Viewing divine nature as Trinity of persons in loving communion and self-gift,[50] he presents the moral domain as one framed in love, relationship and, consequently, in beauty.

Because he grounds his ethical discussion on the rational will, Scotus focuses on love as the main content of the moral law and as the only manner by which the law can be fulfilled. Moral living involves both the content and manner of loving. Here, means and ends coincide. Charity reveals the unity of moral life; joy reveals the heart of moral perfection.

For Franciscans, the moral order transcends the individual self and points toward communion and relationship with others and, ultimately, with God. Understanding God as Triune Communion, participation in divine life is the true human goal. This goal is ultimately a deep relationship of love based upon the nature of God as source of reality. Relationship is the moral goal because the divine is essentially relational, because we are created in the image of God, and because we are invited to enter freely into that relationship.

---

[50] Recall the importance of Richard of St. Victor's vision of Trinitarian life for the Franciscan tradition. See above, Ch. 2, 55.

## III. A CONCRETE CASE TO CONSIDER: DIANE AND HER ILLNESS[51]

Against this background of Scotus's Franciscan moral vision and the centrality of beauty, let us now consider a particular case of moral decision making. This case is taken from Dr. Timothy Quill's experience dealing with a woman dying of leukemia, and appeared in an article in the 1991 *New England Journal of Medicine* on death and dignity.[52]

Diane was diagnosed with leukemia at a relatively young age. She had been raised in an alcoholic family and had led an isolated life. As a young woman, she had vaginal cancer, and through much of her life had struggled with depression and alcoholism. As she gradually took control of her life, she developed a strong sense of independence and personal confidence. She was sober now, and had deeper connections with her husband, son, and friends. At the time of the diagnosis, things seemed to be going well.

Dr. Quill's diagnosis sent Diane into a tailspin. When the bone-marrow biopsy confirmed acute myelomonocytic leukemia, the oncologist broke the news to Diane, hoping to spur her to immediate action. Technological advances in medicine led to hope: intervention was often successful, with cures in 25% of the cases. The oncologist hoped to begin chemotherapy that afternoon. To his surprise, Diane was enraged at his presumption that she would even consider treatment and she was devastated by the diagnosis. All she wanted to do was return home to be with her family; she had already decided that she would forgo treatment.

As her husband and family attempted to reason with her, Diane made it clear that she did not want any treatment, that she would probably die during the treatment and that

---

[51] This case and the discussion that follows originally appeared as part of "Moral Decision-Making as Discernment: Scotus and Prudence," *Moral Action in a Complex World: Franciscan Perspectives* (St. Bonaventure, NY: Franciscan Institute Publications, 2008), 121-42.

[52] Timothy Quill, M.D., "Death and dignity: A Case of Individualized Decision Making," *New England Journal of Medicine*, volume 324 (1991), 691-94.

the suffering involved in chemotherapy would outweigh the slightly longer period of time she would have with them. Her quality of life would suffer as a result of the treatment. In her opinion, a 25% chance of success was not high enough for her to risk the time she had left.

While Dr. Quill was dismayed at her fatalism, he came to understand it and began planning for hospice care. At this moment, Diane surprised him with her desire to maintain control of herself and her own dignity as long as possible. When this was no longer feasible, she wanted to take her own life in "the least painful way possible." Diane's fear of a lingering death would clearly interfere with her ability to enjoy the time remaining. Until she had the assurance of her own ability to end things when she wanted, she knew no peace. Dr. Quill referred her to the Hemlock Society.

The following week, Diane phoned with a request for barbiturates to help her sleep. Dr. Quill knew well that this was the preferred method offered by the Hemlock Society and, while he tried to make sure she was not suffering from depression or in despair, he "wrote the prescription with an uneasy feeling." He also claims that he felt strongly he was "setting her free to get the most out of the time she had left, to maintain dignity and control on her own terms until her death."[53] He met with her regularly for the next few months, but gradually came to see that the time was approaching. They tried to minimize the pain and suffering as best they could, but it was too much for her. She was more terrified of suffering than she was of taking her own life.

The morning she died, Diane said goodbye to her husband and son, and asked them to leave her alone for an hour. When they returned, they found her body on the couch, lying still and covered with a favorite shawl. She appeared peaceful. When they called Dr. Quill, he contacted the medical examiner to report that she had died from "acute leukemia." He did not report the actual cause of death, but only the condition that resulted in death. Quill concludes his story as follows:

---

[53] Quill, "Death and dignity...," 694.

So I said "acute leukemia" to protect all of us, to protect Diane from an invasion into her past and into her body, and to continue to shield society from knowledge of the suffering that people often undergo in the process of dying.[54]

What are we to make of this complex situation, in light of the aesthetic moral vision of a Franciscan like John Duns Scotus? In such a set of circumstances, what could Diane have done differently? What could Dr. Quill have done differently? What aspects might have promoted something more beautiful than what actually occurred?

In looking at this situation, one following Scotus's approach would highlight the following key aspects. First, her state of mind and heart was one of fear and despair. Clearly, the affection for possession was dominating her decision making. It was a challenge for her to act with rational freedom. In addition, she chose isolation from her family in this decision, rather than building up the relationship with them. Rather than allow them to serve and care for her, it was important to her to "retain control as long as possible." Her sense of self depended upon this type of independence, and this type of autonomy.

A second element that Scotus's approach would consider involves the options that were identified by her and her doctor. There seem only to be violent courses of action: chemotherapy vs. suicide. Who was advocating for additional alternatives, those which might promote Diane's peace and harmony, her final letting go of the need to control this situation in all its dimensions? Where were the voices seeking to soothe and calm her fears? Might there have been other options, involving her husband, her son, and her friends? Significant in her mode of decision making and action was her desire to "go it alone" and only get help from the one person who could give her what she wanted: the doctor.

Diane was motivated by her own terribly wounded sense of self-preservation. She tried to make the best decision she

---

[54] Quill, "Death and dignity…," 694.

could, balancing her pain, her desire not to suffer and cause suffering to her husband and family, her willingness to take full responsibility for her own actions. Several of these motivations are praiseworthy. But Scotus would ask: did her actions fully achieve the moral goal she intended? Could she have acted differently? Were her alternatives so stark and limited?

What of her husband and son? They may have acted out of respect for her wishes to be left alone for some time. They may not have realized what she intended to do. But even if they had, they may have experienced the type of helplessness often known to caregivers, who have done all they can to support the person at the threshold of death. Their act of respect for Diane at this critical moment in her life may have seemed to them heroic: perhaps what they wanted to do was to stay with her.

While we would certainly look upon Diane and her family with compassion, Dr. Quill seems to fare less well under the Scotist lens. Who was he and what was he doing? A medical professional, he stood outside the emotion of the situation. He did not act with the integrity of one whose vocation is to promote life. In addition, here was a man who continued to disregard his own emotional ambivalence, who continued to assist someone in despair, who continued to do what she asked. His uneasy feelings plagued him throughout, from the first mention of the suicide, to the prescription for the barbiturates, to the falsifying of the medical report. As he states, "The family or I could have been subject to criminal prosecution, and I to professional review, for our roles in support of Diane's choices." "Support for Diane's choices" – this seems to be the way modern moral theories, Kantian or Utilitarian, would have viewed their role in this tragic situation. Diane was the morally mature agent, she was the autonomous person, she had a right to make this choice. Their role was to help her do what she wanted in this matter.

Let us be frank: there is not a great deal of beauty or harmony to be identified in this moral scenario. Diane was depressed, the family was helpless, the doctor was weak. For another course of action, perhaps there needed to be a different cast of characters: persons who could lift her up and take appropriate control on her behalf, persons whom she trusted, persons who could surround her with love and care, persons who would not leave her alone during the final hours, persons who simply refused to leave her alone when they had every reason to believe she would give in to her fear and despair. A stronger moral community, stronger and richer moral relationships were needed far earlier in Diane's life than when she was diagnosed with leukemia.

What can we draw from this brief reflection on complex moral decision making? What are the elements of moral discernment that the Franciscan tradition would highlight for us today?

The first would be this: **Be expansive and inclusive!** Widen the moral situation, create a larger circle of members, of options, of viewpoints. Moral decision making is not simply a function of personal autonomy and individual rights. Diane's life and final days might have been more peaceful if others around her had helped her to see beyond the narrow set of options she viewed, because of her despair and fears.

A second moral element might be: **Emotions are morally relevant!** Diane, the doctor, her husband and son all seemed to put their emotions on hold as they attempted to deal with this situation. Diane was intent on "maintaining control" right up to the end. Diane's husband and son left her alone when she asked them to leave. What were they feeling? Where was their connection? Dr. Quill refused to listen to his "gut" – he gave her what she wanted. And yet, Diane's negative emotional state was really driving the entire situation.

A third moral element would be: **Be creative! Don't play things conservatively ... take moral risks!** Diane's family could have acted more dramatically to build and sustain their relationships with her. They could have stepped forward and attempted to act on her behalf. Everyone in this situation was far too passive; Diane was in total control. This was not healthy for her, nor was it a harmonious communal scenario. Who was acting in such a way that beauty was brought to birth in this situation?

A fourth moral element would be: **Be faithful!** At a certain point, her husband and son, for whatever reasons, left Diane. Alone she entered into the despair, to the realm of hopelessness. She acted in the best way she could, but where were the others?

A final moral element would be: **Know when to act!** Everyone in this situation remained passive throughout the entire development of the illness. What was her husband thinking and feeling? What was he doing? Where were the moral artisans in this situation? The most significant action was taken by Dr. Quill when he falsified the medical report. This is perhaps the most dissonant note of all. Why, if he had acted well, did he need to lie?

Like contemporary moral thinkers, the Franciscan approach views the moral person as one who stands at the center of the moral discussion, both as agent and as object of love and care. But, unlike the contemporary culture, the moral person is not understood only as an autonomous agent, but rather as the person in relationship to others and within a community affected deeply by her choices and actions. Scotus provides us with a moral vision that is both personalized and creative. It seeks to promote the development of moral persons who are sensitive to beauty around them and alert to the opportunities for creative response in particular situations. His theory calls for the highest level of personal and intellectual training and development, better to hear the Spirit's call. Such moral artisans can be creators of beauty in the world.

In *Speaking from the Heart,* Rita Manning identifies the moral goal of modernity as the development of the unencumbered self.[55] Diane was certainly an example of this independent, autonomous, objective moral agent. This is the self capable of objective judgment, of standing back and assessing a situation, or so she thought. This notion of the self

---

[55] A term she borrows from Michael Sandel. See Rita C. Manning, *Speaking from the Heart: A Feminist Perspective on Ethics* (Lanham, MD: Rowman & Littlefield Publishers, 1992), 2-4.

is found both in Kantian and Utilitarian discussions. Such a self has only one purpose: to become the autonomous moral agent, capable of free decisions and of defending his or her rights in any situation. In the context of libertarian models of freedom, such a self is limited only by the exercise of others in their search for freedom and happiness. Susan Sherman writes, "Within feminist ethics, there is a widespread criticism of the assumption that the role of ethics is to clarify obligations among individuals who are viewed as paradigmatically equal, independent, rational and autonomous."[56]

Like many contemporary writers, Scotus sees the moral order as going far beyond the individual self to point toward communion and relationship with others, but ultimately with God. In this, his Christian and Franciscan identity plays a key role. Understanding God as Triune Communion, he sees participation in divinity as the true human goal. This goal is ultimately a deep relationship of love based upon the nature of God as source of reality.

This type of Trinitarian foundation has clear implications for an environmental ethic as well. If we are called to imitate divine life, then we are called to an expanding life of inclusive love: for other persons, for developing cultures, for our beautiful world, for all being that gives praise to God. Moral living is not a narrow corner of our life, comprised of the "dos" and the "don'ts." Moral living is a way of being that promotes beauty, life and love throughout all that is. Such a way of being requires responsible use of the goods of the earth.

## IV. Implications and Conclusions

Scotus's choice of aesthetic imagery to explain his Franciscan moral insights has significance today in light of four key aspects. First, an artistic paradigm is holistic and incarnational: it addresses the intricacy at the heart of what is often seen as a moral divide between mind and body, between

---

[56] Susan Sherman, "Feminist and Medical Ethics: Two Different Approaches to Contextual Ethics," in *Feminist Perspectives in Medical Ethics* (Bloomington, IN: Indiana University Press, 1992), 21.

principles and virtuous acts. In an artistic model, learned behavior forms the artisan guided by fundamental moral principles. There is a body of knowledge that belongs to the artist, knowledge he has learned from masters of the craft and from his own experience. In the artistic performance, there is no gap between abstract theory and concrete *praxis* to be overcome, as we try to get from what we know we should do to actually doing it. Acting embodies knowledge. The domain of human *praxis* includes internal and external realms which are not opposed to one another. Together they form that harmonious unity of character called integrity.

Second, the artistic imagery supports the focus on love and beauty, but far beyond that imagined by Elaine Scarry. Both in human moral choices and in the order of divine communion, the aesthetic domain offers the bridge between human experience and divine life. There is no break between this world and the next. True moral living is part of a spiritual journey of artistic training and development, promoting beauty in the world and in the human heart.

What's more, as Scotus affirms, we are all naturally constituted to achieve such artistic excellence. The native freedom of the human will moves toward the good and seeks to love appropriately. The affection for justice finds its object in *bonum honestum*, or the good of value, and in God, the highest and most perfect Beauty.

Third, this imagery integrates the notion of *praxis* around the functioning moral agent as artist of beauty. Like the artist or musician, the moral person follows a high standard. Yet the actions of a moral expert are not different in kind from those of any moral agent. Proper and appropriate moral decision making is itself the goal of all human action. Moral actions have less to do with *what* we love but with *how well* we love one another. Moral living is a way of being in the world. It is not simply a question of choosing, but of choosing well and "rejoicing, loving and hating rightly."[57] Moral education involves the training and development of moral sensibilities.

---

[57] Aristotle, *Politics,* 1340a, 15.

Fourth, moral development is a communal endeavor. It is the work of persons in relationship to one another and to the world around them. It is generous, generative and life promoting. The danger of moral autonomy is, quite simply, that of moral perfectionism where I try to attain all the moral virtues to an eminent degree. In achieving my own perfection, I lose sight of my capacity for failure and for compassion.

It is, indeed, easy to see how such an inclusive and aesthetic moral approach would have significant value for the domain of environmental ethics, a central concern for Franciscan spirituality and for contemporary moral reflection. How we treat the natural order, foundational for our personal and communal experience of beauty, directly manifests our moral attitudes. How we develop that self-restraint necessary for sustainability and proper use of resources is central to moral development over a lifetime. How we broaden our categories of moral concern for others, other nations, particularly the most vulnerable, gives witness to our moral development, far beyond personal autonomy to interpersonal development.

Goodness, like beauty, attracts the natural affection within the will to love generously. In his work, *The Glory of the Lord,* Hans Urs von Balthasar has argued that a culture that loses a sense of what is beautiful is drawn to forget both what is true and what is good.[58] If this is indeed the case, then any attempt to engage in contemporary discussion on moral matters would do well to consider an approach that begins not with moral dilemmas or exceptional cases, with obligations, with laws or rules, but rather with the experience of beauty as foundational to the morally good life.

The purpose of moral living might best be understood as the formation of artisans capable of bringing forth beauty in the contingent order, thus expressing their freedom and creativity in imitation of God. As the following chapters make clear, both the exercise of freedom and the judgments of conscience take their appropriate place within the larger spiritual path of the *via pulchritudinis.* Such an artistic approach could indeed provide the basis for a rich and fruitful reflec-

---

[58] Hans Urs von Balthasar, *The Glory of the Lord* (San Francisco: Ignatius Press, 1989), 19.

tion on the moral domain, conceived neither as a realm of un-
yielding absolute principles nor as a field of personal preference. Moral living could once again be understood according
to a broad and inclusive frame that promotes the integration
of what is best in rational human loving and spiritual aspirations.

# 4

## GENEROSITY IN ACTION:
## FRANCISCAN PERSPECTIVES
## ON LOVE AND FREEDOM

### THOMAS A. SHANNON

*The Franciscan moral vision emphasizes
a dynamic realization
of creative and loving freedom
in relation to God's love.*

*The Franciscan moral vision
is more properly understood as a wisdom tradition
rather than a scientifically organized system
of analytic thought.*

The previous chapters considered the center of the spiritual vision of Clare and Francis and how that vision was developed theologically. Additionally, we have seen the significance of goodness and beauty within the tradition as providing the basis for the moral vision of Franciscan living. The purpose of this chapter is to provide an in-depth presentation of the Franciscan perspectives on love and freedom. We will focus on the moral theology as found in works of Bonaventure and Duns Scotus, both of whom understand human morality as "generosity in action." This contribution to ethics has a major bearing on Catholic morality today, particularly with respect to social justice, ecology, and economics.

## I. BONAVENTURE'S ETHIC OF LOVE

Probably one of the most familiar bible verses is John 3:16: "God so loved the world that he gave his only Son so whoever believes in him may not die but may have eternal life." This text focuses on God's love for the world and God's desire to save those who believe in the Son. The Gospel of John reflects on the outpouring of God's love for the world. This love is clearly other-directed and seeks to be returned, but the return of this love is through the salvific work of the Son. Such a model of generosity in action provides the critical paradigm for a corresponding human ethic of generosity in action.

In his theology, Bonaventure makes a critical shift from love to goodness by uniting these two realities through his analysis of another text, Luke 18:19: "No one is good but God alone." Bonaventure develops this theme using the critical insight – *bonum est diffusivum sui* (goodness is diffusive of itself). This grounds a major difference between Aquinas and Bonaventure. Aquinas follows Aristotle in identifying God as the Supreme Being. Bonaventure does not reject this insight but complements it by incorporating into it the name of God from the Christian Scriptures: Love. Here Bonaventure develops a "metaphysics of love." "God is Being; but Being in its highest form is self-communicating Love."[1] Zachary Hayes summarizes Bonaventure's position this way:

> If God is the highest Good, and the nature of the highest Good is to be found in the highest form of love, then the mystery of the Trinity becomes the mystery of the primordial, self-communicative love which is

---

[1] Zachary Hayes, "Faith and Reason: Beyond the Prime Mover of Aristotle," Lecture given at St. Bonaventure University, July 14, 2002, 6.

productive within the Godhead before it moves outside to create the universe.[2]

While agreeing with Aristotle and Aquinas that God exists as the primordial reality, Bonaventure goes beyond this
by describing this reality as relational, as a fecundity of love
that communicates itself both internally as the persons of
the Trinity and externally in the free gift of creation that
reaches its high point in the Incarnation. This leads to Bonaventure's use of the symbol of the fountain to express the
richness of divine love and its profound expression of loving
generosity that provides a foundation for our moral vision.
"With this he gives a strong emphasis to the fertility of the
divine, creative love (*fontalis plenitudo*) from which flows the
immanent movements of the divine love-life within the trinity, and from which flows the remarkably rich stream of created reality."[3] This perspective grounds one of the primary
characteristics of the Franciscan tradition: God as a community of persons in a relation of mutuality that is imaged in
human life.[4]

The theology of Bonaventure is permeated with a vision
of love grounded in an understanding of God as Goodness as
we saw in Chapter Two. His development of the theology of
the Trinity is premised on the relation of the persons within
reciprocal relationships of love and self-giving. As Bonaventure says, "Because God is most perfect, he is of the highest goodness; because he is of the highest goodness, he wills
to produce many things and to share himself."[5] In the Bo-
naventurian perspective "God is an outward-moving dynamic Trinity, whose essential life is marked by personal gift."[6]
The practical application follows naturally: "To be is to be

---

[2] Zachary Hayes, *Bonaventure: Mystical Writings* (NY: Crossroad,
1999), 109.

[3] Hayes, *Bonaventure: Mystical Writings*, 7.

[4] Cf. Kenan Osborne, O.F.M., *A Theology of the Church for the Third
Millennium* (Leiden: Brill, 2001).

[5] St. Bonaventure, *Commentary on II Sentences*, I, 2, I, I, resp. Quoted
in Kevin P. Keane, "Why Creation? Bonaventure and Thomas Aquinas on
God as Creative Good," *Downside Review*, 97 (1975): 100-21 at 111.

[6] Keane, "Why Creation?" 112.

diffusive; goodness is being itself."[7] This outpouring is manifest first in the act of creation of the universe. Within this first incarnation of God's love for the other, the Incarnation of the Word then becomes the total outpouring of the Divine to the totally other – the material world – that is ultimately reciprocated in the personal gesture of supreme love of the Incarnate Word's self-giving in the cross. And in the Franciscan tradition, this expression of love will take on a practical form: lives lived in poverty and service as a way of imitating this profound divine generosity.

In this perspective, the act of creation is a continuation of the self-diffusive love of God. God's creativity is grounded in God's own self-communicative love. Creation is an outward expression of God's self-communicative love expressed first in the Word, and then in the Incarnation. As Catherine LaCugna expresses it,

> God goes forth from God. God creates the world, suffuses its history and dwells within us, redeeming the world from within. God makes an eternal gift to the world of God's very self so that we become by Grace what God is already by nature, namely, self-donating love for the other.[8]

Therefore, "Creation reflects the Word of God's self-expression that becomes incarnate in Jesus Christ; thus, creation returns to the depths of the divine love in and through increasing conformity to the incarnate Word."[9] Redemption is more a transformation of the world and in this process humans become a fuller expression of the image in which they were originally created. The need for redemption is still front and center in Bonaventure's world, but the shift is from a justice model to a love or transformation model. Thus, the primal generosity of God within the life of the Trinity and

---

[7] Keane, "Why Creation?" 115.

[8] Catherine LaCugna, *God for Us* (New York: HarperCollins, 1993), 353-54, cited in Delio, "Theology, Metaphysics and the Centrality of Christ," *Theological Studies* 68 (2007): 260.

[9] Ilia Delio, "Theology, Metaphysics and the Centrality of Christ," 266.

externally in creation and in the radical love expressed in the cross shows us how we are to live and provides us with the basis of our moral lives: generosity in action. Or, as Delio expresses it,

> Bonaventure's focus on Christ crucified as the metaphysical center underscores the power of God's unconditional love revealed in the Cross. If God is a Trinity of love, then the Trinity expresses itself in history in the utter self-emptying of the Crucified. God is most God-like on the cross where the metaphysical center shows itself in love unto death.[10]

This transformative power of love as the core of redemption is described in very personal terms by Bonaventure in this section of *The Mystical Vine*:

> When I created you, I conformed you to the likeness of My divinity. In order to re-form you I became conformed to the likeness of your humanity. Do you, who did not keep the form of My divinity which was impressed on you when you were created, keep at least that imprint of your humanity which was stamped on me when you were re-formed. If you did not stay as I created you, at least stay as I have re-created you. If you do not understand how great were the powers I granted you in creating you, understand at least how great were the miseries I accepted for you in your humanity, in re-creating you, and in re-forming you for joys much greater than those for which I hand originally formed you.[11]

Emmanuel Falque states it this way: "... such a truth will take on a performative sense, one that is transforming

---

[10] Delio, "Theology, Metaphysics ...," 271.
[11] St. Bonaventure, *The Mystical Vine*, 24:3.

for the subject that states it or it will not exist."[12] Zachary Hayes's formulation is:

> The life of grace and the imitation of Christ are a process of responding to the divine offer and the example of Christ. And the human person is changed in that process. We become like what we love. And if it is the divine, self-sacrificing love, we will become human beings to truly reflect such love in the world of human relations.[13]

This perspective also grounds the Franciscan characteristics that focus on a dynamic realization of creative and loving freedom in response to God's love present in the world.

This theme of generosity and self-giving is also derivative from the Pauline kenotic theology that states, simply but effectively, the core mystery of such generosity. Even divinity is not to be clung to, but is willing to totally give of itself to the other:

> His state was divine,
> Yet he did not cling
> To his equality with God
> But he emptied himself
> To assume the condition of a slave,
> And became as men are,
> And being as all men are,
> He was humbler yet,
> Even to accepting death,
> Death on a cross.[14]

Bonaventure captures this in his metaphor of God as a fountain-fullness, an ever-renewing source of refreshment

---

[12] Emmanuel Falque, "The Phenomenological Act of Perscrutation in the Proemium of St. Bonaventure's Commentary of the Sentences," *Medieval Philosophy and Theology* 10 (2001): 18.

[13] Hayes, *Bonaventure: Mystical Writings*, 121.

[14] Phil 2:6-8, in *The Jerusalem Bible* (Garden City, NY: Doubleday, 1996).

and generativity. In the mystery of the Trinity we see the roots of a core element of the Franciscan tradition that sets in motion a profound grounding of an ethic: poverty as a way of expressing the fountain fullness of generosity of God's love for all. But this is not a vision of poverty primarily as an absence of material goods, though to be sure there are clear lifestyle implications included in this vision of poverty.

Rather this is poverty as love and generosity, poverty as an imitation of the deepest reality of the mystery of God – radical self-giving love, total generosity of self for the other. Thus the entire universe and all in it is a pure gift, an overflowing of the self-diffusive goodness of God. The implication of this is an attitude of disponability, or openness to another, with respect to both the self and one's possessions.[15] The translation of this into daily life is primarily a willingness to release the typical grasp that we maintain on either ourselves or our possessions. Poverty as love and generosity implies an attitude of openness to the other on a variety of levels as we meet the other in different situations. It may require a generosity with respect to the time another needs, a generosity with respect to affirming the value of another, or a generosity in responding to the material needs of another. Poverty as generosity requires an attitude of open heart and hands to others in simple but profound imitation of the divine emptying that we have first received. Franciscan poverty is an imitation of the outstretched arms of Christ on the cross.

As the preceding chapter has noted, the ethic that follows from this thus requires an ongoing process of discernment by the intellectual, affective, and volitional dimensions of the person as a whole. This is because the Franciscan ethic is grounded in the two deepest realities of our being created in the image of God. First, our God is first and foremost a community of love. Second, that love is a fountain fullness of a continual outpouring of that love both within the community of the Trinity and without to all of creation. The Franciscan ethic is thus not simply a method but an engagement of the

---

[15] Thomas A. Shannon, "The Existential Modality of the Person According to Gabriel Marcel," *Insight: Quarterly Review of Religion and Mental Health* 4 (September, 1965): 35-44.

whole person in an act of creative fidelity to the love of God and the expression of this engagement in a life of generous service. The centrality of love with its expression in generosity is grounded in Bonaventure's vision of God as self-diffusive goodness. The implication is that "created beings must be diffusive as their creator is diffusive, for this is what it is to be and for Bonaventure nothing can turn inward without corrupting itself, since the centrifugal movement of diffusion is life itself."[16]

## II. Scotus's Ethic of Freedom and Love

While most know Scotus as a philosopher, there is clearly a theological underlay to his work. Both of these orientations are ultimately founded on his commitment to the Franciscan way of life and insights from Francis and Bonaventure. Though Scotus makes the use of Aristotle more explicit in his philosophy than Bonaventure does, the core of his work remains inspired by and faithful to his Franciscan roots, particularly to its commitment to living in creative and loving freedom in response to God's love. Additionally, Scotus shifts from Bonaventure's emphasis on the goodness of God by returning to John 3:16 ("For God so loved the world ...") as the basis for his reflections on Christology. His Christology, therefore, is critical in understanding his approach to love and freedom. Traditionally, in Western theology, redemption is presented as a form of justice owed to God because of the sin of Adam and Eve. The universe had so departed from its original plan that God had to change direction, as it were, by sending a Redeemer to redeem humans, because only such a divine Redeemer can satisfy the offended justice of God the Father. The love that God shows us is primarily a redemptive love focused on restoring the relation between humanity and God that was destroyed because of sin. Thus, the purpose of the Incarnation is to manifest a redemptive love seemingly

---

[16] Shannon, "The Existential Modality ...," 117.

conditioned upon the sin of Adam, a perspective reflected in the Exultet, the hymn proclaimed during the Easter Vigil.

> O wonder of your humble care for us!
> O love, O charity beyond all telling,
> To ransom a slave you gave away your Son!
>
> O truly necessary sin of Adam,
>
> Destroyed completely by the Death of Christ!
> O happy fault
> that earned so great, so glorious a Redeemer![17]

This theme of the Exultet – that the purpose of the Incarnation was to redeem fallen humanity – is close to a normative paradigm for understanding God's love for us and makes a necessary causal link between the sin of Adam and the Incarnation and Redemption. This liturgical perspective was given additional theological status by Anselm of Canterbury in his theory of satisfaction developed in the text *Cur Deus Homo*. Here, the redemptive paradigm is centered on justice and the satisfaction required in justice for sin. As Anselm says,

> So he who violates another's honor does not enough by merely rendering honor again, but must, according to the extent of the injury done, make restoration in some way satisfactory to the person whom he has dishonored.[18]

Now since sin is a violation of the honor due to God, recompense for that sin must take the form of either punishment or satisfaction. However, the satisfaction can only be made by one who is both divine – and therefore capable of making appropriate satisfaction – and human – the one who

---

[17] Roman Missal, English translation according to the Third Typical Edition, 2011.

[18] St. Anselm, *Cur Deus Homo?*, Book I, ch. 11 (Oxford and London: John Henry and James Parker, 1865).

is required to make the satisfaction. Only the person of Jesus who is both God and human is capable of this act of reparation and, therefore, the Incarnation is necessary as a precondition for this act of redemption.

The Franciscan tradition developed by Scotus focuses on the primacy of love, the ultimate free gift of self to all of creation. The tradition presents the primacy of Christ, a primacy based on the over-flowing generosity of God who desired to communicate the very depths of God's own self to one other than God. Thus our redemption is not the motive for the Incarnation. The Incarnation represents the supreme overflowing of the love of God into the universe and God's being united to this universe so intimately that the reality of God is personified in Jesus Christ who is the perfect loving and incarnated response of the universe to God.

In one concise argument that is in harmony with the traditions of Gregory of Nyssa, Irenaeus, and other early theologians, Scotus provides an alternative to the *Exultet* and shows why redemption is not the motive for the Incarnation:

> Consequently, we can say that God selected for his heavenly choir all the angels and men he wished to have with their varied degrees of perfection, and all this before considering either the sin or the punishment of the sinner. No one therefore is predestined simply because God foresaw another would fall, lest anyone have reason to rejoice at the misfortune of another.[19]

Thus, the Incarnation is the reality of the self-communicative love of God that reaches its perfection in one other than God: Jesus Christ. Zachary Hayes frames the issue in this way:

> God creates so that Christ may come into existence. So that Christ may exist, there must be a human race.

---

[19] Allan B. Wolter, *John Duns Scotus Four Questions on Mary* (St. Bonaventure, NY: Franciscan Institute Publications, 2012), 28-29.

But a human race needs a place in which to live. So it is that, for both Bonaventure and Scotus, though for each in a distinctive way, a cosmos without Christ is a cosmos without its head.[20]

Thus, our salvation is the completion of what God intended from the beginning: union with the cosmos personally expressed in the return of love from Christ, the supreme reconciliation of the opposites of divinity and matter. As Delio expresses it,

In short, the primacy of Christ tradition underscores a positive relationship between Creation and Incarnation in such a way that love and not sin is the reason for Christ, a love which binds together all things in the unity of God.[21]

Scotus thus presents a love that is dynamic, overflowing, and generous. As Scotus says: "For the highest Good can freely communicate of himself and show himself as generous not out of necessity but as free in his generous communication."[22] The God of Scotus is a gift-giver, one who seeks not only to give of God's deepest self, but one who gives precisely to be united with the recipient. This is a personal love that communicates itself to that which is totally other – the material – and in doing so, confers the gift of that created matter's becoming conscious of itself so that it can respond to such a gift of love from the depths of creation as a person. The highest expression of this is found in the Incarnation, the infusion of the divine with the human and the human with the divine. Thus:

---

[20] Zachary Hayes, O.F.M., "Christ, Word of God and Exemplar of Humanity," *The Cord* 46 (1996): 6, quoted in Ilia Delio, "Revisiting the Franciscan Doctrine of Christ," *Theological Studies* 64 (2003): 3-23.

[21] Delio, "Revisiting the Franciscan Doctrine...," 23.

[22] Ox I, d. 41, q.u.X, 699b, quoted in Giovanni Iammarrone, O.F.M. Conv., "The Timeliness and Limitations of the Christology of John Duns Scotus for the Development of a Contemporary Theology of Christ," *Greyfriars Review* 7: 239 note 41.

> The Incarnation represents not a divine response to a human need for salvation but instead the divine intention from all eternity to raise human nature to the highest point by uniting it with divine nature.[23]

This reveals both creation and Incarnation as the deepest expressions of the love of God that is freely given. Such perfect love "is not possessive, but self-transcending and creative of relationship. It takes the lover out of himself in union with the beloved. It is an act whose dynamism never ends."[24]

## A. Steadfast Love in Action

Scotus's analysis of aspects of freedom provides an exceptionally rich understanding of freedom as a core locus for morality, particularly since this dimension of freedom leads beyond considering freedom as primarily or exclusively a choice between alternatives. Such a freedom, as William Frank notes, is "freedom beyond choice"[25] and it provides a way to see the unity of both intention and act in making a moral choice. A core feature of this is Scotus's concept of *firmitas*: "the will's ability to adhere to that in which consists its perfection."[26]

Scotus gives this citation from Augustine's *Enchiridion* to elaborate his position,

> 'It was fitting that men should be made in the first place with the power to will both good and evil – if good, not without reward; if evil, not without impunity.' That is to say, in that first state, man is capable of both merit and demerit. And he [Augustine] continues, 'In the afterlife he will not be able to will evil and yet he will not be deprived of its free will. In fact, his will be much freer in that it will in no way be subject

---

[23] Delio, "Revisiting the Franciscan Doctrine ...," 9.

[24] Mary Beth Ingham, *Scotus for Dunces: An Introduction to the Subtle Doctor* (St. Bonaventure, NY: Franciscan Institute Publications, 2003), 107.

[25] Quoted in Ingham, *Scotus for Dunces*, 68.

[26] Ingham, *Scotus for Dunces*, 80.

to sin.' And he [Augustine] adds a proof, as it were. 'For the will is not to be blamed nor should we say that it was no will or that it was not free, when we so will to be happy that we not only do not want to be miserable, but are quite unable to will this. Just as our soul is at present unwilling to be unhappy, so then it will for ever be unwilling to be wicked.'[27]

Scotus also cites Anselm's *Free Choice:*

'Whoever has what is appropriate and advantageous in such a way that it cannot be lost is freer than he who has this in such a way that it can be lost.' From this he [Anselm] concludes: 'The will then which cannot cease to be upright is freer.'[28]

Scotus himself continues by arguing:

Action that has to do with the ultimate end is most perfect. But firmness (*firmitas*) pertains to the perfection of such an action. Therefore, the necessity that is to be found there does not do away with, but rather demands what is needed for perfection, namely freedom.[29]

---

[27] John Duns Scotus, *God and Creatures: The Quodlibetal Questions*, translated with an introduction, notes and glossary by Felix Alluntis and Allan Wolter (Princeton: Princeton University Press, 1975), 377-78. The citation is from Augustine, *Enchiridion*, c. 28, n. 105, in *PL* 40, 281; *CCSL* 96, 106.

[28] John Duns Scotus, *God and Creatures*, 378. The citation is based on Anselm's, *De libero arbitrio*, c. 1. See S. Anselmi, *Opera Omnia*, Vol. I, ed. Franciscus Schmitt (Edinburgh: Thomas Nelson & Sons, 1946), 208.

[29] This reading of Quodlibet 16:32 is based on alternate manuscripts proposed by William A. Frank in his doctoral dissertation *John Duns Scotus' Quodlibetal Teaching on the Will* (Ann Arbor, University Microfilms International, 1982), 70, note 25. The translation is cited from *Duns Scotus on The Will And Morality*, trans. and ed. Allan B. Wolter (Washington, DC: The Catholic University of America Press, 1986), 15. Here Wolter accepts the revised reading proposed by Frank and provides a corrected translation for the text in God and Creatures, 378. The Latin text of Scotus is as follows. *Et primo sic: Actio circa finem ultimum est actio perfectissima; in*

What is significant is that freedom "expresses the ability on the part of the will to achieve perfection through the active union with its beloved."[30] Such a conception of freedom far outstrips our commonplace understanding of freedom as the ability to choose. From the perspective of steadfastness or *firmitas*, freedom is "understood as the ability to adhere to its object in a self-actualizing action, the love-product of which is in no way prefigured in the will nor coerced by the object."[31] Thus, freedom for Scotus is not limited to free choice only. But, here there is a dramatic difference between divine freedom and human freedom.

God, in a single, perfectly free act of love, chooses God's own self as the only perfect good commensurate with the very nature of God and this act expresses the fullness of God's free love. Thus, "[t]he only response of an infinite will that befits the infinite beloved is a love exhausting, as it were, the lover's capacity of love and the beloved's capacity to be loved."[32] This means that God's freedom is a freedom beyond choice.

On the human level, however, we are aware that any choice we make is only one of many possible acts and does not in fact express the fullness of our freedom. This means that this choice is not infinitely perfect. Thus, we always experience freedom as a series of particular, limited choices. We are aware that we could have chosen otherwise and that such a choice would have given a different degree of perfection: "choice is simply basic freedom in inferior conditions."[33] While willing, our will is never fully actual, for it is contingent. Yet, for all that, we can approach our perfection through our steadfastness in cleaving to the object of our love. According to Scotus "(t)he perfection of freedom connotes a perse-

---

*tali actione firmitas in agendo est perfectionis, igitur necessitas in ea non tolit sed magis ponit illud quod est perfectionis; si est libertas.*

[30] Frank, *Quodlibetal Teaching*, 82.

[31] Frank, *Quodlibetal Teaching*, 85.

[32] William A. Frank, "Duns Scotus's Concept of Willing Freely: What Divine Freedom Beyond Choice Teaches Us," *Franciscan Studies* 42 (1982): 73.

[33] Frank, "Duns Scotus's Concept of Willing Freely ...," 87.

verance and stability in the will's adherence to the good."[34] This grounds the Franciscan commitment to human growth and development as the basis for conversion. The tradition recognizes that while not each and every human act or solution is perfect, human acts and solutions are in fact perfectible. Thus, the human commitment to the pursuit of ever more perfect moral actions results in a process of continuous conversion. While neither denying nor denigrating choice or the significance of the moral act as a consequence of a choice, Scotus's emphasis on steadfastness in the pursuit of perfection, or *firmitas*, highlights what we would term continuity in moral development through continued practice and performance. This leads to an emphasis on the inherent value of the good and the ensuing perfection that comes from continued adherence to it. Scotus's concept of *firmitas* gives us a way of affirming the moral significance of the act, but more important, of appreciating the transformative possibilities that emerge from the constant adherence to the particular good achieved through continual practice. Freedom understood as *firmitas* leads us beyond the individual act to a deeper examination of the good at stake and to an evaluation of the individual act in relation to the whole of one's life. That is, the individual act receives its meaning and significance from its relation to the project of one's life which is characterized by steadfast adherence to the good. The Scotistic concept of *firmitas* gives moral priority to the constancy of the commitment to the good, not the isolated act apart from the totality of one's commitment, thus also grounding the moral integration of actor and act.

One's moral intention comes from one's steadfastness in the good (*firmitas*) rather than from an individual, isolated act, thus uniting in a profound way both intention and the act. Thus again, the Franciscan ethical tradition focuses not on a method or to a set of specific rules but on the good and to continually living in generosity. Thus the tradition offers a holistic vision of life that integrates both one's commitment

---

[34] Frank, *Quodlibetal Teaching*, 87.

to the good as well as living out that commitment through generosity of action.[35]

## B. Anthropological Perspectives

Scotus's thought also presents an interesting grounding for the experience of self-transcendence. As also discussed in the previous chapter, this is based on his distinction between the *affectio commodi*, the inclination to do what is to my advantage, and the *affectio justitiae*, the inclination to do justice to the intrinsic reality of a particular being or situation. In the former, nature seeks its self-perfection, whether in the individual or the species. Seeking what is to one's advantage actualizes the potential instilled in one by virtue of what the being is. That is, it is quite natural for all beings to seek out their own perfection. That is what they are designed to do and that is what their job is, so to speak. From the viewpoint of a nature, this quest for perfection is a good because it fulfills the nature by enabling it to become what it is. Scotus, however, contrasts nature to will. A nature is a principle of activity by which an entity acts out or realizes its essence and is the reason why an entity acts as it does. A will, on the other hand, "is not of itself so determined, but can perform either this act or its opposite, or can either act or not act at all."[36] Thus, the reason why this act was done as opposed to another is that the will is the will and can elicit an act in opposite ways.

The *affectio justitiae* is one of the many gifts given us by God and is the source of true freedom or liberty of the will, as well as a restraint on the *affectio commodi*. The *affectio justitiae* allows us to transcend nature and natural causal determinism and go beyond ourselves and our individually

---

[35] For further reading, see *Manual de Teología franciscana*, ed. José Antonio Merino y Francisco Martinez Fresnada (BAC: 2003), particularly Chapter 7 *Teologia Moral y Politica* by José Parada Navas, 415-72.

[36] *Quaestiones Metaphysicam* I, q. 15, Article 2, in Wolter, *Will and Morality,* 151.

defined good.[37] The *affectio justitiae* is the capacity to see the value of another being.

> To want an act to be perfect, so that by means of it one may better love some object for its own sake, is something that stems from the affection for justice, for when I love something good in itself, then I will something in itself.[38]

Paradoxically then, if a free agent acts merely according to nature, it acts "unnaturally" with respect to seeking its total good, since to seek what is "*bonum in se* is not to seek something that 'realizes the potential of a rational nature.'" It is somehow to transcend "the *natura*" and thus to have a mode of operation that sets the rational agent apart from all other agencies."[39] What Scotus is arguing here is that while it is good to seek the fulfillment of our own nature, there is another dimension of reality that will bring us to a state of perfection beyond our own nature.[40] This is seeking the good in itself or, to put it in theological language, seeking our ultimate good who is God. Thus, Scotus moves from the constraints of our nature that limit us to self-perfection to an openness to the better or best that will take us beyond our nature to our supernatural perfection: life in God. This then translates to a life lived in imitation of God which, for the Franciscan tradition, is a life of generosity in action.

---

[37] "Similarly, as Anselm and Scotus insist, the dignity of rational creatures, the crown of moral life, lies in their capacity for self-determined commitment to something else – to right reason, or to God loved above all and for his own sake, or to both, even to a heroic degree at the cost of life and happiness." Marilyn McCord Adams, "Ockham on Will, Nature, and Morality," *Cambridge Companion to Ockham*, ed. P.V. Spade (Cambridge: Cambridge University Press, 1999), 245-72, at 267.

[38] *Ordinatio*, supp. dist. 49, qq. 9-10, in Wolter, *Will and Morality*, 477.

[39] John Boler, "The Moral Psychology of Duns Scotus: Some Preliminary Questions." *Franciscan Studies*, 50 (1990): 31-56.

[40] "If willpower were constituted by the affection for advantage alone, it would lack the ecstatic reach required for moral virtue or merit, which Scotus takes to be the glory of created rational agency." Adams, "Ockham on Will, Nature, and Morality," 253.

The will's seeking justice grounds our capacity to transcend our own self-interest. For Scotus, the *affectio justitiae*, which is the key to understanding both freedom and steadfastness, allows us to understand freedom as "a positive bias or inclination to love things objectively or as right reason dictates."[41] That is, the proper focus of moral analysis is not the individual act or choice, but the inclination as a whole. And, such an inclination focuses on fidelity to the good in itself, not on an inclination which focuses on the specific act of choosing that good, nor the necessary appreciation of what is good for the fulfillment of the nature of the agent. The focus of moral analysis is not, therefore, simply centered on the individual act but on the good to which we wish to adhere and which is manifest in this particular act, a perspective also developed in the previous chapter. Key to this moral analysis are the joint concepts of practice and performance, which blend and integrate action and intent within the moral agent. Through the constant practice of acting virtuously, one learns more and more about the moral core of a particular virtue. And, the more skilled one becomes at the performance of what is morally good, the more steadfast one's adherence to the good becomes. Consequently, there is not a separate intention and a separate act, but a seamless performance of one's holding fast to the good.

Scotus here affirms that we have the capacity to value an entity for its own sake, independent of its personal or social utility. As he would phrase it, we have the ability to transcend the capacity to do justice to ourselves by doing justice to the good itself. The strong claim is that we are capable of recognizing the good and choosing it, at a given instance, even though such a choice may run counter to our personal self-interest or what fulfills our own nature. Valerius Messerich writes:

---

[41] Wolter, "Native Freedom of the Will as a Key to the Ethics of Scotus" in *The Philosophical Theology of John Duns Scotus*, ed. Marilyn McCord Adams (Ithaca, NY: Cornell, 1990), 152.

The will by freely moderating these natural and necessary tendencies to happiness and self-perfection is
able to transcend its nature and choose Being and
Goodness for their own sake.... Thus the free will is
not confined to objects or goods that perfect self, but
is capable of an act of love.... [L]ove is the most free of
all acts and the one that most perfectly expresses the
will's freedom to determine itself as it pleases.[42]

The conclusion is that one can distinguish at least a good
and a better in human life. What is good in human life is a
life that perfects us, that brings our being to a greater actu-
alization. This is the realization of the *affectio commodi*. And
while this is good, and brings our nature to self-perfection,
what is better is the transcendence of self, either to appreciate what is good or even to curb our legitimate interest in
self-perfection in order to seek the good of others for their
own sakes. This is the realization of the *affectio justitiae*.

While we can affirm self-perfection, such perfection is not
ultimately an end in itself. Rather, we must step beyond the
confines of self and actualize that most free of all acts, an act
of love for our neighbor that ultimately leads to a deeper love
for God. Only then do we find ourselves open to the depths
of reality. And in the steadfast adherence to that beloved, we
realize the fullness of freedom. Scotus's moral order is a relational order with love at the center, and this center is personified in the loving God who first loves us and calls us to
union. This leads to the fostering of reciprocal relationships
which result in an other-centered moral dynamic: love motivated by the value of the other, love culminating in self-sac-
rifice for the other that creates a community in which each
member seeks the good of all. The fullest expression of the
moral life is revealed in relations with others. This is a way
of living characterized by respect and love, not by manipula-

---

[42] Valerius Messerich, O.F.M., "The Awareness of Causal Initiative and
Existential Responsibility in the Thought of Duns Scotus," in *De Doctrina
Ioannis Duns Scoti* 2: *Problemata Philosophica* (Rome: Acta Congressus
Scotistici Internat., 1968), 629-44, at 630-31.

tion or control. It is a life lived in relationships of mutuality in imitation of the very nature of the Triune God.[43]

This moral vision is reinforced in Pope Benedict XVI's encyclical *Caritas in veritate*, "This dynamic of charity received and given is what gives rise to the Church's social teaching, which is *caritas in veritate in re sociali*: the proclamation of the truth of Christ's love in society."[44] Love is the grounding of the social ethic of the Church. Additionally, Pope Benedict, echoing Bonaventure, says of us humans:

> Charity in truth places man before the astonishing experience of gift. Gratuitousness is present in our lives in many different forms, which often go unrecognized because of a purely consumerist and utilitarian view of life. The human being is made for gift, which expresses and makes present his transcendent dimension.[45]

In this capacity for both giving and receiving gifts, Benedict XVI grounds an ethic that expresses the core insight of this chapter: "… if it is to be authentically human, [the human community] needs to make room for the principle of gratuitousness as an expression of fraternity."[46]

## C. The Influence of Love on Moral Action

While Scotus does not operate out of a virtue tradition as is currently being developed by many contemporary ethicists, nonetheless his writings on virtue provide an historical connection to this current development. Scotus sees virtues neither as relating us to our final end nor as even able to help us know our final end. As John Boler notes, "He [Scotus] is maintaining that morality cannot be an extension or refinement of a project of self-realization and/or eudaemonism (as

---

[43] Mary Beth Ingham, "Scotus and the Moral Order," *American Catholic Philosophical Quarterly* 67 (1993): 149.

[44] *Caritas in veritate*, 5.

[45] *Caritas in veritate*, 34.

[46] *Caritas in veritate*, 34.

that Aristotelian theme had been developed in the Middle Ages)."[47] Again this suggests that while seeking the fulfillment of our nature is a good, such a quest can take us only so far. Here Scotus brings in the revelation of our final end as a loving union with God to complement his philosophical understanding of virtue and its role in the moral life.

Following Ingham's analysis,[48] two elements are key: First, "natural goodness based upon virtue is needed as prerequisite for that moral goodness defined as the harmony of all circumstances under the dictates of right reason."[49] This component of natural virtue is not a totally free act, but nonetheless contributes to making such a free choice. Second, Scotus uses a concept of partial co-causality in which two causes "operate together to constitute an effect whose perfection is unattainable by either cause working separately."[50] In this instance, the moral cause, which is the will, operates with the natural cause, which is the habitual act. Here, free choice, or the actual moral act, relies heavily on virtue or the natural inclination to make the morally correct decision. As Ingham phrases it, "Natural virtue is a disposition toward love whose presence enhances, but does not entirely constitute the morally good act."[51] Thus, virtue gives a material basis or grounding for the moral act that is chosen freely under the guidance of right reason. Virtue consists of a natural inclination to the good, but a moral act is a free embracing of that good. Thus, for Scotus, virtue is "more to be identified with motivation than with performance: moral excellence is the perfection of motivation."[52]

What is critical is the interplay between the natural – virtue – and moral perfection – the free choice of the loving

---

[47] John Boler, "Transcending the Natural: Duns Scotus on the Two Affections of the Will," *American Catholic Philosophical Quarterly* 67 (1993): 110.

[48] Mary Beth Ingham, "*Ea Quae Sunt Ad Finem*: Reflections on Virtue as Means to Moral Excellence in Scotist Thought," *Franciscan Studies* 50 (1990): 177-95.

[49] Ingham, "*Ea Quae Sunt Ad Finem* ...," 190.

[50] Ingham, "*Ea Quae Sunt Ad Finem* ...," 190.

[51] Ingham, "*Ea Quae Sunt Ad Finem* ...," 192.

[52] Ingham, "*Ea Quae Sunt Ad Finem* ...," 193.

act. The free choice takes the moral actor beyond the natural goodness of the virtuous act and leads one to the loving choice of the good. As noted by Mary Beth Ingham in the previous chapter, one can do a particular deed – giving an alms to a poor person, for example – but can have a variety of motivations for doing so: to have the person stop pestering you, because you have some extra change in your pocket, or because you want to express your love for this person. Here we move from various levels of natural goodness to the loving choice of the good and with each shift in motivation, our actions become transformed, and for Scotus, this leads to dimensions of human fulfillment that are discovered in revelation. It is precisely in this position on free will that we see a critical shift from the eudaemonistic ethic of Aristotle and Aquinas to the love centered ethic of Scotus in which the virtues play an important part in disposing the moral agent to right action but, nonetheless, must be complemented by the free act of love of the good. As Bettoni phrases it,

> For Duns Scotus, just as for St. Augustine, virtue is not something valuable simply because it is a way of acting that is measured by, and in accordance with nature, as Aristotle teaches, but because of the act of love by which the virtuous act is directed to God.[53]

Thus, for Scotus, while the practice of the virtues brings one to a life of moral integrity and harmony with one's neighbors, such a life, while valuable in itself, is not sufficient for it does not of necessity lead one to one's final end: union with God. Thus, for Scotus, all virtuous acts must be fulfilled by an act of love that moves beyond what we can call the vertical field of natural virtues to a transcendent openness to a life of goodness revealed by God. While practicing the virtues can set us on the road to a life well lived, for Scotus, the goal is the life fully lived and this is found only through acts of love

---

[53] Efrem Bettoni, *Duns Scotus: Basic Principles of his Philosophy* (Washington, DC: Catholic University Press, 1961), 169. Cited in Mary Beth Ingham, "Scotus and the Moral Order," *American Catholic Philosophical Quarterly* 67 (1993): 144, note 47.

that open us to the love of God that is the fulfillment of our lives.

## D. The Decision-Making Process

Scotus also provides a process that one can use to achieve such free acts of love. Ultimately, we need to make a decision and shape that decision as best as we can so that it brings us as close to an act of love as possible.

Scotus's discussion of the Commandments follows their traditional division into two tablets or tables. The first table contains the first three commands which focus on human obligations to God. The second table – commandments four through ten – focuses on our obligations to our neighbor. Scotus's analysis of the second table with its obligations to one's neighbor is helpful for contemporary discussions of morality.

First, Scotus's affirmation of the contingency of the second table of the Decalogue grounds his critical argument that action itself is not sufficient to access its morality. Since Scotus argues that the love of God is the only act morally good under all circumstances (and conversely the hatred of God the only act morally evil under all circumstances), he also argues that an act has to be put into a context of meaning or intentionality before a judgment can be made about its morality. To state it differently, the moral standing of an act together with its consequences require further determination and precision in order to specify the concrete moral dimensions of the act. That is, the act in and of itself is not sufficient for a complete moral assessment. One would also need to know the intention and all the circumstances surrounding the act to adequately assess its moral status.

Second, objective morality is constituted not by the act's defining the intention but by the intention's defining the act. This is so because it is not the case that "the nature of its object determines its moral species: rather it opens it to further moral determination."[54] As Scotus argues, while one would think that the type of act signified by the terms adultery and

---

[54] Quodlibet, q. 18, in Wolter, *Will and Morality*, 215.

theft could not possibly be good, "it is possible for the under-lying act to exist without the deformity, for instance, the act of intercourse or that of appropriating such a thing."[55] From Scotus's perspective, a statement about or a description of the act as such is not sufficient to establish the morality of the act.[56] Attention is now centered on the co-causality of both the intention and the performance of the act, as inte-grated in the performance of the moral agent. Both act and intention are continually refined through practice and per-formance and the moral agent becomes more and more com-mitted to his or her steadfast apprehension and practice of the good that is the center of one's moral life.

Third, three elements are needed to determine the moral suitability of a specific act for a specific agent: (1) the nature of the agent "to act by virtue of intellectual knowledge, which alone is able to pass judgment, properly speaking, upon the appropriateness of the action";[57] (2) the nature of the agent which is the ability to actually "pass judgment upon the act and carry it out in accord with that judgment";[58] (3) the es-sential notion of the act itself which comes from a consider-ation of the circumstances of end, manner, time, and place.

Scotus writes that the "moral goodness of an act consists in its having all that the agent's right reason declares must pertain to the act or the agent in acting."[59] This is fulfilled when "these three notions are given [since] no other knowl-edge is needed to judge whether or not this particular act is suited to this agent and this faculty."[60]

---

[55] Quodlibet, q. 18, in Wolter, *Will and Morality*, 215.

[56] Cf. also Mary Beth Ingham's observation in "Scotus and the Moral Order," *American Catholic Philosophical Quarterly* 67 (1993): 139-40. She wrote that "The central moral issue for Scotus, however, seems to be found not in identifying objects which are good (since all creation is both good and ordered), but rather working out the adequation of loving relative to each object, and thus the increasing control of *affectio justitiae* over *affectio commodi*."

[57] *Ordinatio* 1, q. 18, in Wolter, *Will and Morality*, 213.

[58] *Ordinatio* 1, q. 18, in Wolter, *Will and Morality*, 213.

[59] Wolter, *Will and Morality*, 211.

[60] Wolter, *Will and Morality*, 213.

The Franciscan ethical perspective is thus not simply a methodology but, rather, a way of life grounded in the outpouring of the love of God for the world and humanity most fully revealed in the life of Christ. This way of life seeks to reciprocate this love by living a life of generosity made possible by our acts of love grounded in free and generous steadfastness that lead us on a path of continuous conversion. The Franciscan ethic is profoundly theological in that it is lived within the outpouring of the love of God and profoundly anthropological in that it sees a life of love and generosity as the most profound way of being human.

### III. CONTEMPORARY APPLICATIONS OF LOVE IN ACTION

The ethic of the Franciscan tradition is indeed an ethic of generosity in action. As Hayes notes in a comment on Bonaventure's text, *The Mystical Vine*:

In the midst of the meditation stands the word compassion. In terms of its etymology, the word comes from the Latin *com-pati*. This means, literally, "to bear, to endure, or to suffer with." It names a love, then that is willing to express itself in voluntary suffering for the good of others, as Christ has done. In this way, as Christ's human love in the service of God and humanity was a reflection of the mystery of the eternal Word, so the human love of the disciple of Christ will reflect the mystery of the eternal Word as the one who is totally from the Other, and totally at the service of the Other as it reaches to others. Meditation on the mystery of the cross should move one to a practical love of the crucified Christ which will express itself in the form of caring for others and in personal asceticism that takes its inspiration from the cross.[61]

---

[61] Hayes, *Bonaventure: Mystical Writings*, 125.

This perspective on ethics is, however, not limited to this tradition. For example, a profound expression of poverty as generosity on a social level is the option for the poor and an understanding of justice as participation as developed most profoundly in liberation theology, but also is a vision affirmed by the U.S. bishops in the pastoral letter *Economic Justice for All*.

This understanding of justice marks a significant stage of development in Roman Catholic social ethics. This stage begins with the papacy of Pope John XXIII who, in his first encyclical, *Mater et magistra*, noted the increasing complexity of social life and how the lives of individuals and the institutions in which they lived were more deeply intertwined. John went further by teaching that "the economic prosperity of any people is to be assessed not so much from the sum total of goods and wealth possessed as from the distribution of goods according to norms of justice, so that everyone in the community can develop and perfect himself."[62] Directly addressing the structural question, John noted that:

> [J]ustice is to be observed not merely in the distribution of wealth, but also in regard to the conditions under which men engaged in productive activity had an opportunity to assume responsibility and to perfect themselves by their efforts.[63]

As the contemporary encyclical tradition continued, a more developed sense of justice emerged that continued to focus on structural and institutional issues. *Octogesima adveniens* by Pope Paul VI focused again on the need to create a just social order, but one in the construction of which the poor themselves must be involved. The centrality of justice also for Christianity appears in the document *Justice in the World* from the 1971 Bishops' Synod in which they affirmed:

---

[62] *Mater et magistra*, no. 74. This can be found in David J. O'Brien and Thomas A. Shannon, *Catholic Social Thought: The Documentary Heritage* (Maryknoll, NY: Orbis, 1992), 96.

[63] *Mater et magistra*, no. 82, 97.

Action on behalf of justice and participation in the transformation of the world fully appear to us as a constitutive dimension of the preaching of the Gospel, or, in other words, of the Church's mission for the redemption of the human race and its liberation from every oppressive situation.[64]

This understanding of justice and its relation to graciousness was further developed by the U.S. bishops in their 1986 pastoral letter *Economic Justice for All*. In paragraphs 70 through 74, the bishops make a series of important claims about the nature of justice and its implications. In describing distributive justice, the bishops argue that allocation of income, wealth and power in society needs to be evaluated in light of its effects on persons whose basic material needs are unmet.[65] Of importance here is the inclusion of social power along with wealth and income as elements in an understanding of justice. In discussing social justice, the bishops argue that persons have an obligation to be active and productive participants in the life of society and that society has a duty to enable them to participate in this way.[66] This identifies an important new feature of justice: participation. While the poor must have their needs met, they in turn have the obligation to use their new standing to make their own contribution to society. Justice is a gift received and a gift given. Finally, the bishops note that basic justice calls for the establishment of a floor of material well-being on which all can stand. They argue that extreme inequality is a threat to the solidarity of the community for such because disparities lead to deep social division and contribute to division and conflict.[67]

This understanding of justice finds a natural home in the Franciscan tradition that stresses the generosity that must be at the heart of such a revised ethic of justice. The sense of justice proposed here is not a justice that seeks merely

---

[64] *Justice in the World*, Synod of Bishops, 1971, Introduction, *Catholic Social Thought* ..., 289.

[65] *Economic Justice for All*, no. 70, *Catholic Social Thought* ..., 595.

[66] *Economic Justice for All*, no. 71, *Catholic Social Thought* ..., 595.

[67] *Economic Justice for All*, no. 74, *Catholic Social Thought* ..., 596.

to give to each his or her due, a justice that is blind and impartial, nor a justice that seeks the fulfillment of each and every minute detail of distribution. Rather, it is a justice that gives freely as one has been given, a justice that welcomes the marginalized, a justice that seeks to share. This version of justice is not content with, to use the common metaphors, either making the pie larger or making sure that all receive an equal piece. Though justice as generosity recognizes that productivity and distribution are important elements, it also argues that equally important questions are: Who has access to the pie? Who is invited to the table? Are the needs of the outsiders being taken into account? As Pope Benedict XVI notes in *Caritas in veritate*:

> But the social doctrine of the Church has unceasingly highlighted the importance of *distributive justice* and *social justice* for the market economy, not only because it belongs within a broader social and political context, but also because of the wider network of relations within which it operates. In fact, if the market is governed solely by the principle of the equivalence in value of exchanged goods, it cannot produce the social cohesion that it requires in order to function well. *Without internal forms of solidarity and mutual trust, the market cannot completely fulfil [sic] its proper economic function.*[68]

A very specific example of the narrowness of many traditional accounts of justice occurred during a class on affirmative action. After prolonged and painful discussion, one of the students finally asked in a very exasperated tone: "Why do they think they can have our jobs?" This is clearly not an attitude of generosity or selflessness, but an attitude of strict accounting and numerical equality, to say nothing of the attitudes of racism and protectionism underlying the question.

We know that generosity is often difficult to practice. In times of economic difficulty, charities are among the first to

---

[68] *Caritas in veritate*, 35. Italics in original.

suffer. Many do not want to support social programs that help the unemployed and uninsured, the marginalized and the immigrants, or support badly needed health care reforms. Support for such programs unfairly taxes future generations, the critics claim. Here Pope Benedict XVI observes:

> Consequently, projects for integral human development cannot ignore coming generations, but need to be marked by solidarity and *inter-generational justice*, while taking into account a variety of contexts: ecological, juridical, economic, political and cultural.[69]

## IV. Conclusion

Adopting and living out the vision of ethics inspired by the Franciscan tradition puts us in contact with several different elements of the larger Catholic tradition. First is a critical paradigm shift with respect to salvation. The Franciscan tradition shifts our perspective from being saved from sin to being made whole for participation in the love of God, which implies the "healing and wholeness of God's creation, and this wholeness is ultimately the transformation of created reality through the unitive power of God's creative love."[70] Such a perspective can also be seen, in the insight offered by Ingham, as a shift from the beatific vision to that of a beatific embrace.[71] Or, to follow the suggestion of Zachary Hayes, we can speak of a redemptive completion:

> Completion refers to the process of bringing creation to its God-intended end which is anticipated already in the destiny of Christ. Redemption refers to the necessary process of dealing with all the obstacles that stand in the way.[72]

---

[69] *Caritas in veritate*, 48. Italics in original.

[70] *Caritas in veritate*, 18.

[71] Ingham, *Scotus for Dunces*, 109.

[72] Zachary Hayes, "Christ, Word of God and Exemplar of Humanity," *The Cord* 46.1 (1996): 16.

Second, Bonaventure's emphasis on the Trinity as a community of relationships, as developed in Chapter Two, gives us an extremely important way to think about ourselves as already existing in a community. Much traditional reflection on the Trinity focuses on the individual persons and their roles in salvation history. Such a focus, while obviously having its merits, also highlights in a way the individuality and separateness of the Divine Persons. The focus on individuality and distinctness of role can be translated into seeing ourselves as separate and distinct persons, as autonomous beings who, while having a relation to others, primarily have our own distinctness and personhood. The vision of Bonaventure, reflected in the Franciscan commitment to relationships, suggests the priority of the community and an understanding of persons in relation to membership within that community. Thus, for Bonaventure, the individual understands his or her deepest meaning of self in already given relationships with a community. Individuality is not destroyed or diminished, but is given a much richer understanding through its being founded in mutual reciprocity. Our own communities and our own relationships reflect the primal community and relationships within the Trinity. Thus, our primary self-understanding is of a self-in-relation, a self constituted by relations with others, a self whose core is realized in self-giving. Bonaventure's reflections on God as community provides rich ground for understanding ourselves, the significance of human community, and can help correct the excesses of an exaggerated autonomy or libertarianism that places the human in isolation.

Third, the Franciscan tradition on Christology that sees the Incarnation desired for itself as God's deepest and most total gift to the totally other shows us the profound mystery of the universe as gift and as the ground of a dynamic interpersonal reality. But, this orientation also understands that creation is in a process of transformation. It did not come pre-formed at the very beginning of its existence, but rather had to evolve to a point at which it reached a critical moment of self-consciousness in the presence of humans. This transformation still continues on the material level as the universe and all in it continue to evolve, but there is also a deeper personal transformation open through incorporation into the continuing salvific work of Christ.

Fourth, the emphasis on love and generosity in both Bonaventure and Scotus points the way to a new understanding of a foundation for ethics: an ethic of generosity. This ethic finds its inspiration in Bonaventure's understanding of God as a fountain fullness, a never-ending spring that nourishes and refreshes all who come in contact with the primal source of generosity. It draws inspiration from Scotus's understanding of God as a center of generosity and constant loving presence flowing from divine liberality. This is an ethic that finds full expression in Francis's deepest sense of poverty as total generosity, total liberality with all that has been given him, whether material or spiritual. It finds contemporary expression in the option for the poor that recognizes the privileged position the poor ought to have in our own lives and the life of our community. It will find expression in implementing Scotus's insight that, to be fulfilled, we must do more than fulfill our natural structure. Rather, we are not to hold on to that structure through seeking its fulfillment only, but must transcend it in a spirit of generous and transformative love for the other. Thus, for the Franciscan tradition, justice is not a matter of weighing claims to ensure equality, nor a matter of ensuring that each has his or her own, much less seeking an eye for an eye. Rather, the key contribution of the tradition is justice as transformative generosity. Such a vision is born within the primal mystery of the communal love within the Trinity, revealed most fully in the mystery of the cross and Resurrection, and modeled in the life of Francis and Clare.

Thus, we should not be surprised to see two levels of transformation at work simultaneously. One is expressed with the ongoing evolution of the material world with its dynamic of modification and adjustment, the inherent movement of the evolutionary process. Here, creation is growing and maturing and developing, but in ways that may be unclear, in ways that may involve considerable pain as new paths are taken. On the personal level, this process of transformation also occurs as we attempt to implement the reality of generosity and self-transformative love in our own lives and communities. This too is an evolution of the spirit that requires new paths, considerable pain, and the tension between competing understandings of self and community. But in both cases, we will experience the growing pains in creation, indeed, the sign of the cross within creation as it were, and we seek to fulfill our common and ultimate destiny of full transformation through the incorporation of the cosmos and our social world into the full body of the resurrected Christ.

Finally, the Franciscan tradition does not provide a specific ethical methodology, though there are clearly methodological elements in the tradition. Rather, the tradition offers us a way of life that is grounded in the created order but transcends that order through acts of love and generosity that unite us with our final end of life in the community of love that is the Trinity. The tradition offers a fundamental option of love and generosity that is grounded in Scotus's concept of *firmitas*, or steadfastness. This attitude orients all of our actions to our final ends and puts us in daily and direct contact with the love God has for us, which is revealed in both creation and the Incarnation. The tradition thus encourages us not to calculate what is mine and what is others,' or what are fair shares, or what the risks or benefits might be, or what the consequences are. Rather, the tradition offers us a vision of life that asks us to respond to others as God has first responded to us – in love and generosity. We clearly need to work out the details of such a life, but the tradition offers us the foundation of love and generosity on which to build such a life.

# 5

## ACTING OUT OF LOVE
## A FRANCISCAN UNDERSTANDING OF CONSCIENCE

### THOMAS A. NAIRN, O.F.M.

*The Franciscan moral vision
recognizes each person as an image of God.
Since each person
reflects the creativity of God in an individualized way,
each person should be treated with profound respect.*

From the spiritual vision of Francis and Clare and from
the profoundly Trinitarian and Christological theology of the
Franciscan intellectual tradition there has arisen a moral vision that attempts to form its adherents into "lovers of divine wisdom."[1] We have already seen how this wisdom tradition describes the moral life both as a life surrounded by
and devoted to beauty, and as generosity in action, highlighting freedom in love. In this chapter, we will build upon these
foundations and investigate what it means to act out of love
by analyzing the Franciscan understanding of conscience.
Beginning with the debate regarding conscience that has
occurred in the years since the close of the Second Vatican
Council, the chapter will suggest that the Franciscan moral

---

[1] St. Bonaventure, *Itinerarium Mentis in Deum*, Prologue, 4, in *Works
of St. Bonaventure*, II, trans. Philotheus Boehner, O.F.M. and Zachary
Hayes, O.F.M. (St. Bonaventure, NY: The Franciscan Institute, 2002), 39.

tradition represents a middle ground in this debate. It will explain the tradition's use of the term "conscience" and of a related term, *synderesis*, placing these ideas into a larger theological and moral context of natural law and the virtues. It will then discuss how the Franciscan moral vision acknowledges the limitations of moral judgment, including the possibility of error, moral failure, and sin. Returning to contemporary moral theology, the chapter will close by suggesting four implications of the tradition and their relevance for today.

## I. The Contemporary Debate

An area in moral theology that has developed significantly since the Second Vatican Council has been the understanding of personal conscience. The final Council document, *Gaudium et spes*, described conscience as "the most secret core and sanctuary" in which the person "is alone with God, whose voice echoes in his depths." It continues by explaining that conscience "reveals that law which is fulfilled by love of God and neighbor" and finally suggests that "in fidelity to conscience, Christians are joined with the rest of humanity in the search for truth."[2] At the time these words were written, they seemed revolutionary, and in the intervening years they have posed a challenge for moral theologians regarding precisely how to incorporate this social, dynamic understanding of conscience into moral theology.

Catholic theologians and philosophers have addressed this challenge in a variety of ways. Their reflections have, in fact, led to a debate regarding the nature of conscience and its function in the life of the faithful Christian. Sydney Callahan, for example, has described conscience as "that personal activity that is uniquely characterized by going beyond analysis and exploration to morally committing ourselves to what

---

[2] See *Gaudium et spes*, 16. Note how compatible this description is with the characteristics of the Franciscan moral vision. Note also that the Council's understanding of "fidelity to conscience" is closely related to Duns Scotus's notion of *firmitas* discussed in Chapter Four.

we avow we ought to do or what ought to be done."[3] Similarly, Walter Conn has explained that conscience is "the actively involved personal agent struggling to reach a concrete understanding and practical judgment as to what course of action he or she should take to respond in a creative and fully human way to the values in this particular situation."[4] On the other side of the debate, moralist Germain Grisez has insisted that for "faithful and clearheaded" Catholics, the right of conscience can never be in conflict with the Church's Magisterium.[5] This debate, whose roots are in the Second Vatican Council, continues to the present day.

These conflicting understandings of the meaning of conscience led to other debates regarding its role and function in the moral life: Is a judgment of conscience determined by the individual, and, if so, can it be equated with personal opinion? Do all opinions of conscience count equally? Or is the proper function of conscience that of deducing moral conclusions from absolute ethical principles? Is conscience merely subjective judgment? Or does it know objective truth? Is conscience infallible, prone to error, or something in between? Is the contemporary emphasis on personal conscience simply another symptom of the moral relativism of our age?

As Franciscans attempt to answer these and similar questions, we find an important resource in the Franciscan intellectual tradition itself, especially in the writings of St. Bonaventure. As we will see, the Franciscan tradition offers a middle course among these contemporary alternatives. In fact, it resonates beautifully with the image of conscience from the Second Vatican Council. Judgments of conscience are not simply determined by the individual. Bonaventure, for example, describes conscience as "God's herald and messenger." He maintains that conscience "does not command things on its own authority by merely subjective judgment,

---

[3] Sydney Callahan, *In Good Conscience* (New York: HarperCollins Publishers, 1991), 23.

[4] Walter Conn, *Christian Conversion: A Developmental Interpretation of Autonomy and Surrender* (New York: Paulist Press, 1986), 93.

[5] See Germain Grisez, "The Duty and Right to Follow One's Judgment of Conscience," *Linacre Quarterly* 56, 1 (February 1989): 13-23.

but commands them as coming from God's authority."[6] Neither is the judgment of conscience simply a logical deduction from moral principles. He acknowledges the complexity involved in the exercise of what the tradition has called practical reason.

## II. BONAVENTURE'S UNDERSTANDING OF CONSCIENCE AND *SYNDERESIS*

Even though it may seem that the notion of conscience has become especially important in the last century, the term has had a long history that actually pre-dates its use in Christianity.[7] There was a continuing vigorous discussion about the nature and function of conscience both among Patristic theologians and among those of the Middle Ages.

As we look to the Franciscan moral tradition,[8] we see that conscience was an important concept for St. Bonaventure, who developed his understanding of the term early in his theological career, following closely the theological lead of his mentor, Alexander of Hales. Bonaventure develops several of the moral notions put forth by his mentor, including Alexander's understanding of *synderesis*, virtue, natural law, and the fact that the moral life itself is a response to God, the Highest Good. Bonaventure's most complete discussion of conscience is found in Distinctio 39 of the Second Book of his *Commentary on the Sentences of Peter Lombard*, one of his earliest works.[9] Distinctio 39 is divided into two articles, the

---

[6] St. Bonaventure, II Sent, d. 39, a. 1, q. 3, ad 3 (II, 907b).

[7] It is especially the Stoic philosophers who developed the understanding of what we now call conscience. See, for example, the *Manual of Epictetus* or Seneca's *Epistulae Morales*.

[8] This chapter will investigate the understanding of conscience in the theology of Bonaventure. John Duns Scotus did not use the term conscience in his philosophy or theology, although, as we have seen, he did write extensively about moral judgment.

[9] The *Commentary on the Sentences* is a very early work of St. Bonaventure, composed between 1250 and 1252. To help put this in a more complete perspective, it may be helpful to place this in the context of other important dates in the theologian's life. He received his "license to teach publicly" from the University of Paris in 1248 and was solemnly awarded

first explaining Bonaventure's understanding of conscience proper and the second dealing with a related concept called *synderesis*. A second source for Bonaventure's understanding of the term is the third part of his short theological text, the *Breviloquium*, dating from 1257.

Prior to examining Bonaventure's understanding of conscience, however, it is helpful to review again the general style of Bonaventure's theological writings that was introduced in Chapter Two. When compared to the way that contemporary theologians explore the issue, his description of conscience can seem at first to be distant and strange. The structure of his answers may look even artificial and contrived. This "strangeness" arises partly from Bonaventure's frequent use of triads, that is, his enumerations of three related elements. This is not simply a literary style on the part of the saint. He uses triads for theological reasons, demonstrating his adherence to the first characteristic that was discussed in the Introduction, the Franciscan belief that on the human level – and on the level of all creation – there is a mirroring of the internal Trinitarian life of God. As we have already seen,[10] Bonaventure believed that all creation was a vestige or "footprint" of the Triune God and therefore to be true to its nature must lead to God in a three-fold way. The human person is also the very image and likeness of God. (Combined with footprint, this becomes another triad). If the Trinity created the universe and all creatures, then anyone must be able to see in creation in general and in humanity in particular not simply an image of God but more specifically an image of the Trinity.

Consequently, before reflecting on conscience and human freedom, we should first understand the inherent Trinitarian or triadic structure itself of the human person that demonstrates the love of the Triune God in whose image humanity is created. While this triadic logic may seem foreign to the

his doctorate from the same university in October of 1257, having already been elected General Minister of the Franciscan Order in February of the same year. In the Middle Ages, the *Sentence Commentary* was the text by means of which one became a Master of Theology (*magister*).

[10] See above, Chapter Two, 51-87, especially 84.

contemporary reader,[11] it is an essential part of Bonaventure's philosophical and theological enterprise. As strange as this may sound to our ears, it can nevertheless assist those of us living today to appreciate more fully Bonaventure's amazing awareness of the Trinity who creates all and maintains all in existence. With this in mind, we turn first to St. Bonaventure's understanding of conscience and then to a related medieval concept called *synderesis*.

As we make our way through these elements of Bonaventure's thought, it might be helpful to keep a concrete case in mind. In this chapter, we will continually refer to the following scenario:

> Jim receives a phone call that his mother has just been rushed to the local hospital. When he arrives, he is greeted with the news that she has suffered a severe stroke. The doctors don't know how long the brain was deprived of oxygen or how much damage has been done. Jim's mother is in a coma. At this point things don't look good, but there is still a lot that the doctors are doing to stabilize her and to prolong her life. They want Jim's input. Years ago, his mother named him as her agent when she filled out an advance directive for health care. Although Jim welcomed becoming his mother's agent at the time, the weight of the task now feels very heavy. To make matters worse, Jim suddenly remembers a conversation he had with her just a couple weeks ago, just after she had visited a close friend in the intensive care unit of the same hospital – the same intensive care unit where she is now located – and she made him promise that he would not let her end up like her friend, co-

---

[11] Such a triadic logic is not totally absent in contemporary philosophy. The metaphysics of the American pragmatic philosopher Charles Sanders Peirce, for example, makes use of what he calls Firstness, Secondness, and Thirdness. See, for example, Charles Sanders Peirce, "A Guess at the Riddle," *The Essential Peirce: Selected Philosophical Writings*. Volume One (1867-1893) (Bloomington, IN: Indiana University Press, 1992), 244-79.

matose and surrounded by tubes in such a sterile and seemingly unfriendly environment.

This case is a fairly common occurrence given the complexity of health care today and the reluctance of people to discuss in detail their concerns regarding life-sustaining treatments. Can the Franciscan moral tradition's understanding of conscience help Jim with the decisions he may now have to make?

## A. Conscience

The very words that Bonaventure uses to describe conscience may also seem foreign to our ears. He calls it a "*habitus* of the cognitive potency."[12] This description already places the reader in a sphere quite different from that of today's philosophy or theology. First of all, although the term *habitus* may sound similar to the word "habit," they are not exactly the same. In the Middle Ages, the term *habitus* was an important moral term used to denote a predisposition (often developed through practice, and here it relates to our contemporary understanding) that occasions a particular way of acting. Either a virtue or a vice, for example, would be considered a *habitus*, as would preferences for certain ways of acting that have nothing to do with virtue or vice (such as always wanting ice cream for dessert or preferring to drive to a destination using local roads rather than the highway). Secondly, Bonaventure maintains that conscience is a process that is concerned with cognition, that is, with knowing and understanding. It is therefore something reasonable, although this does not mean that it is the result of a strict deductive logic. According to Bonaventure, this element belongs to practical reason rather than theoretical or speculative reasoning.[13]

---

[12] St. Bonaventure, II Sent, d. 39, a. 1, q. 1 con. (II, 899b).

[13] As is the case with other medieval theologians, when St. Bonaventure speaks of the practical reason, he is talking about what a person morally ought to do. This is distinguished from speculative or theoretical reason. It is the latter form of rationality that involves deduction from the

Using his triadic logic, Bonaventure then explains more precisely how conscience is a cognitive habitus by suggesting that the term "conscience" can actually have any of three different meanings: (1) sometimes it is the *habitus* of the practical intellect by which we know God's law, specifically the natural law; (2) at other times it is that *habitus* that enables us simply to be conscious or aware in a general way; and (3) at still other times it is that which directs human judgments regarding what one should or should not do in one's actual concrete circumstances.[14] These meanings are connected with three distinct but related tasks: As suggested above, Bonaventure first links conscience with knowledge, especially knowledge of the natural law. This forms an important foundation for his understanding of conscience and will be described in greater detail later in this chapter. Secondly, he links conscience with consciousness or awareness. Finally, he emphasizes that at least some element of conscience must be linked with concrete human judgments. In discussing this last element he moves toward the understanding of conscience articulated by ethicists like Callahan and Conn described earlier in this chapter. For Bonaventure, all three elements are important, but his actual analysis moves primarily between the first and third elements of the triad mentioned above, while always presuming the second element.

As we look at the first description of conscience, we notice that for Bonaventure, conscience is first of all a capacity for discovering the general principles of natural law that govern human behavior. He never equates conscience with mere personal opinion. Rather, conscience involves first and foremost a search for truth, the general truth about human behavior and practical reason that involves a deep understanding of what it means to be a human person.

To appreciate this element of conscience, we need to investigate further what Bonaventure means by natural law. As simple as this question seems, it is a difficult one to an-

---

principles of logic. Practical reason, involving the contingent, cannot arrive at the same degree of certitude as speculative reason does.

[14] Bonaventure, II Sent, d. 39, a. 1, q. 1 con. (II, 899a and b).

swer. Most commentators concede that in the saint's writings, the term "natural law" has in fact many inter-related meanings,[15] as is the case with most medieval theologians. We have already seen that, for Bonaventure, nature itself is "a book in which the creative Trinity shines forth."[16] He thus relates natural law to the "first book"[17] in which the created universe itself leads one to contemplate the diffusive goodness of God. Following Alexander of Hales,[18] Bonaventure's description of natural law brings together both reason and will working in concert. For example, quoting Augustine (and ultimately St. Paul's Letter to the Romans), Bonaventure describes natural law as "the impression made in the soul by the divine law."[19] It is the law of God written on the human heart. Elsewhere, he specifies natural law further and identifies it with the Golden Rule written on the heart, that people should do to others what they would want done to them.[20] In fact, this identification of natural law with the Golden Rule occurs quite frequently in the saint's writings.[21] Still elsewhere, Bonaventure describes natural law in a very narrow sense, as an ordering principle that arises from human nature. For example, John Quinn suggests that for Bonaventure, "natural law consists in the first principles of moral

---

[15] See, for example, Christopher M. Cullen, *Bonaventure* (New York: Oxford University Press, 2006), 104. See also, Jean Porter, *Natural and Divine Law: Reclaiming the Tradition for Christian Ethics* (Grand Rapids, MI: Wm. B. Eerdmans Publishing Co., 1999), 140.

[16] Bonaventure of Bagnoregio, *Breviloquium*, II, 12, 1, in *WSB*, IX, trans. Dominic V. Monti, O.F.M. (St. Bonaventure, NY: Franciscan Institute Publications, 2005), 96. Also, see above, Chapter Two, 51-88.

[17] See the discussion of nature as God's "first book" in Chapter Two, 72 and 84.

[18] See *Summa Fratris Alexandri*, III-II, Inq 2, Q 1.

[19] Bonaventure of Bagnoregio, *Disputed Questions on Evangelical Perfection* q. 4, a. 1, con. in *WSB*, XIII, trans. Robert Karris (St. Bonaventure, NY: Franciscan Institute Publications, 2008), 215.

[20] Bonaventure, II Sent, d. 39, a. 1, q. 2 (II, 901a). When we begin to look to what St. Bonaventure says about conscience, we encounter an immediate difficulty. See 164 note 9.

[21] There is a similarity between Bonaventure and Duns Scotus in this respect. Recall that, for Duns Scotus, the principles of natural law lie in a harmonic relationship with the first principle of love. See above, Chapter Three, 99.

truth, or the primary dictates of human nature, which are the right rules of human conduct in relation to both God and neighbor. The human will is bound innately to right action by the natural law, even before it is known by the intellect."[22] Michael Crowe suggests that for Bonaventure natural law is "the order [that] God, in his wisdom, has established for all creatures."[23] Note that none of these descriptions actually contradicts any of the others. Rather each description tends to deepen and enrich the understanding of the multiple facets involved in knowing the natural law. This layering of understandings of critical terms is also typical of Bonaventure's theological enterprise, as is true for scholastic theology in general.

While these descriptions of natural law might be helpful in understanding Bonaventure's theology, they lead to further questions: If natural law is written on the human heart, how do we come to know it? Is it merely the result of some sort of vague intuition or feeling? How explicit can natural law be? How can it obligate us even before it is known to our intellect (as Quinn suggests)? According to Bonaventure, there are three ways in which natural law obligates the person.[24] He relates this triad to salvation history. Bonaventure begins by speaking about natural law as God's plan for humanity when God first created human nature. Since God created humanity in God's very image and likeness,[25] natural law was both explicit and implicit for Adam and Eve prior to original sin. Those obligations of natural law that ordered the person to God were explicit, and those ordered to the rest of humanity were implicit. After the Fall, as the human image and likeness to God became tarnished,[26] the obligations

---

[22] John F. Quinn, "St. Bonaventure's Fundamental Conception of Natural Law," in *S. Bonaventura 1274-1974*, Vol. 3 (Grottaferrata, Italy: Collegio S. Bonaventura, 1973), 579.

[23] Michael Bertram Crowe, *Changing Profile of the Natural Law* (Leiden, the Netherlands: Kluwer Law International, 1978), 119.

[24] See, for example, III Sent. d. 37, a. 1, q. 3 (III, 819-820).

[25] Gen 1:26.

[26] The word "tarnished" is used deliberately. According to Bonaventure, God's image is never destroyed. Bonaventure explains that after the Fall, human nature was infected in two ways, "the mind with ignorance

of natural law became more implicit in the two precepts of natural law: Do unto others as you would have them do unto you, and do not do unto others what you would not have them do unto you. Finally, the written Law of Moses made explicit these implicit natural law obligations. This is especially true with the Ten Commandments.

For Bonaventure, natural law and God's revealed law are not mutually exclusive. As Jean Porter has shown, for Bonaventure, as for the Medieval theologians in general, the interplay among Scripture, natural law, and human reason was the source for moral normativity. Each of the three played a part in interpreting how the other two were to be understood.[27] Bonaventure further explains that the most general sense of natural law is what is in fact contained in the Law and the Gospel. He goes on to say that its more precise sense is what right reason dictates. Finally, its most precise sense is what tradition has described as natural law proper.[28] Therefore, although the obligation that natural law imposes is implicit in the understanding of human nature itself, it is even clearer for the one who follows the Gospel. Understanding the Gospel gives the person keener insight into human nature, and therefore into natural law itself.

Bonaventure also suggests that conscience as knowledge is both innate in the person and unerring.[29] In our own day, Douglas Langston explains this in the following way:

Not only does [conscience] never make a mistake about the truth of very general practical principles,

---

and the flesh with concupiscence. The result is that humans, blind and bent over, sit in darkness and do not see the light of heaven without the aid of grace together with justice to fight concupiscence and without the aid of knowledge together with wisdom to fight ignorance" (*Itinerarium mentis in Deum* 1, 7). See, Boehner and Hayes, 51. See also *Breviloquium*, III:6, (Monti, 112-15).

[27] See Porter, *Natural and Divine Law*, 140.

[28] Bonaventure, IV Sent, d. 33, a. 1, q. 1 (IV, 747-48). When Bonaventure speaks of the Roman jurists, he is speaking especially of the jurist Ulpian, whose famous definition of natural law was what humans have in common with the animals.

[29] Bonaventure, II Sent, d. 39, a. 1, q. 2 con. (II, 902b).

but it also can never be lost to any person, no matter how morally corrupt that person may become.[30]

This exercise of conscience reveals to the person the precepts of natural law written in the heart. Note, however, that Bonaventure is talking here about the most general principles of natural law. What he is describing would not be far different from the statement of many anthropologists (and even some sociobiologists) today that there are certain general principles or prohibitions that tend to be roughly identical across cultures, for example general principles regulating family or community life or the prohibition against some forms of murder. There are also parallels between Bonaventure's understanding and that of the Second Vatican Council, especially its explanation that the conscience is "the most secret core and sanctuary" of the person where one "is alone with God whose voice echoes" in the depths of one's heart.[31]

For Bonaventure, this first understanding of conscience as general knowledge of the natural law is unerring not because of some human power but rather because such knowledge ultimately comes from God. One is dependent here upon the saint's philosophical understanding of knowledge as illumination.[32] By means of this concept, Bonaventure suggests that God empowers the human person to know the natural law similar to the way natural light allows a person to see images. This is similar to that intellectual illumination by means of which God enables the person to discover the truth of the principles of the speculative reason.[33]

---

[30] Langston, *Conscience and Other Virtues* (University Park, PA: University of Pennsylvania Press, 2001), 26. More will be said about this later in this chapter.

[31] *Gaudium et spes*, 16.

[32] Following St. Augustine, the Franciscan school asserted that knowledge of the truth demands steadfastness and unchangeability. Since creatures are changeable, these characteristics can be found only in the mind of God. Therefore certain knowledge can come to the human person only by divine illumination. Bonaventure compares this to natural light, which is necessary for one to see.

[33] See Bonaventure, II Sent, d. 39, a. 1, q. 2 con. (II, 903a).

Returning now to Jim's situation, we see that this first element of Bonaventure's notion of conscience already comes into play. The question for Jim is not simply what he wants to do or even what he thinks his mother wants to do. Rather, Bonaventure would claim that there are certain general principles of natural law itself that need to be respected in any decision that Jim makes. Following Bonaventure's lead, Jim might begin his moral deliberation by trying to understand these general principles. In the broadest sense, he might make use of the Golden Rule: If he were in such a situation as his mother, how would he want to be treated by those who care for him? This very general understanding could then be made more specific by means of the Decalogue, especially the Fourth and Fifth Commandments. In speaking of the Fourth Commandment, Bonaventure himself mentions the reverence, obedience, and kindness that are owed to parents.[34] In speaking of the Fifth Commandment, Bonaventure actually talks about appropriate end-of-life care and cautions people to avoid what he calls "murder done in a transferred sense."[35] Finally, Jim might acknowledge even more explicit principles of the natural law, such as the dignity of the human person or respect for life, which serve as mediating principles to guide his behavior.

It is clear, however, that these general principles in themselves do not offer complete guidance for Jim. There remains the issue regarding how he should move from these general principles to concrete moral judgments. To engage in this task, we need to look to the third element of Bonaventure's triad. Since conscience deals with the practical reason, and therefore the concrete behaviors of contingent persons, it is never simply an abstract intellectual exercise. It must also relate to the person's will and even emotions.[36] In this, Bo-

---

[34] See Bonaventure of Bagnoregio, *Collations on the Ten Command-ments*, Collation V, in *WSB*, VI, trans. Paul J. Spaeth (St. Bonaventure, NY: The Franciscan Institute, 1995), 73-74.

[35] Bonaventure uses this term to mean that a person maliciously omits something in order to cause the death of a person. See *Collations on the Ten Commandments*, Collation VI, (Spaeth, 88).

[36] Bonaventure, II Sent, d. 39, a. 1, q. 1 con. (II, 899b).

naventure shows his reliance on the basic characteristics that were discussed in the Introduction to this book. He acknowledges human contingency, taking seriously the possibility of human growth and decline (Characteristics Five and Six). He also takes into account the whole person, intellectual, affective, and volitional (Characteristic Seven). It is the third element of conscience that addresses these contingent and changing elements of human experience.

Even though knowledge of the general principles of natural law is important for the movement of conscience, the goal of such decisions of conscience is to arrive at a moral judgment regarding what needs to be done here and now. Bonaventure acknowledges that there might be various degrees of specificity in answering this question. For Bonaventure, the movement from very general principles to what a person ought to do here and now is somewhat complex, involving

> the application of the very general principles to situations that may be either general or particular. A general situation is one that covers a variety of cases.... Whenever anyone is faced with a specific choice ... he is presented with particular application of the very general principle obviously connected to the general application of this principle.[37]

This application of the general rule to the circumstances is not simply the product of strict logical deduction. There are elements of applying the general rule to a specific situation that are acquired through experience. Langston remarks:

> We have at birth the ability to see the truth of certain very general principles, and we can neither lose this ability nor improve it. Yet we can improve our ability to bring to our attention very general practical principles the truth of which we can endorse or reject. Clearly, the more experience we have, the more

---

[37] Langston, *Conscience and Other Virtues*, 26.

terms and concepts we possess, and consequently the
more principles we can consider.... In short, although
conscience is innate to all people, it can be improved
(or weakened) in its exercise.[38]

The complete movement of conscience, therefore, involves
both one's knowing the general principles of morality and
also one's ability to analyze and utilize these principles in
determining what one ought to do in the particular concrete
circumstances one finds oneself. Rather than simply a logical
deduction, this movement involves complex moral reasoning,
questioning what the appropriate behavior may be. Furthermore, conscience can either grow or decline. It is dynamic,
adapting to new information and actually changing with new
experiences, since experience can change both the person's
knowledge of the general principles of natural law and her
or his ability to apply those principles to particular issues. It
has been noted: "The dynamism Bonaventure posits is cru-
cial for a theory of conscience. The fact that the content of
conscience changes in reaction to experience and teaching is
essential to any proper understanding of conscience."[39] This
links him closely to the spiritual vision of Francis and Clare
described in earlier chapters.

If we return to Jim's situation, we can see how his own
level of maturity and previous experience might affect his
movement from the general principles of natural law to his
judgment regarding what he must do in light of his mother's
illness, both for good and possibly ill. On the one hand, his
memory of his mother's conversation may restrict his ability
to view the real alternatives. On the other hand, physicians
might help him understand the variety of choices he actually
has and the relative pros and cons of the various choices. As
a Catholic, he might understand that, while the value of life
should be protected, it is not necessarily protected by simply
prolonging biological life as an absolute. He will be guided by
the teachings of the Magisterium. Furthermore, a spiritual

---

[38] Langston, *Conscience and Other Virtues*, 29.
[39] Langston, *Conscience and Other Virtues*, 36-37.

mentor might discuss with him the *Catholic Ethical and Religious Directives* that state: "The use of life-sustaining technology is judged in light of the Christian meaning of life, suffering and death. In this way two extremes are avoided: on the one hand, an insistence on useless or burdensome technology even when a patient may legitimately wish to forgo it and, on the other hand, the withdrawal of technology with the intention of causing death."[40] Following the method of Bonaventure, Jim may prudently weigh the benefits and burdens to his mother of the various treatment options which the physicians suggest. Since he also understands that practical reason deals with the contingencies of human life, he will understand that such decisions will not be exact, such as the result of a mathematical formula. Yet, he can trust that he is indeed able to make these decisions with some confidence.

## B. Virtue and the Virtues

If one's conscience is able to grow or decline, what ensures that learning and experience aid conscience in growth? To answer this question, we must look to Bonaventure's understanding of virtue. In both Bonaventure's earliest work, *The Commentary on the Sentences*, and his last work, *The Collations on the Six Days of Creation*, there is a discussion of the virtues. He began his analysis by entering the medieval debate concerning the very nature of virtue and explained his own position in relation to those of Aristotle and Peter Lombard.[41] Using his now familiar three-fold division, Bonaventure explained that there are three understandings of virtue: the common understanding, the proper understanding, and the "more proper" understanding.[42] For him, the common un-

---

[40] United States Conference of Catholic Bishops, *Ethical and Religious Directives for Catholic Health Care Services: Fifth Edition* (Washington, DC: USCCB, 2001), Introduction to "Part Five: Issues in Care for the Seriously Ill and Dying."

[41] A major difference between the two was that for Aristotle virtue was a perfection or strength of human nature – part of human nature itself – while, for Peter Lombard, it was the result of grace, which God works within us without us.

[42] Bonaventure, II Sent, d. 27, dub 3.

derstanding is that of Aristotle, which claims that virtue is a power or perfection. The "proper" understanding is also attributed to Aristotle, and that is "a habit of the will consisting in the mean, determined by right reason, insofar as a wise person will determine it."[43] Bonaventure acknowledges, however, that the "more proper" understanding of virtue is that of Peter Lombard, that it is a "quality of the mind, by which one lives uprightly and of which no one may make bad use, which God works in us without us."[44] Bonaventure thus understands that the virtuous life is the result of God's grace.

In the *Collationes in Haexaemeron*, Bonaventure's last work, he explains this further by criticizing Aristotle's understanding as that of one who has not yet moved from darkness into God's light.[45] Since the Fall, sin has wounded the human person. The saint therefore posits a three-fold task for virtue: (1) Virtue orders the soul to its proper end, (2) it rectifies the wayward affective dispositions (or emotions), and (3) it heals them.[46] The person's final end that Bonaventure discusses is union with God. In this context, he stresses the importance of faith, "without which the virtues are worthless."[47] Such ordering, rectifying and healing is accomplished only by grace. Bonaventure explains: "Faith – that has hope and charity together with good works – heals the soul, and, once it has been healed, cleanses and lifts it up and makes it into the likeness of God."[48]

Following Augustine, Bonaventure maintains that charity is the form of the virtues. He explains:

Charity itself is the root, form, and end of the virtues, relating them all to the final end and binding them all to one another simultaneously and in orderly fashion.

---

[43] Bonaventure is quoting from Aristotle's *Eudemian Ethics*, Book II, ch. 6.

[44] Peter Lombard, *The Sentences*, c 1, n1, though part of the definition is found in St. Augustine's sermon on Psalm 118, Sermon xxvi.

[45] See *Collations in Haexaemeron*, VII, 5. I, in *Works of Bonaventure*, V, trans. Jose de Vinck (Patterson, NJ: St. Anthony Guild Press, 1970), 111.

[46] *Haex.*, VII, 5 (De Vinck, 111).

[47] *Haex.*, VII, 6 (De Vinck, 112).

[48] *Haex.*, VII, 13 (De Vinck, 116).

Hence charity is the weight of a properly ordered attraction and the bond of perfect union. It maintains order as regards the different objects of love, in our desire for them and their effect on us. At the same time it possesses oneness in the habit by having only one end and one object which is most to be loved, which is the reason for our loving all things destined to be tied with the bond of love within the one Christ as a body to the head – a body containing all those to be saved.[49]

In this way, charity gives life to the virtues and, in fact, to one's entire moral life. Without charity, the moral life remains incipient and imperfect.[50]

This understanding of the primacy of charity gives Bonaventure a lens through which to examine the other virtues, especially the four cardinal virtues of prudence, justice, temperance, and fortitude. On the one hand, he acknowledges that each of the virtues relates to the Aristotelian mean (his second, "proper," meaning of virtue), that is the middle ground between two vices:

The Philosopher says that 'virtue is an intermediate point between two extremes....' Prudence is the driver of the virtues. Wherefore prudence says: I have found the proper measure; and temperance acts as a watchman and says: I too wanted this; and justice acts as a distributor, willing not only for itself but also for the other; and because many adversities occur after that, fortitude acts as a defender, lest the proper measure be lost.[51]

---

[49] *Brevil.*, V, 8, 5. (Monti, 202-03).

[50] See Cullen, 98. Similarly, in his General Audience of March 17, 2010, Pope Benedict XVI explained that St. Francis showed with his whole life the primacy of love. Similarly, Bonaventure uses this inspiration to understand the primacy of love.

[51] *Haex.*, VI, 12 (De Vinck, 100).

Bonaventure adds: "Each is dependent upon the others. For temperance must be prudent; justice must be strong; while prudence must be sober, just, and strong."[52]

The cardinal virtues, however, are always dependent upon the theological virtues, especially charity. Bonaventure maintains that the virtues find their origin in faith, are lifted up by hope, and are fulfilled by charity. He explains that without faith, hope, and charity the cardinal virtues are "without clothing" and adds that these virtues must always be "clothed with the gold of love."[53] Finally, dependent upon the spirituality of St. Francis, Bonaventure insists on adding virtues which are not typically listed as such.[54] One such virtue is that of humility. He maintains that this virtue is the very foundation of "all Christian perfection" and describes it as "the gate of wisdom, the foundation of justice, and the dwelling place of grace."[55] His addition of the virtue of humility expresses another important characteristic of the Franciscan moral tradition (Characteristic Six) that acknowledges an Augustinian vision, recognizing human limitation, including the real limitations of human reason.

Returning once more to the case we have been discussing, Jim might understand that the section of *The Ethical and Religious Directives* mentioned above involves an understanding of the life of virtue. He might see that what he needs to do is discover the mean between the extremes of euthanasia, on the one hand, and an insistence on useless or burdensome technology on the other. Jim might realize that, in his deliberations, he will be helped by his having developed the cardinal virtues of prudence, justice, temperance, and fortitude. He may acknowledge that the virtue behind all of his deliberation is love, especially the love for his mother. Finally, he might, in humility, accept the limits of his own

---

[52] *Haex.*, VI, 13 (De Vinck, 101).

[53] *Haex.*, VII, 15 (De Vinck, 117).

[54] See, for example, Cullen, 103-04.

[55] See *Disputed Questions on Evangelical Perfection*, I, concl. (Karris, 41). Bonaventure refers to John 14:6 and acknowledges Christ as the way, the truth and the life. Humility thus relates to grace, since Christ is the way; relates to the truth of justice, since Christ is the truth; and to a taste for wisdom, since it recognizes that Christ is the life.

contingency and realize the limits that the human condition places on his own decision making.

## C. *Synderesis*

For Bonaventure, the cognitive element in the process of conscience (which, as we have seen, he tends to equate with conscience itself) involves both the person's knowing the general principles of natural law and the ordered movement from those general principles to concrete judgments regarding what one ought to do here and now. Bonaventure states, however, that what conscience cannot do is to motivate the person to desire to be good and to do the good. We have already investigated how the life of virtue can affect this desire. Following his mentor, Alexander of Hales, Bonaventure adds that it is *synderesis* that provides the person with the actual motivation. For him, there is a close relationship among conscience, virtue, and *synderesis*. Virtues are developed in relation to the dictates of conscience and in turn they are manifestations of the drive to the good that is *synderesis*.[56]

*Synderesis* is an odd word for most contemporary people. It is not used in ordinary speech – not even in most theoretical discussions about conscience. The term *synderesis* seems original to St. Jerome and entered the medieval lexicon by means of Peter Lombard's *Book of Sentences*. In commenting on the four living creatures in Ezekiel's vision (Ez 1:4-14), Jerome identified the human face with the rational part of the human being, the lion with the emotional part, and the ox with the appetitive part. Finally, he identified the eagle with that "which the Greeks call *synderesis*, that spark of conscience which was not even extinguished in the breast of Cain after he was turned out of paradise, and by which we discern that we sin, when we are overcome by pleasures or frenzy and meanwhile are misled by an imitation of reason."[57]

---

[56] See Langston, *Conscience and Other Virtues*, 35.

[57] Quoted in Langston, *Conscience and Other Virtues*, 9. Since there is no such word as *synderesis* in the Greek language, the word itself seems most likely to be a misspelling of the Greek word for conscience, *synedesis*.

Bonaventure remains faithful to Jerome's thought when he describes *synderesis* as the "spark of conscience." This language, however, created some controversy in medieval theology. For medieval theology, the question "How does *synderesis* relate to conscience?" was a very important one. Some theologians believed the two terms were identical, while others insisted that they had to be different. To the former group, those who believe that the "spark of conscience" must be identical to conscience itself, Bonaventure replied:

> It must be said therefore that it is called the 'spark' because conscience cannot move or disturb or, if you will, goad a person except by means of synderesis, which is like a stimulus or a flame. Just as reason is not able to move except by means of the will, neither is conscience able to move except by means of synderesis.[58]

In contrast to conscience, which he describes as cognitive, the saint maintained that *synderesis* is part of the affective or emotional dimension of the person. In explaining the concept in this manner, Bonaventure was stating something rather similar to that of some contemporary moral theologians who acknowledge that "the foundational moral experience is an affective response to value."[59]

Making use again of his triadic logic, Bonaventure proposes that *synderesis* has three functions: to motivate the person to do the good, to help fight against temptation, and to protest against any evil that may have been committed.[60] Each of these functions has a role in Bonaventure's fully developed understanding of decisions of conscience. The first element is lacking in many contemporary theories that tend

---

[58] Bonaventure, II Sent, d. 39, a. 2, q. 1 ad 3 (II, 910b).

[59] See, for example, Daniel Maguire and A. Nicholas Fargnoli, *On Moral Grounds: The Art / Science of Ethics* (New York: The Crossroad Publishing Company, 1991), 19. This discussion is also reminiscent of Duns Scotus's explanation of the relationship between the *affectio commodi* and the *affectio justitiae*, which we first encountered in Chapter Three, 110.

[60] Bonaventure, IV Sent, d. 50, p. 2, a. 2, q. 2, ad 4 (IV 1052b).

to understand conscience as having to do merely with a person's preferences. Bonaventure suggests on the contrary that conscience is meaningful only for the person who genuinely desires the good, as we showed in the discussion of virtue. For Bonaventure, the only reason to make a judgment of conscience is because the person both wants to be good and is actively pursuing the good.

By means of the second element in the triad, Bonaventure explains how one pursues the good in an appropriate or fitting way: One must always maintain the right priorities. There never is simply one good. Goodness for him is what arouses human desire, but there are at least two understandings of the good: temporal and eternal.[61] Each of these goods produces a different kind of love in the person. That which is eternal inspires the theological virtue of charity; that which is temporal, if pursued only for itself, arouses what Bonaventure calls a lesser and misplaced love. As we have already seen, for Bonaventure (as for Francis before him), the true purpose of creation is to elicit in people a movement toward God as their final end. Pursuing temporal goods for themselves therefore involves a diversion from what is the ultimate Good that "turns away, distracts, and traps" the soul.[62] It is *synderesis* that helps the person to use the created world as a means to the eternal rather than be distracted from one's true purpose.

Bonaventure offers an analogy: In his *Commentary on Ecclesiastes*, he compares the created world to a ring that is given a bride by the bridegroom. The ring is the sign of the bridegroom's love and elicits a loving response in the bride. He continues:

---

[61] This relates to the natural and the supernatural end of the person and the discussion of the three meanings of the term virtue discussed in the previous section.

[62] *Commentary on Ecclesiastes*, 1, 33, in *WSB*, VII, trans. Robert Karris, O.F.M. and Campion Murray, O.F.M. (St. Bonaventure, NY: Franciscan Institute Publications, 2005), 120. Bonaventure is quoting Hugh of St. Cher's *Commentary on Ecclestiastes*.

The love is chaste when she loves the ring as a memento of her husband and on account of her love for her husband. The love is adulterous when the ring is loved more than the husband, and the husband cannot regard such love as good.[63]

So too, the person needs to appreciate the created world most importantly as a gift and memento of our loving God. Creation is properly loved when it brings the person closer to God and not when it is loved merely in itself.

The saint describes the final constituent of this triad as protesting against the evil that a person may have done. In this sense, Bonaventure understands *synderesis* as involving what is often called the "consequent conscience," that function of conscience that contemporary theologians have often called the "guilty conscience," the element of conscience that protests one's wrong doing. In this way, *synderesis* accuses the person of not living up to her or his principles. We will investigate this element of *synderesis* more fully in the next section.

Prior to that discussion, however, it may be helpful to return to Jim's moral judgment involving his mother's medical care. By means of his notion of *synderesis*, Bonaventure conveys that there is an important moral question prior to the question of "What should I do?" That question may be simply stated as: "Why even be moral at all?" In trying to answer this question, Bonaventure explains that if people are to be true to their deepest humanity, they must acknowledge that part of what it means to be human is to have moral principles and to act in accordance with them. Deep within, most people have an abiding sense of right and wrong. In fact, we speak of those who seem to lack such a sense as sociopaths, recognizing that something is psychologically as well as morally wrong with them. Timothy O'Connell has described this sense as "an abiding human characteristic, a general sense of value, an awareness of personal responsibility that is utterly

---

[63] *Commentary on Ecclesiastes*, Introduction, q. 1, 1 (Karris and Murray, 78).

emblematic of the human person."[64] As Jim acknowledges this sense of responsibility, Bonaventure's notion of *syndere-sis* can provide for him an answer to one of the most funda-mental questions in moral theology: "Why are you concerned about being good and doing good?" For a faithful Christian, the answer would encompass both an understanding of what it means to be a human person in general and what it means to be a person of faith. The Franciscan moral tradition sug-gests that a major part of the reason for being moral is to act in response to God's love by living a life that embodies love of God and neighbor.

Finally, Bonaventure maintains that *synderesis* can nev-er be extinguished in the person, not even by sin. He nuances this statement by adding that for the sinner the first two parts of the triad that make up *synderesis* may in fact be lost, that is, *synderesis* no longer motivates the person to the good, nor does it fight against temptation. Even though these two important functions are no longer present, Bonaventure maintains that *synderesis* itself is not totally extinguished. The third feature of *synderesis* remains as that prick of con-science that "murmurs in response to their guilt."[65] This will be described more fully in the next section.

## D. Moral Decisions, the Possibility of Error, and the Reality of Sin

In Bonaventure's moral theology, when a person makes a good moral decision, conscience and *synderesis* work together to achieve the good end. Bonaventure explains that the ob-ject of a person's moral deliberation is not simply what one wants to do but rather what one knows one should do in light of who God is calling one to be. Reminiscent of Conn's defini-tion of conscience, it is a fully human response to value. The dynamic that has been discussed in previous chapters again becomes evident here: The exercise of conscience is in actual-

---

[64] Timothy O'Connell, *Principles for a Catholic Morality: Revised Edi-tion* (New York: Harper and Row, 1990), 110.

[65] Bonaventure, II Sent, d. 39, a. 2, q. 3 con. (II, 914b).

ity the *praxis* of the fully mature moral agent acting in accordance with creative love in a rational response to concrete circumstances. This response is not based on personal whim but, rather, rooted in one's perception of reality. Bonaventure would agree with the Second Vatican Council that by means of conscience "one detects a law that one does not make up but which holds the person in obedience."[66] The saint stresses that when one makes a moral decision,

> conscience is like God's herald and messenger; it does not command things on its own authority, but commands them as coming from God's authority, like a herald when he proclaims the edict of the king.[67]

Having investigated the notions of conscience and *synderesis* on one hand, and acknowledging the movement between that action of conscience by which the person comes to know the general principles of natural law and that action of conscience that raises the question regarding what must be done here and now, we see that for Bonaventure, decisions of conscience are complex ones, dependent upon the principles of natural law "written on the heart," but also dependent upon learning and previous experience. Although the saint acknowledges that there are elements of the process of coming to a moral decision that are unerring, he also maintains that conscience can make a mistake. He also speaks about moral failure and sin.

As we have already seen, the activity of conscience cannot simply be a mechanistic or purely logical application of general principles to current circumstances. Using still another triad, Bonaventure explains what happens when conscience uses its innate knowledge of natural law, experience, and learning to determine what ought to be done in the current circumstances. Conscience may actually dictate any of three sorts of actions: (1) those in conformity to God's law, (2) those

---

[66] *Gaudium et spes*, 16.

[67] Bonaventure, II Sent, d. 39, a. 1, q. 3, ad 3 (II, 907b). As a follower of St. Francis, who called himself "the herald of the great King," Bonaventure would most definitely appreciate the notion of conscience as a "herald"!

which in some sense even go beyond God's law, and (3) those which do not live up to God's law or are contrary to it.[68] The first of these three possibilities is the most straightforward: conscience simply reveals to us what is commanded by the law of God. In the second possibility, conscience may dispose a person to go beyond the letter of the law, as she or he tries to discern God's will in the given circumstances. Contemporary readers might see this in a way similar to Karl Rahner's insistence that there is an individual ethical reality of a positive kind which is untranslatable into a material universal ethics based on natural law.[69]

The third element of the triad deals with moral failure. In Bonaventure's explanation, it is clear that the first two dictates of conscience stem from the fact that the conscience is God's herald and messenger. To clarify this, we again return to the decisions that Jim needs to make regarding his mother's medical care. Immediate decisions may entail further decisions at a later time. Will his mother survive the immediate effects of the stroke? If so, in what sort of state will the stroke leave her? What sorts of care will she need? The decisions that Jim makes now in dealing with the immediate situation may entail more decisions afterward. His mother's illness will affect who Jim is now and who he will become. As Jim tries to be faithful to what he believes God is calling him to be as a faithful son to his mother, some of his decisions will be rather straightforward, like the first element of this triad. Some of his decisions, however, will probably be more complicated, and Jim might see himself called to go beyond the strict duties a son has to his mother. Jim may adopt a type of spiritual discernment process to sort out both kinds of decisions. There may also be the possibility that Jim would simply like to get out of having to continue to make these decisions at all. He may try to find a way out. In fact, he may decide that the easiest thing for him to do is to make

---

[68] Bonaventure, II Sent, d. 39, a. 1, q. 3 con. (II, 906b). This question is also the source of the other quotations in this paragraph.

[69] See Karl Rahner, "On the Question of a Formal Existential Ethics," in *Theological Investigations*, Volume 2 (New York: The Seabury Press, 1963), 217–34.

a decision that will entail the least burden upon himself. By including the third element of the triad, that of acting contrary to God's law, Bonaventure acknowledges the possibility of moral failure.

Bonaventure gives three explanations for moral failure: the darkness of blindness, the lustfulness of pleasure, and the hardness of obstinacy.[70] We have already seen that the saint believes that decisions of conscience arise from the combined activities of reason, emotion, and will. It should not be surprising, therefore, that for him, error can be traced to any of the three, thus impeding the proper movement of conscience.

The first form of moral failure, "darkness of blindness," refers to some sort of defect in the intellect or reason by means of which a person recognizes as good what is actually wrong. Contemporary Catholic authors would probably speak here of ignorance, or of an erroneous conscience. For example, in dealing with his mother's illness, Jim might misunderstand the Catholic teaching about respect for life and demand that the doctor do everything physically possible to keep his mother's heart beating even to the extent of demanding futile treatment that is tremendously burdensome to his mother.

Bonaventure describes the second element, "lustfulness of pleasure," as a form of weakness in which the person is so taken up with his or her own pleasure that "a sense of guilt has no place."[71] Casual readers might infer that the saint means only sexual pleasure, but this is not the case. Contemporary theologians would probably expand on Bonaventure's formulation and speak simply of an exaggerated self-interest. Returning to Jim, let us say that his mother survives this immediate crisis, but never fully recovers. She needs long-term care, and Jim finds a nursing home for her. At first, he visits her often, but is never really comfortable with these visits. He does not like being around the other people in the institution, and he does not like to be reminded

---

[70] Bonaventure, II Sent. d. 39, a.2, q. 2 con. (II, 912b).
[71] Bonaventure, II Sent. d. 39, a.2, q. 2 con. (II, 912b).

that his once vibrant mother now seems to be only a shell of her former self. Although she speaks with him and knows who he is, her conversations are halted as she keeps forgetting the correct word, and she speaks more and more about a past that does not include him. His visits to her become less and less frequent. Eventually, he stops visiting her at all, and she wonders what happened to her son. We might say that, because of the personal pain, Jim has made a wrong moral choice, but it is equally true that it is possible that Jim may mistakenly convince himself that what is actually wrong is really right. He can become a victim of his own self-deception as he tells himself that it is better for his mother if he no longer visits her since his visits only confuse her and do no good.

The "hardness of obstinacy" is different from the previous two elements because, in this case, the person is not mistaking what is wrong to be good. Rather, she or he is freely choosing evil, knowing in fact that it is wrong. Bonaventure states that, in this third understanding, *synderesis* is impeded, though not destroyed, so that it is not able to motivate the person to the good. *Synderesis* survives merely to "murmur against the sinner's guilt."[72] In some ways, this last element can seem distant from the mentality prevalent in contemporary people which tends to "medicalize" people who choose evil not as being truly vicious but rather as mentally ill. Several contemporary ethicists, however, have begun to return to an Aristotelian understanding and have begun again to speak of some people as "vicious."[73] Returning again to Jim, he might determine that it would be easiest for him if his mother were simply out of the way. Without regard for law or morality, he might simply choose to end her life himself because he can.

By the time we come to this third understanding of moral failure, we are in the realm of sin. For Bonaventure, sin is not a positive essence but rather a corrupting influence that "contaminates the will," having no essence apart from the

---

[72] Bonaventure, II Sent, d. 39, a.2, q. 2 con. (II, 912b).
[73] See, for example, Candace Vogler, *Reasonably Vicious* (Cambridge, MA: Harvard University Press, 2002).

good in which it inheres.[74] He is following Augustine here in acknowledging that evil is not something positive, but rather the absence of the good where the good ought to be. Moral failure is the result of original sin. Bonaventure shows that original sin corrupted the three faculties that comprise the working of conscience: reason, emotions, and will. Speaking of the sin of Eve, he explained: "In her craving for superior knowledge, she rose to pride; this drew her into gluttony, which in turn cast her down into disobedience. The first was a thought, the second a feeling, and the third a deed."[75] Bonaventure then reminds his readers that "every sin is an imitation of original sin."[76] It is "the act of disordering God's universe, of turning away from the Good to grab hold of lesser goods."[77] We return to Bonaventure's notion of *synderesis*. He reminds his readers that temporal things are first of all gifts and mementos of a loving God to be used toward our final end. They are never simply ends in themselves. Ilia Delio has shown that this plea remains important today:

> Bonaventure's understanding of sin speaks clearly to our modern world, at least in the western hemisphere. With an emphasis on materialism, information gathering, success, power and prestige, there is a compulsion to strive for some, if not all, of these attractions without limit.... Yet such frantic seeking apart from God can only lead to the illusion of the self. In many ways, it leads to a false and private self which wants to exist outside the reach of God's will and God's love, outside of life. Such a self cannot help being anything but an illusion.[78]

---

[74] Cullen, *Bonaventure*, 137.
[75] *Breviloquium*, III, 3, 2. (Monti, 105).
[76] See *Breviloquium*, III, 8, 6. (Monti, 121).
[77] Cullen, *Bonaventure*, 136.
[78] Ilia Delio, *Simply Bonaventure: An Introduction to His Life, Thought, and Writings* (Hyde Park, NY: New City Press, 2001), 76-77.

Given these tendencies, people today may experience the reality of moral failure even more than in Bonaventure's time.

### III. Implications: The Franciscan Understanding of Conscience and Its Relevance for Today

Even though certain elements of Bonaventure's description of conscience might sound strange to contemporary ears, the contours of his moral vision do indeed have relevance for today. We can extract from his explanation of conscience four important implications for a contemporary Franciscan understanding of moral theology today.

First, Bonaventure's notion of conscience builds upon the characteristics of the Franciscan moral vision that were discussed earlier. By means of his triads, he shows in a very special way how human life mirrors the internal Trinitarian life (Characteristic One) and how this is realized in creative and loving freedom in response to God's love (Characteristic Two). His process of moral decision making is actually a form of spiritual discernment, engaging the whole person – intellect, emotions, and will (Characteristic Seven), acknowledging human learning and growth (Characteristic Five) on the one hand, but human limitations and sin on the other (Characteristic Six). Bonaventure's approach demands humility regarding both human assessments and human actions. It can therefore be described as a middle tradition between the two understandings of conscience mentioned at the beginning of this chapter, incorporating both polarities in tension (Characteristic Ten). This tension is a hallmark of Bonaventure's theological imagination and suggests to his readers that living in this creative tension is an important element of the moral life.[79] What Bonaventure's notion of conscience offers contemporary Franciscans, in fact, is a

---

[79] See, for example, Ewert H. Cousins, *Bonaventure and the Coincidence of Opposites: The Theology of Bonaventure* (Chicago: Franciscan Herald Press, 1978).

process by means of which one demonstrates one's integrity and moral seriousness about Christian life and discernment.

Second, as a middle tradition, Bonaventure's vision offers important correctives to some contemporary descriptions of conscience. As opposed to those methods in moral theology that emphasize solely the deductive element of conscience on the one hand or its intuitive element on the other, Bonaventure's idea of conscience is holistic, taking fully into account all three elements of intellect, emotions, and will. In fact, his emphasis on the affective element of conscience through the discussion of *synderesis* seems more contemporary than many treatises of the past century. Yet, although he genuinely incorporates the emotional element into this process, he is emphatic that conscience itself remains cognitive. It is a process of discernment in search for truth. In fact, he continually calls conscience "God's herald and messenger."[80] Nevertheless, this cognitive process is never simply an exercise of deductive logic. Bonaventure speaks of the importance of learning and of previous experience in developing one's conscience. The use of conscience is always an exercise of practical reason, not theoretical reason.

Third, Bonaventure's enterprise demonstrates the importance of the Catholic wisdom tradition in moral theology. The full scope of this wisdom tradition is best understood by returning to the moral decisions that Jim must make concerning his mother and analyzing how Bonaventure's understanding of conscience can be of help to him. Although the saint describes conscience as the herald and messenger of God, his morality, like that of Blessed John Duns Scotus, is not simply a form of divine command theory. The first element that Bonaventure stresses is that the object of a decision of conscience is not simply what Jim or his mother wanted or desired. For the saint, decisions of conscience must be guided, first of all, by the general principles of natural law, shown especially in the Golden Rule. These principles are then made more specific, as, for example, in the Ten Commandments. For Bonaventure, however, one cannot move di-

---

[80] See also Bonaventure, II Sent, d. 39, a. 1, q. 3, ad 3 (II, 907b).

rectly from general principle to specific action. The element of personal experience is also important. It takes a certain level of maturity to engage in this movement, and this maturity will result in better moral decisions. The same maturity will accept the limits of one's own experience and knowledge. It accepts the fact that, in making moral decisions, we also necessarily rely on an authority greater than that of our own person. Although Bonaventure wrote during a period of history when the understanding of the ecclesial *Magisterium* was just beginning to develop, for contemporary Franciscans, such reliance would obviously include reliance upon the *Magisterium* of the Church.

Fourth, Bonaventure does not simply call one to personal responsibility, but more especially calls one to act as a person of faith. It is by means of conscience that people respond to God's love already given by embodying in their decisions of conscience the love for God and neighbor. This is never automatic, however. As the life of virtue is a reality for Bonaventure, so too is the possibility for moral failure. Since conscience brings together reason, emotion, and will, any of these three can thwart the movement of conscience. Ignorance can affect our cognition, the desire for pleasure (or self-centeredness) can overpower our affective response to value, and an inclination to sin can lead us to choose evil.

Bonaventure does not offer his reader a foolproof way of always making the correct moral decision; no such foolproof way exists. What he does offer is the possibility of moral wisdom, often the result of trial and error.[81] His understanding of conscience takes the search for moral truth seriously, but it is not simply deductive. It acknowledges the importance of human experience, but is not a form of intuitionism. It maintains that the person must grow and change, but is not relativistic. His understanding of conscience joins together cognitive and affective elements and subsumes both of these under virtue. In doing so, he shows us the importance of wisdom, humility, and especially love for moral decision making.

---

[81] In this, he is like John Duns Scotus. See above, Chapter Four, 123-160.

It is a dynamic model of moral reasoning and judgment that has been valid for over 700 years and remains so today.

PART III

# 6

## THE FRANCISCAN MORAL VISION AND CONTEMPORARY CULTURE

THOMAS A. NAIRN, O.F.M.
THOMAS A. SHANNON

*The Franciscan moral vision incorporates
within it a tension that arises out of respect
for both sides of several polarities—
the institutional and the charismatic,
the universal and the particular, the past and the future, the
act and the person. It acknowledges that this tension
is part of living as a pilgrim in this world.*

Although the Franciscan spiritual tradition has had significant and lasting influence within the Church, its intellectual tradition has not gained widespread recognition. Even though its moral tradition is a rich one, it has frequently been considered to be at the margins of contemporary Catholic moral theology. Nevertheless, this tradition may be especially timely today. The opening years of the twenty-first century have proven to be fractured. The world has experienced major terrorist attacks and an economic downturn of proportions it had not seen since the early twentieth century. Political discourse among nations and within the United States has become increasingly polarized, and many today experience even religion as divisive rather than unifying. Wherever one turns, there seems to be increasing antagonism and division. Against this cultural backdrop, one can describe the Franciscan moral vision as a middle or mediating tradition, incorporating within itself both sides of various polarities. By living within the tension created by these polarities, it can provide a fitting alternative to many contemporary points of view.

The previous chapters analyzed the Franciscan moral tradition and, in doing so, used contemporary ethical issues and situations to illustrate elements of the tradition. This chapter and the one that follows will move a step further by trying to bring the Franciscan vision into dialogue with contemporary culture and ethics. This chapter will begin by investigating some of the contours of contemporary culture, especially contemporary Western culture – a fascination for freedom and autonomy, an acknowledgment of relativity, and an appreciation of the growing complexity of contemporary life – and explaining how the Franciscan moral vision can be seen as a counterpoint to some dominant philosophies of today. It will then articulate constituents of the contemporary Franciscan moral stance. It will conclude by describing aspects of the theological anthropology that serve as a basis for a contemporary Franciscan vision.

## I. CONTEMPORARY CULTURE

This book began by explaining the spiritual and theological vision that was embodied in the example and writings of Francis and Clare of Assisi and later developed by the great medieval Franciscan theologians, especially St. Bonaventure and Blessed John Duns Scotus. However, we do not see the world in the same way as did Francis or Clare or Bonaventure or Scotus. Even if we are not Westerners, many of us have been influenced for good or for ill by the history of Western culture, especially that of the eighteenth-century Enlightenment. Many of us have been formed by the culture of the United States with its Enlightenment values of democracy, self-reliance, individualism, and autonomy. As we evaluate the Franciscan moral vision and its relation to contemporary culture, we need to analyze some dominant elements of today's Western culture: a fascination for freedom, an acknowledgement of relativity and relationality, and an appreciation of the complexity of the modern world. Even if our own cultural framework is not that of the West, this analysis may help us become more aware of our own points of view and the frameworks out of which we view reality. Such awareness will help us become more attentive and critical readers of the core elements in the Franciscan moral vision and open a dialogue between the great historical framers of that vision and contemporary ethics.

## A. Freedom

### 1. Freedom as Autonomy and Choice

One of the hallmarks of contemporary Western culture has been its emphasis on freedom of choice. Rooted originally in the Enlightenment desire of seeking freedom from religious domination, this emphasis upon choice soon expanded to other areas of life, for example, the freedom to choose one's government. More recently, freedom has come to be understood simply and exclusively as the ability to choose among many competing options. In the last fifty years, this understanding of freedom as choice – aided by post-modernism – further evolved into the position that a person's choices should not be questioned by others, let alone judged by them. That one made one's choice authentically became the sole criterion by which any choice was to be evaluated.[1]

This mindset led in turn to a strong emphasis on the individual. Freedom came to serve as the social context for self-discovery and self-identification. Since I can choose what I want, my choices become the core expression of who I am

---

[1] See, for example, Christian Smith, *Lost in Transition: The Dark Side of Emerging Adulthood* (New York: Oxford University Press, 2011), 21-27.

and further define who I wish to be. While not implying that individuality is simply the sum of one's choices, one can say that such freedom of choice provides the grounding for the current emphasis on the importance of self-determination. Who I am and become is not determined by my family, my social or economic class, or my education. Rather I believe that I have the freedom to become who I choose to be – even to *continuously* choose to be someone different. American culture especially has come to be seen as a culture of second chances, as this continuing freedom to choose re-creates individual identity. The strong social corollary of freedom of choice is the opening up of the social landscape for constantly creating new opportunities.

Democracy became the social expression of personal freedom of choice. Social contract theorists of the modern period developed the idea of government by the consent of the governed. Although it took generations for its extension to all races and genders, the reality of "one person one vote" triumphed. Each person was to examine the issues, participate in discussion, evaluate the candidates, but ultimately, in the privacy of the voting booth cast his or her vote expressing a personal verdict on the issues at hand. Government and social policy were truly to be with the consent of the governed.

The single word that best captures this understanding of freedom is autonomy. Implicit in this concept are the expectations that people will make their own choices and live by them. Each person is responsible for his or her choices, and so becomes the master of his or her life and destiny. Autonomy has been the foundation for much of Western culture and a powerful motivator for individuals to seek out their personal destiny. In the United States, the legal community began to define autonomy as the "right to be let alone."[2] The cultural assumption continues to be that, whatever the life event, I alone will decide – an assumption that has had immense implications for several forms of contemporary morality.

---

[2] This definition, first found in Thomas M. Cooley, *The Elements of Torts* (1888), 29, was quoted by Justice Louis Brandeis, in "The Right to Privacy," *Harvard Law Review* 4, 5 (December 15, 1890).

## 2. The Isolated Individual

One result of identifying freedom of choice with the multiplicity of personal options has been expanding the social and economic frameworks that supply these options. In many stores today, one can find brand after brand of the same product. The number of choices offered does not make consumers freer but can in actuality cheapen choice by virtue of the sheer number of options that are offered. This multiplicity of choices can lead to indifference: In light of the vast number of options we have, we choose randomly because we have no real basis on which to make the decision. Every option is simply that — an option, no better or worse than other options. Since we can always choose again, we do not need to ask whether this particular choice is good, bad, or indifferent. Our choices become simply preferences that we can reorder at any time, each individual choice having little or no meaning.

Ironically, the number of options can actually lead to a lack of freedom and a general dissatisfaction with our ability to choose. Seemingly unlimited options result in no choice at all because we cannot sufficiently examine the alternatives. This can result in indecision rather than choice. Rather than exercising freedom, I experience frustration. Although I think I am free, I do not act with personal freedom.

The notion of autonomy can also lead us to assume that we are self-made persons, the products of our choices, our work, our efforts, our ambitions. We believe that we alone are responsible for who we have become. But this affirmation of self-reliance is often illusory. Our choices are never simply autonomous. Indeed, they are often tethered to forces that direct both the range of our choices and even our identities. The range of options from which we choose is often determined by factors beyond our control. Rather than autonomous individuals, we become the victims of the marketers of "new and improved" products and of consumer culture.

A final consequence of understanding freedom exclusively as choice and a desire to be a self-made person can be isolation and abandonment. Having made our choices, we are left with them. Having relied upon oneself, the individual has no one else to turn to for assistance. Since I have made myself I do not need anyone else, I stand alone. I have no reason to want or expect help, for I must make all decisions by myself. Having chosen, I now live with my choices, at least until the next time I choose, it is my choice after all. I have no one to whom to turn in case of need or crisis. Culture recognizes an element of truth here in the expression: "You've made your bed, now lie in it."

### 3. The Franciscan Perspective: Individuality as Gift from God and Freedom as Commitment to the Good

As we explored the Franciscan moral vision, we encountered an understanding of freedom that is quite different from that discussed above. The Franciscan moral tradition, especially in the writings of Blessed John Duns Scotus, has demonstrated a profound respect for the individual. Scotus's principle of *haecceitas*, for example, explains that individuation "must be intrinsic, unique, and proper to the being itself.... It must be incapable of reproduction ... the undivided individual of each being. It can only be known by direct acquaintance, not from any consideration of common nature."[3] The tradition thus emphasizes the irreplaceable value of each individual created by God.

The Franciscan moral vision also emphasizes the possibility of a dynamic realization of creative and loving freedom of each individual in response to God's love (Characteristic Two). The Franciscan tradition does not explain freedom in terms of the number of options from which we make (often indifferent) choices but rather as the commitment to the good. This sort of freedom is not simply doing what one wants but grows out of a profound self-mastery. It is not an attribute of

---

[3] Mary Beth Ingham, *Scotus for Dunces: An Introduction to the Subtle Doctor* (St. Bonaventure, NY: Franciscan Institute Publications, 2003), 52.

the isolated individual but rather is exercised in communion with and for others.

In the Franciscan tradition, the moral life is a lifelong journey of ongoing conversion centered on the human capacity to respond freely and generously to the good. Bonaventure, for example, maintains that freedom is not the fact of having a multiplicity of choices but rather involves *what* we choose and *how* we choose.[4] In his understanding of freedom, humility is more important than autonomy, and it is the virtues that guide moral decision making rather than mere personal preference. Similarly, Scotus discussed freedom in the moral life in terms of a balance of the two moral dispositions, the *affectio commodi*, our desire for happiness, security, and self-fulfillment and the *affectio justitiae*, our affection for justice that inspires us to search for goods of lasting value, which Scotus calls the seat of our freedom.[5] In each of these understandings, freedom grows and develops not in isolation from others but by searching for truth together with others in community by being grasped by the beauty of the good. Morality and aesthetics are related.

## B. Relativity

An important distinction that emerged in the mid-twentieth century was that between an "open" and a "closed" society. As developed by philosophers such as Henri Bergson[6] and Karl Popper,[7] this notion contrasts open societies, which are non-authoritarian and respectful of freedom, with closed ones, which, they contend, confuse social customs with unchanging natural laws. Within the context of an open society, the notions of history and development become more important. Applying this broad understanding to the field of

---

[4] See Ilia Delio, *Simply Bonaventure: An Introduction to His Life, Thought, and Writings* (New York: New City Press, 2001), 125.

[5] See *Ordinatio* II, d. 6, in Allan B. Wolter, *Duns Scotus on the Will and Morality* (Washington: CUA Press, 1997), 298-99.

[6] Henri Bergson, *Two Sources of Morality and Religion* (Notre Dame: University of Notre Dame Press, 1994) [original English version, 1935].

[7] Karl Popper, *The Open Society and Its Enemies*, 2 volumes (Princeton, NJ: Princeton University Press, 1962) [original English version, 1945].

theology, some thinkers have contrasted contemporary historical understandings with what they call an older "classicist" mentality.[8] This general movement has raised questions concerning how one is able to comprehend reality itself. Twentieth-century philosophers drew what they considered to be the logical conclusion: If personal experience is important to one's understanding of the world, then each person's thought and evaluation is relative to that of every other person. Given this understanding, many asserted the relativity of all standards, norms, moral principles — and even truth itself. Everything was seen as relative to one's culture, history, and social location.

## 1. Diversity and Respect for the Other

The understanding that points of view are perspectival and therefore not absolute has led to an advancement of knowledge, especially in the sciences, both physical and social. It has led to many notions that are simply taken for granted in Western culture today: an embrace of pluralism, the celebration of diversity, a healthy criticism of ideological reasoning, evidence-based research, and a suspicion of authoritarianism. This in turn has led to greater participation by diverse populations in the political process and has often forced the dominant culture in a given society to acknowledge its own hubris, admitting that its advantages have often come not because of the power of its ideas but rather simply because of power.

Contemporary Western society has accepted pluralism in a way not seen before. Catholic theology itself has similarly acknowledged the fact of diversity. In the past fifty years major schools of theological thought have emerged around certain seminal thinkers – for example, Karl Rahner, Bernard Lonergan, Joseph Ratzinger, or Hans Urs von Balthazar. The latter part of the twentieth century also gave rise to theolo-

---

[8] See Bernard Lonergan, "The Transition from a Classicist Worldview to 'Historical Mindedness,'" in William F.J. Ryan and Bernard J. Tyrrell, eds., *A Second Collection* (New York: Herder and Herder, 1974), 1-9.

gies from sources not previously mined. Today one can speak of Latin American liberation theology, African-American theology, feminist theology, African theology, Asian theology, womanist theology, and Latino/a theology. Traditional theologians from Europe and North America have also begun to realize the perspectival nature of their own theology and to understand that a tremendous contribution to theology occurs when these diverse elements of the Christian community reflect together upon their experience of God.[9]

As the thoughts and ideas of those on the margins make their way into dialogue with the dominant culture, cultures begin to see themselves through the eyes of others. "What everybody knows" comes to be understood as what my group, in its cultural and historical particularity, believes to be true. Cultures come to understand that their world views are limited. Studies become more qualified, conclusions more humble. The acknowledgement of the possibility that my dialogue partner might have something important to teach me can lead in turn to healthy criticism of my own ideas and presuppositions. This can lead to a greater openness to new ideas and to welcoming the cultural, philosophical, and even theological expressions of others, acknowledging that in the very diversity of perspectives comes the possibility of a fuller and more appropriate understanding of the world, of my faith, and even of God.

## 2. Relativism

The issues surrounding the question of relativity in the twentieth and twenty-first centuries have also raised significant difficulties. An emphasis on the merits of a plurality of ideas and methods can easily lead to the conclusion that any method or idea is just as good as any other idea or method. Relativity and relationality, which emphasize the richness of a variety of traditions, can often turn into relativism. If any

---

[9] See, for example, Stephen Bevans and Roger Schroeder, *Constants in Context: A Theology of Mission for Today* (Maryknoll, NY: Orbis Books, 2004).

idea is as good as any other, then there really is no reason to choose one idea or option as better than any other – except for some private, personal reason. This notion is evidenced in contemporary culture in expressions such as "that may be good for you but not for me" or "that's just your opinion." I no longer speak of things as better or worse, except in reference to me. As relativism is joined with freedom understood as autonomy, choice simply becomes arbitrary. If all standards are only idiosyncratic, then there can be no discussion of the good beyond personal preference.[10]

Relativity can lead to a certain superficiality both in discourse and in relationships. If those elements which are deepest in me are simply my private ideas or values and have no relevance to others, then there is no real basis for forming community around such values,[11] much less for any public discussion about the merits of the values. There is little hope for true dialogue. Whatever I share cannot have "objective" value for the other. This attitude has been enshrined in some forms of post-modernism, a major philosophical school of the last part of the twentieth century. This school of thought has challenged the very foundations of Western philosophy. It asks whether one can truly distinguish knowledge from ideology, progress from decline, truth from falsehood. Such a philosophical stance maintains that, even though I can evaluate something as preferable to me, I cannot suggest that any choice be normative for others.

Even the contemporary culture's attention to diversity can be illusory. Rather than respecting true diversity, the stance of relativity often attempts to make Western liberalism paradigmatic for all peoples and all cultures. What is taken as globalization can more accurately be seen as expanding Western hegemony. As indifference to the content of one's free choices can lead to abandonment, the indifference of relativism can lead to fragmentation. All of us wear many hats: we may be students or teachers, members of the work

---

[10] See Smith, *Lost in Transition*, 27-35.

[11] See, for example, George Lindbeck, *The Nature of Doctrine: Religion and Theology in a Post-Liberal Age* (Louisville, KY: Westminster John Knox Press, 1984).

force, administrators, vowed Franciscans, Secular Franciscans, married, parents, single, members of a variety of voluntary groups, members of social clubs. We know that each
of these groups has its own standards of behavior, and the
rules of some groups may even contradict those of others.
It becomes easy to believe that since no group can maintain
its standards beyond the group, standards themselves are
valid only within a particular group. I adopt the values of the
group only when I am part of that group. I end up with one
morality when I am at home, another when I am at work,
a different morality when I am with my friends, and still a
different one when I am in church. None of these is better or
worse than any other.[12]

### 3. The Franciscan Perspective: Relationality and Love

Since the Franciscan moral vision, rooted in the spiritual
experience of Francis and Clare, has not been the dominant
theological vision of the Church, Franciscans are probably
more aware than many others in the Church that there are
a variety of valid philosophical and theological alternatives
that can enrich theology. Along with some contemporary
philosophers such as Alasdair MacIntyre,[13] this tradition is
comfortable speaking about the importance of perspective
and about the necessity of philosophical traditions for the
grounding of philosophical ideas. Where the Franciscan vision parts company with many contemporary philosophies,
however, is that it acknowledges that some perspectives and
some traditions are better than others. It understands with
much of contemporary philosophy that the richness of relationality arises from human desires, but, as we have seen, it
also maintains that only God can satisfy these desires with
infinite communion, relationship and harmony. Furthermore, the Franciscan tradition maintains that, while a crude

---

[12] For a further analysis, see, for example, Jeffrey Stout, *Ethics After
Babel: The Languages of Morals and Their Discontents* (Boston: Beacon
Press, 1988).

[13] See Alasdair MacIntyre, *Whose Justice? Which Rationality?* (Notre
Dame, IN: University of Notre Dame Press, 1988).

autonomy and relativism can lead to fragmentation, the true freedom and relationality that leads to harmony and community can only be based on the foundation of love of God and neighbor. As we have seen, although both Bonaventure and Scotus acknowledge that human desire and delight are "essential guides" along the way of morality,[14] these guides are not ends in themselves but rather part of a Franciscan personalist vision of moral living, responding to the love of God and others.

## C. Complexity

### 1. Complexity and Technological Progress

One of the contributions of modern science has been the dazzling variety of technologies that has made contemporary life more convenient. Improvements in farming equipment have made planting and harvesting easier for millions of farmers and as a result agricultural products have become relatively plentiful. Manufacturing has transformed the lives of many on the planet within the last century, making products available and affordable to people around the globe. Transportation technologies have made long range travel relatively inexpensive. Communications technologies allow people in remote areas of the world to be in contact with one another. Computing technologies have brought to millions the Internet with the capacity to collect and analyze vast amounts of data. It is still difficult to realize that the computing power in a low-end cell phone today vastly outstrips the computing power of the most advanced computers developed fifty years ago.

Advances in the pure sciences have also been astounding. The move from learning the basic structure of the DNA molecule to splicing genes to decoding the human genome was accomplished in a half century, thanks in part to continued rapid developments in computing power. In fact, our current understanding of progress itself is related to the growth

---

[14] See above, Chapter Three, 118.

of technology along with its greater and greater complexity. The computer and its offspring such as the Internet have become symbols of just how complex our technologically dependent world has become.

We have come to accept a world that is increasingly more complex both technologically and culturally. The assumption that progress and continual change is beneficial has become an engine of contemporary Western society, which has attempted to export this conviction to other cultures as well. As we become accustomed to a greater array of technologies and become more competent in using them, we also come to believe in the promise that technology offers.

Technology increases our options. Because of technology, we typically accomplish today what was considered impossible as recently as fifty years ago. As Daniel Callahan has stated (not without irony), "Where choice is, technology is. Where technology is, choice is transformed."[15] Similarly, technology promises greater relationality. Global communication, for example, is now commonplace, creating a world in which communities are linked in many complex ways by instantaneous communication. In fact, some have suggested that complexity itself is relationality.[16] Finally, technology promises us greater control. Yet as complexity grows, we in fact become more and more dependent upon technology to help us understand and manipulate the complex, relational world we experience and to negotiate the complex choices we must make.

## 2. Complexity, Fragmentation, and Disruption

Although globalization and technological advances have brought benefits to people throughout the world, they have also occasioned significant social disruption. Technology's promise of greater relationality, for example, has often been

---

[15] Daniel Callahan, *The Troubled Dream of Life: In Search of a Peaceful Death* (Washington, DC: Georgetown University Press, 2000), 69.

[16] Karen Brennan, et al., "On the Complexity of Technology and the Technology of Complexity" (Vancouver, BC: Proceedings of the 2007 Complexity Science and Educational Research Conference), 57.

illusory. The complexity of contemporary life has occasioned as much fragmentation as relation. Given the developments in communications technologies, with numerous information sites on the Internet, many of which representing a particular ideological or commercial bias, we should not be surprised that the same event can be evaluated quite differently, depending upon the information source a person has used to receive the information. Rather than creating greater homogenization, technology and globalization often contribute to greater heterogenization.[17] Communication technologies have created the possibility of interacting solely with like-minded people all over the globe. Although at first this might seem like greater relationality, the result can rather be greater fragmentation, with many individuals interacting only with others of similar persuasion. Even though such interaction may be with others who are geographically and culturally different, it is with those who are ideologically the same. This results in global society's fragmenting into a multitude of small voluntary associations based on similar ideology. One group can offend another group but never challenge it.[18]

The complex choices that technology presents has also had the effect of making those choices more difficult, leading many to believe that they are simply not able to make the choices that are asked of them. They become more and more dependent upon the help of experts to make these complex choices. Some patients and family members, for example, fear the medical choices that technology has foisted upon them. They feel simply unprepared to make them. At the same time, others praise technology as having increased "consumer choice in healthcare," and they advocate that the "consumer" must be allowed to choose among all competing options, including, for example, "aid in dying."[19]

---

[17] See Vincent J. Miller, "Where Is the Church? Globalization and Catholicity," *Theological Studies 69*, 2 (June 2008): 415-17.

[18] Miller, "Where Is the Church?" 418.

[19] See, for example, Thomas Nairn, "Reclaiming Our Moral Tradition," *Health Progress* 78, 6 (November/December, 1997), 37.

The belief that any change is necessarily progress along with the increasing dependence upon technological solutions in an increasingly complex world have lead many to question the promise that technology offers. Both socially and religiously, many express their dissatisfaction with freedom, relativity, and complexity as interpreted by liberal Western culture. From the social side, many choose to highlight or to rediscover their ethnic identities. In political philosophy, many are calling for a return to stability and social order. Religiously, thinkers are pointing out the problem of open-ended freedom and asking whether their theological counterparts have forgotten the doctrine of original sin.

### 3. The Franciscan Perspective: Beauty and Morality

Catholic moral theology must engage the complexities of contemporary life.[20] The Franciscan tradition — as a "middle" tradition — can serve a mediating role in analyzing both the potentiality and the dangers associated with decision making in today's complex world. In the Franciscan tradition, the movement from self out to love of God and neighbor is both a moral and an aesthetic task. As we have seen, it is the experience of beauty that opens the person to generosity and to the greater promise of the moral life. Beauty expands our vision, allowing us to see ourselves, others, and the world differently — allowing us to become ever more inclusive in our acts of justice and love, accepting the other, rather than withdrawing into our own ideologically homogeneous conclaves. This expansive vision is at home with the aspirations and desires that motivate the contemporary dreams of freedom and relationality.

It maintains, however, that these desires, as proper as they are, are fully appreciated only in a larger context that allows us to apprehend and appreciate Goodness itself. For Bonaventure, this appreciation of beauty is at the core of the

---

[20] See, for example, James T. Bretzke, *A Morally Complex World: Engaging Contemporary Moral Theology* (Collegeville, MN: Liturgical Press, 2004).

Franciscan spiritual tradition. Speaking of St. Francis, he says:

> In beautiful things he contuited Beauty itself and through the footprints impressed in things he followed his Beloved everywhere, out of them all making for himself a ladder through which he could climb up to lay hold of him who is utterly desirable. With an intensity of unheard devotion he savored in each and every creature – as in so many rivulets – that fontal Goodness.[21]

Similarly, Duns Scotus demonstrates a harmonic moral vision that arises out of a sustained consideration of divine graciousness and the abundant beauty of the natural order.[22] Without such a proper ordering of these desires, the contemporary dreams of humanity turn into a nightmare. The Franciscan appreciation of beauty and goodness offers an opportunity to integrate the diverse and often conflicting elements of contemporary culture into a coherent vision that is ethically and aesthetically satisfying, a vision that begins and ends with God.

## II. The Franciscan Vision as a Moral Stance

The Franciscan moral tradition incorporates within its vision respect for both sides of an array of polarities. It respects the tension of living as a pilgrim in this world (Characteristic Nine). It offers a coherent vision that values the individual, but it grounds the individual in community. It affirms the value of choice but maintains that proper choices are directed to the good. It affirms diversity but acknowledges a relationality beyond diversity that is rooted in solidarity

---

[21] Bonaventure, "The Major Legend of Saint Francis," 9.1, ed. Regis Armstrong, Wayne Hellmann, and William J. Short, *Francis of Assisi: Early Documents*, Volume 2, *The Founder* (Hyde Park, NY: New City Press, 2000), 596.

[22] See above, Chapter Three, 127-28.

and the mutuality of love. These elements are constitutive of the Franciscan moral stance.

## A. What Is a Stance?

The concept of a stance or horizon is rooted in contemporary philosophy[23] and is understood as that which brings consistency to one's knowledge and values. It is one's overall orientation to life. Everyone has a way of seeing and interpreting things, and often this is unreflective — it is simply the way we were taught to see the world. The analysis of one's stance or horizon attempts to reflect upon why we see the world in a particular way. A stance is formed through the interaction between a subjective dimension and an objective dimension, which fashions the way one looks at reality.[24] The subjective dimension consists in our commitments, lived values, and held beliefs. The objective dimension comprises "the range of data that comes into view for us to interpret, judge and act on."[25] It is the continual dialogue between these two poles that structures our understanding of reality. In a way similar to the earth's horizon, our stance or horizon sets limits to what we know or are able to experience. One's stance, however, can also open new horizons and disclose new opportunities.

Although there is no direct translation from one's stance to a specific resolution of an ethical issue, a stance or horizon nonetheless provides a critical context in which such considerations are made. Thus a stance can help us perceive the contours of an ethical issue and give us the resources that can help to resolve it.

---

[23] For a fuller discussion of a moral stance see James J. Walter, "What does Horizon Analysis Bring to the Consistent Ethic of Life?" in Thomas A. Nairn, O.F.M., ed., *The Consistent Ethic of Life: Assessing Its Reception and Relevance* (Maryknoll, NY: Orbis Books, 2008): 3-15.

[24] Walter, "... *Consistent Ethic of Life?*," 9.

[25] Walter, "... *Consistent Ethic of Life?*," 9.

## B. The Franciscan Moral Vision as an Ethical Stance

There are many dimensions to a given stance. On one level, in relation to what we have discussed above, there are certain elements that are culturally or historically specific. On this level, there is usually no question of good or bad, since such stances are the result of complex historical and cultural factors that have combined in particular ways in the development of a particular culture.

On a more fundamental level, however, we can compare and contrast ethical stances in terms of "better" and "worse." Theologian David Tracy, for example, has discussed this ability to compare and contrast in terms of what he calls "criteria of relative adequacy," consisting on the one hand of criteria of appropriateness (both to contemporary experience and to the tradition, either religious or secular) and on the other hand of criteria of intelligibility (coherence and existential meaning or truth).[26]

In this sense, the eleven characteristics presented in the Introduction[27] to this book as central elements of the Franciscan tradition are foundational to the Franciscan ethical stance. They are not only descriptive of the Franciscan spiritual and theological tradition but are also normative for contemporary Franciscan moral vision and action.

## C. Elements of the Franciscan Stance: Clustered Commitments

From what we have discussed above, it should be evident that the Franciscan moral vision is deeper than a set of external rules or norms. It is rather based on the way Franciscans see themselves, others, the world, and especially God. The eleven characteristics of the Franciscan moral vision can be further specified by discussing several themes that have

---

[26] David Tracy, *The Analogical Imagination: Christian Theology and the Culture of Pluralism* (New York: Crossroad Publishing Company, 1981), 238-41.

[27] See above, Introduction, 16-17.

been part of this study. These themes constitute the way Franciscans see the world and serve as a basis for normative judgments made in the Franciscan moral tradition. As Walter suggests:

> When we seek to thematize or make explicit in consciousness the contents of a stance – that is, to make explicit both the subject and object poles of the decision maker's stance – we attempt to make explicit the very foundations of the normative judgment itself and its justifications. In other words, the normative judgment – that is, judgments about what kinds of virtues we need to live the moral life well, or judgments about the rightness of actions, or judgments about moral obligations – arises from within the context of a normative stance, and so the stance is actually the ground and justification of the normative judgment itself.[28]

From what we have discussed above, it should not be surprising that certain related themes are central to the contemporary Franciscan ethical stance. We will now analyze them in related clusters of personhood, relationality, and community; love, beauty, and graciousness; and generosity, poverty, and transformation.

### 1. Personhood, Relationality, Community

A constant of the Catholic moral tradition has been the fact that humans are created in the image and likeness of God. We have noted, however, that, particularly for the Franciscan tradition, the God in whose image the human person is created is the Trinity, that is the communion of three divine persons united in a mystery of eternal self-communicative love:

> The Father is the source or fountain fullness of infinite goodness because the Father is primal, unoriginate,

---

[28] Walter, "… *Consistent Ethic of Life*?," 9-10.

and hence self-diffusive. The Son is that person eternally generated by the Father's self-diffusive goodness (*per modum naturae*), the total personal expression of the Father, and thus Word and Image of the Father. The Word is the complete expression of the mystery of God in one who, while God, is other than the Father. The Spirit proceeds from Father and Son in an act of loving volition (*per modum voluntatis*) on the part of the Father and Son. The Spirit is that freedom-in-love between the Father and Son, who perfects their love in a holy and eternal union.[29]

In the Godhead it is this eternal reciprocal relation of love and self-giving that establishes the relation among persons. Love, which is the very nature of God, establishes the divine community and serves as the divine model for human community.

Since God's love is expansive and overflowing, it reaches out beyond God's own self and empties itself into what is other than God – creation. God's love is the birthplace of all creation. Thus it should be no surprise that community is intrinsic to the very nature of humanity, for we are created by the Trinity and are images of it. For the Franciscan tradition this understanding of community extends to all of creation – inanimate as well as animate. The entirety of creation becomes the footprint (*vestigium*) of God. Francis's "Canticle of Creatures," for example, is not mere anthropomorphizing of nature but a genuine recognition of the concentric nature of God's ever expansive love rippling throughout all of creation. For Franciscans, the ultimate reason for community is because we are created in the image of a God whose deepest nature is itself communal. The contemporary Franciscan vision continues to affirm and celebrate this today by its recognition of the relational and communal nature of all reality.

---

[29] Ilia Delio, "Religious Pluralism and the Coincidence of Opposites," *Theological Studies* 70, 4 (December 2009): 827-28.

## 2. Love, Beauty, Graciousness

We have seen throughout this study that in the Franciscan tradition the highest form of being is self-communicating love. This is the dynamic that pulses through the life of the Trinity and is the love that wills the world and humans into existence. Thus this love is a sharing love that gives freely so that others may receive it and continue to live in this love by sharing it with others. This is the gift of God's own self that reaches an apex in the Incarnation. This is the very foundation of the Franciscan moral vision.

In line with its Augustinian roots, the Franciscan stance sees beauty as a reflection of order and proportion. Within the inner life of God there is the order of relations between the persons of the Trinity united through the proportion of their relations to one another. Each is the complement of the other in a harmonious dynamic exchange of love. In creation, this sense of proportion is modeled through the order within creation and the proportion of composition of material reality. This grounds Bonaventure's teaching on exemplarity and is a means of our experiencing the beauty of the Creator. A sense of proportion or harmony of composition is a further development of the understanding of beauty. Elements joined proportionately work harmoniously and bring a sense of well being to the whole. Thus, beauty is

> that surprising brilliance or clarity that arrests and liberates our attention, evoking awe and wonder and opening us to the eternal. Beauty does not merely please and attract us, it also derails and releases from obsessive and deadly attention to the self or the routines of survival, and summons us to reach like Michelangelo's Adam, for the other and the divine.[30]

---

[30] Patrick T. McCormick, "A Right to Beauty: A Fair Share of Milk and Honey for the Poor," *Theological Studies* 71, 3 (September 2010): 703. This seminal article presents the role of beauty in constructing a social ethic.

The understanding of beauty as order, proportion, and an opening to the transcendent cuts across the grain of much of contemporary culture in which beauty is at best "in the eye of the beholder."

## 3. Generosity, Poverty, Transformation

For Francis, Clare, and their followers, an important attribute of God in whose image we are created is a generosity, grounded in the goodness of God, that overflowed in an unimaginable love for the other. In his contemplation of this ever renewing fountain fullness, Francis discovered the deep relationship between love and poverty. God's love revealed in the person of Christ is a totally self-emptying love. It is fully actualized in the Crucified One who holds nothing back even in the face of rejection. While such a notion of love clearly has implications for understanding poverty as a renunciation of material possessions, it also grounds a deeper understanding of poverty itself as total generosity. This was the love that Francis modeled in his poverty. It was, to be sure, a material poverty, but it was especially a poverty of generosity in that possessions and wealth were to be used for others. This was the love that Francis demonstrated through his humble service, whether in preaching to the animals, in working among the lepers, in his rebuilding churches both physically and spiritually, and in his preaching by example. He held nothing back for himself.

The contemporary Franciscan tradition understands that such a poverty of spirit leads to moral transformation, not as a result of notions of progress but rather because of personal conversion, allowing oneself to respond more readily to God's graciousness by following the example of Christ, the Word made flesh. This Word "contains all things that God can and does create."[31] This is the story of the perfecting of creation,

---

[31] See Zachary Hayes, *The Hidden Center: Spirituality and Speculative Christology in St. Bonaventure* (New York: Paulist Press, 1981), 131. See Bonaventure, *Defense of the Mendicants* 2, 12. José de Vinck and Robert Karris, *WSB*, XV (St. Bonaventure, NY: Franciscan Institute Publications, 2010), 61.

of human completion. It is a story, however, that knows that there is no human completion without the gratuity of God's grace and without the exacting project of human self-mastery. Humans "enter into the movement of the Trinitarian life by entering into the life movement of the Son in as far as they personalize the fundamental value of His life in their own."[32] In imitation of Christ, this project of self-mastery depends upon the self-giving love that was shown on the cross.

In a culture that accepts the sheer number of choices as the indication of freedom, this Franciscan vision continues to maintain rather that it is "how we choose and what we choose [that] makes a difference – first, in what we become by our choices and second, what the world becomes because of our choices."[33] In the Franciscan stance, it is Christ crucified who is central to Christian moral living and to the transformation of society.

## III. Implications: The Contemporary Franciscan Understanding of the Moral Person

How then can one describe the contemporary Franciscan understanding of the moral person?[34] First, in keeping with its tradition, the contemporary Franciscan moral vision exhibits a profound respect for the individual. We have seen several examples of this respect for the individual demonstrated in the Franciscan tradition. The tradition insists that God did not simply create abstract human beings, but rather individual men and women, each precious in their distinctiveness. This is the value inherent in Scotus's principle of *haecceitas*.

Second, the Franciscan moral anthropology acknowledges that the person is created out of love and created for love.

---

[32] Hayes, *The Hidden Center*, 133.

[33] Delio, *Simply Bonaventure*, 125.

[34] For a more complete discussion of the contemporary Franciscan understanding of the person, see Dawn Nothwehr, *The Franciscan View of the Human Person: Some Central Elements* (St. Bonaventure, NY: The Franciscan Institute, 2005).

This aspect of the Franciscan moral tradition ensures that the emphasis on the individual does not become individualism. The human person, as other creatures, is a footprint of God. Moreover, humans are created in the very image of the Trinity. Out of this notion of the person as footprint and image comes the idea that persons are related one to another and in fact are related to all of creation. We have already seen that for Francis all creation was brother and sister. This notion of relationality permeates the contemporary Franciscan moral vision and has implications both for the understanding of the entire world as creative gift of a generous God and of an understanding of human solidarity. The person has been created by God in her or his individuality but at the same time can fulfill himself or herself only in community with others.

Thirdly, the contemporary Franciscan moral vision understands that, although morality necessarily encompasses moral rules and norms, it is much more than simply a set of rules. We have already seen that neither Bonaventure nor Scotus would maintain that Franciscan morality is simply a deductive application of general principles to concrete circumstances. Although both theologians respect normativity, they recognize the importance of experience and learning in the formation of the moral life. Similarly, the contemporary Franciscan vision maintains that morality, while respectful of norms, is more specifically a way of life into which one is called. It is a way of life that involves both personal and social morality, demanding a response to the love that God has shown us by means of an outwardly directed love of God and neighbor. It is a way of life that is a matter of continuous conversion.

# 7

# FRAMING ENGAGEMENT
# WITH SOCIETY

## JOSEPH P. CHINNICI, O.F.M.

*The Franciscan moral vision embodies
a distinct social vision that intersects
the personal with the political,
the individual with the communal,
the singular life of virtue
with the anticipation of the Reign of God for all.*

In our previous chapters we have discovered that the Franciscan moral tradition in its theological foundations places a high premium on understanding God as a love communion of three-in-one, the active reading of our own experience in the light of God's gift, and our free and generous response to this relationship which is discovered to be present in time, history, and all created things. Founded on the continual relationship between Trinitarian communion and creation, the Franciscan moral imagination affirms bonds of fraternity not only between the members of the Church and the adherents of the movement itself but also with every creature that exists. We have argued that the term "poverty," reflecting Trinitarian life itself, conveys self-emptying love and the willingness to share with anyone in need. The tradition cultivates a certain epistemology of "contuition," the seeing of all things in the light of God's gift and a certain personal orientation: namely, the cultivation of moral self-awareness and the free choices of a self-moving and conscience-centered actor, whose affection for the love of God, neighbor, and self grows throughout life. This tradition, really a Christian penitential humanism, also makes public ethical demands. It affirms our responsibility both individually and communally to discover rationally and to choose freely engagement with the contemporary world in a way that gives witness to the unity of all that exists in a God who is an "economy of communion."[1]

Today we recognize that the "public realm" or "society" of which we speak is both national and global in nature. The Arab Spring in its political and economic dimensions has rippled across Europe, Asia, America, and Africa; protests in Spain, Greece, India, Europe, South Asia, Mexico, Israel have indicated global dissatisfaction with established democratic processes and their ability to achieve an equitable justice which includes all peoples; the Occupy Wall Street movement has argued for the inadequacies of the prevailing political-economic systems.[2] The Pontifical Council for Justice and Peace itself issued a universal call for "Reforming the

---

[1] The vision as will be seen has much in common with that elucidated in Benedict XVI, *Charity in Truth, Caritas in veritate* (Vatican City: Libreria Editrice Vaticana, 2009), Chapters 3-5. For Trinitarian foundations see *Caritas in veritate*, 54-55; John Paul II, *On Social Concern, Sollicitudo rei socialis* (Washington, DC: United States Catholic Conference, 1988), 35-45. For "penitential humanism" see Joseph P. Chinnici, O.F.M., "Penitential Humanism: Rereading the Sources to Develop a Franciscan Urban Spirituality," in Ken Himes, O.F.M., ed. Roberta A. McKelvie, O.S.F., *Franciscans in Urban Ministry* (St. Bonaventure, NY: Franciscan Institute Publications, 2002), 109-28.

[2] For background see Niall Ferguson, Charles S. Maier, Erez Manela, Daniel J. Sargent, *The Shock of the Global, The 1970s in Perspective* (Cambridge, MA: Harvard University Press, 2010); Nicholas Kulish, "Protests Rise Around Globe as Faith in the Vote Wanes," *The New York Times* (Wednesday, September 28, 2011), A-4; Cara Buckley and Rachel Donadio, "Rallies Across Globe Protest Economic Policies," *The New York Times* (October 16, 2011), A-4; Michael Kimmelman, "The Power of Place in Protest," *The New York Times*, Sunday Review, 1, 6-7.

International Financial and Monetary Systems in the Context of Global Public Authority." In it we read,

> The economic and financial crisis which the world is going through calls everyone, individuals and peoples, to examine in depth the principles and the cultural and moral values at the basis of social coexistence. What is more, the crisis engages private actors and competent public authorities on the national, regional and international level in serious reflection on both causes and solutions of a political, economic and technical nature.[3]

Perhaps the time has come when "a new trajectory of thinking" will be received:

> in order to arrive at a better understanding of the implications of our being one family; interaction among the peoples of the world calls us to embark upon this new trajectory, so that integration can signify solidarity rather than marginalization. *Thinking of this kind requires a deeper critical evaluation of the category of relation.*[4]

The purpose of this chapter is to engage the Franciscan moral vision more directly with the public realms of politics and economics. To be sure, an answer to the call for a "reform in the principles and the cultural and moral values at the basis of social coexistence" will not be achieved. The Franciscan tradition leaves more room for human freedom and development in knowledge and practice than any one set of answers can do. But it is the conviction of the authors

---

[3] Pontifical Council for Justice and Peace, "Towards Reforming the International Financial and Monetary Systems in the Context of Global Public Authority," Vatican City, 2011, citation from Preface, available at: http://www.vatican.va/roman_curia/pontifical_councils/justpeace/documents/rc_pc_justpeace_doc_20111024_nota_en.html.

[4] *Caritas in veritate, Charity in Truth*, 53, referring to Paul VI, *Populorum progressio*, 85. Italics in original.

of this volume and of many others that a rediscovery of the Franciscan tradition in the areas of politics and economics has much to contribute to the contemporary discussion.[5] Embedded in it, as we have argued in this book, is a rethinking of the deeper dimensions of the "category of relation," a rethinking which has the possibility of touching the global relationships between people and the relationships between people and their environment.

Unfortunately, both because of its internal history in the Church and its focus on the virtue of poverty, which has little resonance in the popular understanding of that term in both the developed and developing worlds, the Franciscan moral vision has often been confined to the sacristy of a private religious asceticism. In actual fact, however, the ethical approach presented here necessitates both a social project and a public asceticism. Within the Church, it provides a healthy complement to more dominant approaches which emphasize the sanctity of private property, natural law, and the rights of human dominion. It requires its adherents through clear thinking and disciplined action to make fraternity, freedom, and the communion of goods visible in the world. It argues for a new ethics of sustainability. Here, the human being is not simply a *homo oeconomicus* whose actions are based on autonomy and self-interest, nor solely a *homo consumens*, who is a "protagonist of a culture of having." More fundamentally, he or she is, rather, a *homo creatus et donator*, someone who in his or her fullness is made in the image of God and is therefore capable with grace of freely producing spiritual

---

[5] Some of the public dimensions of Franciscan sociology, economics, and politics have only recently been highlighted by European scholars and will be cited throughout this essay or listed in the bibliography. For an introduction in English see Giacomo Todeschini, *Franciscan Wealth, From Voluntary Poverty to Market Society* (St. Bonaventure, NY: Franciscan Institute Publications, 2009); Daria Mitchell, O.S.F., ed., *Poverty and Prosperity: Franciscans and the Use of Money*, Washington Theological Union Symposium Papers, 2009 (St. Bonaventure, NY: Franciscan Institute Publications, 2009).

and material gifts so as to mutually exchange "goods" with all members of the same human family.[6]

The first section of this chapter, "Engaging History," shows that the foundation for the dynamism of a Franciscan moral imagination is a continuing commitment to engage in the process of historical change. "Elements of a Basic Stance," the second section, describes in very general terms key principles which comprise the Franciscan stance as applied to the public sphere. "The Dynamism of Human Moral Life in Politics and Economics" then considers the moral vitality inherent in the Franciscan approach to the political and economic spheres of life. Throughout the chapter some comments will be made relating the tradition to contemporary social challenges. At the outset it is important to recognize that no one Franciscan thinker has presented a systematic overview of these elements. Dramatic shifts occurred as the Franciscan movement became part and parcel of the institutional structures of the Church and society. Philosophical approaches varied from generation to generation. Still, when reinterpreted from today's standpoint, some disparate but typical stances unify the tradition's overall orientation toward life in the public square. As noted in Chapter One, the profile that emerges is a "trajectory of thought," a "thought style," an "interpretive frame," or an "ethical stance" rather than a "system" of moral theology as it touches political economy.[7]

## I. ENGAGING HISTORY

Understanding the distinctive character of a Franciscan moral orientation for public life requires that a person

---

[6] For a contemporary parallel of an "economy of communion" and the broad interpretation of *homo donator* see Luigino Bruni, ed., *The Economy of Communion, Toward a Multi-Dimensional Economic Culture*, trans. Lorna Gold (Hyde Park, NY: New City Press, 2002), and in the same volume Luigino Bruni, "Toward An Economic Rationality 'Capable of Communion,'" 41-67.

[7] "Thought style" is taken from Mary Douglas, *How Institutions Think* (Syracuse, NY: Syracuse University Press, 1986); *Thought Styles* (London: SAGE Publications, 1986).

appreciate the social upheaval that marked the tradition from the beginning. The entire thirteenth century, particularly in Italy, but in other parts of the West also, was an era in which the inherited tripartite classifications of people by profession and religious status (those who pray, those who fight, those who labor; the clerical, the monastic, and the lay divisions of the Gregorian reform) was breaking apart under the pressure of demographic growth, a new commercial economy, the growth of the cities, and the entrance of the poor as active agents on the stage of history. In such a situation an emergent merchant and professional class, highly literate and politically engaged, participated in the formation of new structures of civil government.[8] As traditional social structures weakened and the inherited bonds of kinship dissolved, significant questions of theodicy emerged: How is God present in this new world? Does God care for the marginal person? What does the prevalence of suffering and injustice say about the goodness of God? How does the Church speak to this new political and economic order? Here, the boundaries of personal, communal, and ecclesial identity became ambiguous, and, tied as it was to an inherited feudal structure and sociology of classes, the Church underwent an intensive period of internal struggle and reform. Social deviance and theological heresy became preoccupations for some, while others engaged in practices and discussions which attempted to meet the needs of this new world. The Franciscan moral tradition which evolved sought to develop a public performance which would bridge the gap between people's experience, their knowledge of the world, the new political and economic relationships, and the Gospel revelation of God's presence in history. This moral tradition developed fully within the context of the Church and consciously rejected alternate moral cosmologies.

With the initial breakup of the traditional world, the twelfth century had already seen a shift in moral sensibility

---

[8] For a good introduction see Lester K. Little, *Religious Poverty and the Profit Economy in Medieval Europe* (Ithaca, NY: Cornell University Press, 1983).

away from abstract norms and established laws toward an ethic based on intentionality. In the thirteenth century, the birth of the communes witnessed a corresponding sense of civic engagement, responsibility, the centrality of conscience, and the actions of the will. Identification with those who were poor became particularized, part of an individual's personal responsibility for those socially visible "on the side of the road." A new "religious person" marked by a "pauperistic spirituality" entered onto the scene.[9] Some discovered the presence of Christ in the poor and asked new moral questions. What virtues, for example, should mark public life? Could a merchant be saved? What was a just price? Who belonged to the society being constructed? What norms should govern the relationships between men and women?[10] The whole could be described as an "anthropological turn" as the locus of faith and the encounter with the holy shifted slightly from mediating structures and traditional patterns of relationships toward direct encounter with the Word of God, personal experience, individual choice, and the struggle to form new communities of peace and support within a volatile situation. The Franciscan movement was intricately tied to these general developments. As one historian summarized, "It is in this telling tension between the joyful acceptance of the world and the rejection of its perversion that people must find their salvation, in the dialectic between receptivity and reaction."[11]

This context of social mutation is important as a starting point for understanding the Franciscan approach to public

---

[9] Grado G. Merlo, "La Conversione alla povertà nell'Italia dei secoli XII-XIV," and Antonio Rigon, "I testamenti come atti di religiosità pauperistica," in Enrico Menestò, ed., *La Conversione alla Povertà nell'Italia dei Secoli XII-XIV* (Spoleto: Centro Italiano di Studi Sull-Alto Medioevo), 3-32, 391-414.

[10] See as one example Sylvain Piron, "Perfection Évangelique et Moralité Civile: Pierre de Jean Olivi et L'Etique "Economique Franciscaine," in Barbara Molina e Giulia Scarcia, eds., *Ideologia del Credito Fra Tre e Quattrocento: Dall'Astesano ad Agnelo Da Chivasso* (Asto: Centro Studi sui Lombardi e sua creditor nel Medioevo, 2001), 103-43.

[11] Jacques LeGoff, *Saint Francis of Assisi*, trans. Christine Rhone (London and New York: Routledge, 1999), 130.

life. When the tradition is alive, it stands fully within an historical situation marked by both established inheritances and currents of innovation. In its most vital stages it has been marked by a willingness to engage new questions, new political and economic structures, new aspirations, and new moral dilemmas. History and time are constituent elements of God's revelation. The human being is a poor *viator,* a pilgrim or traveler along the way who, we hope, makes choices which lead to a society of peace and justice that lies ahead. His or her social vision is marked neither by nostalgia for a primitive golden age nor by a rigidity which takes a particular political or economic or socio-moral arrangement as absolutely normative. A reading of the "signs of the times" thus pushes the moral imagination toward a public ethic which is situated within the contingencies of life, rooted in the past but always moving forward.[12] It has a critical, growing edge.

The sources describe Francis of Assisi as a "man of the future."[13] Always embedded in the circumstances of life, Francis encouraged his followers to live not *ad tempus,* according to a merchant's calculus of time centered on personal reward, but *ad Deum,* according to a life directed in service to God's will.[14] Bonaventure, following the ancient definition of theology, privileges the scriptural revelation within its historical unfolding. God's incarnate embrace of

---

[12] The historical and anthropological turn is indicated in Ovidio Capitani, "Verso una nuova antropologia e una nuova religiosità," in *La Conversione alla Povertà,* 447-71.

[13] See the classic essay "Francis, Man of the World to Come," in Cajetan Esser, *Repair My House,* ed. Luc Mély, O.F.M, trans. Michael D. Meilach, O.F.M. (Chicago, IL: Franciscan Herald Press, 1963), 15-45.

[14] See *Earlier Rule* 22:19-26 and his consistent eschatological interpretation of *servus* based on Matt 24:46 in Regis J. Armstrong, O.F.M. Cap., J.A. Wayne Hellmann, O.F.M. Conv., William J. Short, O.F.M., eds., *Francis of Assisi, Early Documents,* Volume 1: *The Saint* (NY: New City Press, 1999), 80, 134 (hereafter cited as *FA:ED* 1). For background, Jacques LeGoff, "Merchant's Time and Church's Time in the Middle Ages," in *Time, Work, and Culture in the Middle Ages* (Chicago: University of Chicago Press, 1980), 29-42, where he argues that the Church's time belongs to God whereas the merchant's time is measured, calculable, rationalized, and secular.

every age of the human journey calls people toward a moral perfection which lies only in the future and provides a deep structure to the human being's and indeed all of creation's *itinerarium in Deum* (journey into God).[15] The ethic of Peter Olivi engages his situation through a reading of history,[16] and Scotus's more philosophical reflections occur within a developmental and eschatological framework.[17] The entire trajectory focused on God's economy in history is rooted in Augustine and, as such, critiques a social and moral order which claims too close a connection between divine law, natural law, and human law, or between the Church and the kingdom of God.[18] The role of the Holy Spirit and the appropriation of God's will become central for those who are traveling through time. Within the context of a contingent world which is constantly changing, God's continuously creative action and the human choice to enter freely into this gratuitous relationship become a central moral dynamic for the construction of an eschatologically driven political economy. Taking this starting point seriously in our present situation would require that practitioners of the tradition engage in a positive but critiquing way the questions of globalization, neo-liberalism, multiculturalism, relationship to the natural environment, and the political and economic

---

[15] Alfonso Pompei, "Teologia della Storia della Salvezza in San Bonaventura da Bagnoregio," in *Bonaventura da Bagnoregio, Il pensare francescano* (Roma: Miscellanea Francescana, 1993), 334-47.

[16] David Burr, "Bonaventure, Olivi and Franciscan Eschatology," *Collectanea Francescana* 53 (1983): 23-40.

[17] See Scotus, Ord. IV, d1, q.3, n.8, in *Opera Omnia* 16 (Paris: Ludovicum Vivès, 1894), 136, as cited and applied to ethics in Allan B. Wolter, O.F.M., "Native Freedom of the Will as a Key to the Ethics of Scotus," *The Philosophical Theology of John Duns Scotus*, Marilyn McCord Adams, ed. (Ithaca: Cornell University Press, 1990), 162; Wolter, "Scotus' Eschatology: Some Reflections," in Michael F. Cusato, O.F.M., F. Edward Coughlin, O.F.M., eds., *That Others may Know and Love, Essays in Honor of Zachary Hayes, OFM* (St. Bonaventure, NY: The Franciscan Institute, 1997), 305-48.

[18] For background see R. A. Markus, *Saeculum. History and Society in the Theology of St. Augustine* (New York: Cambridge, 1970), Chapter 4; "Conversion and Disenchantment in Augustine's Spiritual Career," reprinted in Markus, *Sacred and Secular, Studies on Augustine and Latin Christianity* (Aldershot, Hampshire, Great Britain: Variorum, 1994).

adjustments which are required to reveal the Gospel message in a world which is called toward a better future. While not presenting a specific roadmap, this historical engagement with politics and economics is shaped by some key elements of a basic stance.

## II. Elements of a Basic Stance

## A. The Discovery of Elsewhere

As part of a vast movement for change and a penitential reformation in the ordering of life, the Franciscan movement seeks to discover and make socially valuable "someplace else," what Giacomo Todeschini has identified as the "elsewhere."[19] On a political and economic level, the moral tradition includes in the human contract those people who are excluded from the prevailing social contract. Todeschini argues that the increased development of a monetary economy associated with the world of the merchant championed an organized and calculable world of exchange which measured value in terms of possessions and productive usefulness. This evolving commercial system became enshrined in civic relationships, laws, codes of behavior, and the hopes and aspirations of the new class. Membership in this civic arrangement, in which the Church itself was partially embedded, was based primarily on property, money, and the concrete public display of wealth. The poor, the useless, the politically and economically powerless were those who did not fully belong either to a society organized by orders and classes or to those whose public recognition depended on "cash value."

By rejecting money, property, and ownership and codifying this rejection in the central value of "voluntary poverty" or "living without anything of one's own" (in Latin, *sine proprio*), Francis of Assisi and his companions attempted to argue for a different definition of belonging, one which was based

---

[19] What follows owes a good deal to Todeschini, *Franciscan Wealth*, Chapter II.

on the "surplus gratuitous value" of all things. It is telling that the trajectory of Francis's own conversion narrative was marked by "leaving the world" of relationships shaped solely by commercial values and entering into a new field of familial relationships dictated by the "Spirit of the Lord and Its holy activity."[20] This is the Gospel world of an ever expanding circle of creatures in whom is discovered an innate dignity: the lepers, Clare and the sisters, the men and women of the marketplace, the poor, the non-believers, inanimate creatures. In this new world, people and things could not be measured solely by their usefulness, productivity, or even religious allegiances. All creatures possessed a value "given from above" by the Creator. The civic project became the inclusion of these "others" in the social contract by voluntarily companioning those who were not useful and productive, caring for the suffering human being, distributing goods so that everyone was given a basic human dignity, and focusing on the human condition of being "brother" and "sister" to all – whether animate on inanimate.

While the institutionalized growth of the Franciscan movement and its insertion into the pastoral structures of the Church obscured the immediate presence of the "elsewhere" so evident to Francis and his companions, a social vision which included the poor and valued simplicity marked the movement's function in the medieval city and Church. Economically speaking, the members of the Order, particularly through the lay confraternities which gathered around the friars, the practices of penance which were enjoined, and the establishment of places of exchange, served as a conduit whereby the goods of the society circulated between "those who had" and "those who had not." On an abstract level the anthropology of Bonaventure joined everyone in a common bond of human "ontological poverty" which required a permanent acceptance of and response to God's gift; his Christology highlighted the following of the one who made himself voluntarily poor by becoming a human being with other human beings, that is, the one who practiced

---

[20] Citation from *Later Rule* 10:8 in *FA:ED* 1, 105.

solidarity with humankind (II Cor 8:8-9 became a key text). In Bonaventure's social vision, "the possessor of a superfluity of earthly goods is morally bound, in justice, to come to the assistance of the needy by distributing his surplus goods."[21] On a popular level, the biographical narratives of Francis which formed the bulk of the oral and literary tradition communicated the importance of the "elsewhere" in the formation of the social contract. Embedded in these examples were both a reforming critique and an ethical ideal which called for conversion. For example, in a work from the 1250s, when a brother is caught disparaging a poor man, Francis replies: "Brother, whenever you see a poor person, a mirror of the Lord and his poor mother is placed before you. Likewise, in the sick, look closely for the infirmities which he accepted for our sake."[22] To see the "elsewhere" was to recognize a fellow member of the Body of Christ.

This vision of a universal *fraternitas* in which each creature has intrinsic value and all are called equally to a life of penance – a discovery of "elsewhere" – has already been alluded to in earlier chapters of this book. The practice of living voluntarily "without anything of one's own" implies a break from the prevailing order and also points to the much more positive ordering of all relationships toward a social pattern dictated by belief in the Trinitarian communion of persons. God's identity is one of self-diffusive goodness and a vestige of this God can be found in each creature, while an image of this God is discovered in each human being. Framed in terms of a contemporary social ethics, the Franciscan life which performs its belief in God offers not only a social critique but also a continuous searching for the "elsewhere" which society has ceased to value, as well as a commitment to

---

[21] Citation from Bernard Cullen, "Property in the Writings of St. Bonaventure," Christian Wenin, ed., *L'Homme et Son Univers au Moyen Age* (Louvain-La-Neuve: Éditions de L'Institut Supérieur de Philosphie, 1986), II, 829.

[22] Thomas of Celano, "The Remembrance of the Desire of A Soul," 85, in Regis J. Armstrong, O.F.M. Cap., J.A. Wayne Hellmann, O.F.M. Conv., William J. Short, O.F.M., eds., *Francis of Assisi: Early Documents*, Volume 2, *The Founder* (New York: New City Press, 2000), 303.

a life of making that "elsewhere" publicly valued.[23] However weakly it is lived at any given time, the "elsewhere" remains a component part of a stance that lives uneasily with established but exclusionary arrangements of social order. Negatively put, in any given political and economic situation the Franciscan moral stance begins with the question: Whom does this arrangement exclude from human flourishing? Today, the best of Catholic social thought considers deeply the growing disparity between rich and poor in the United States and the challenge of a global ethic which touches the systemic economic and cultural relationships created by the international monetary system.[24]

## B. Paradise

It is one thing to develop a public hermeneutic of the elsewhere, it is another to describe the society into which one is inviting people. One historian has called this society the "Franciscan utopia in the medieval Church," but perhaps the term "paradise," more biblical and theological, captures the reality better.[25] This future homeland was the society which God intended from the beginning, and its chief image came through reflection on the original "garden paradise" described in Genesis or the heavenly Jerusalem of the Apocalypse. Monastic spirituality had enshrined these *topoi* and their values were appropriated by Francis, Clare and their companions as a public project in the marketplace of the city.[26] The images resonated with the ideals described

---

[23] For parallel comments see John Paul II, *Sollicitudo rei socialis*, 40, on solidarity and the Trinitarian model of human society.

[24] See for example, John A. Coleman and William F. Ryan, eds., *Globalization and Catholic Social Thought, Present Crisis, Future Hope* (Maryknoll, NY: Orbis Books, 2005).

[25] André Vauchez, "L'Utopie franescaine dans l'église medievale," *Lumiere et Vie* XXXIII (Avril-Mai-Juin, 1984): 39-47. For use of the term "paradise" see *Earlier Rule*, 22:1, *FA:ED* 1, 82.

[26] For the association of these images with the monastic spirituality of desire see Jean Leclercq, O.S.B., *The Love of Learning and the Desire for God, A Study of Monastic Culture*, trans. Catharine Misrahi (New York: Fordham University Press, 1961, 1982), 53-70.

by Augustine in his influential work *The City of God*. The saints gave them an eschatological orientation. In concrete terms, for the Franciscan movement, centered as it was on the theological vision of the Trinity, the society toward which people were moving was one marked at its very beginning by the sharing of all things in common (again the positive understanding of poverty) and by the equality of each person in a community of loving relationships (fraternity). Such a view implied something about dominion, ownership, and the simple use of things, three major elements in a political economy. Although this understanding of "paradise" and its concrete manifestations would be constantly fought over both within and without the Order, the Franciscan schoolmen preserved the vision in intellectual terms in their commentaries on Lombard's *Sentences*. For the purposes of this essay, two key elements, the foundational starting points for constructing a Franciscan political economy, may be highlighted.

### 1. Omnia esse communia
### ("Everything is common to all")

Alexander of Hales in his *Commentary on the Sentences* situates the discussion of the common possession of goods in the questions dealing with the natural law as it is ordered to the neighbor.[27] To be noted immediately is that he is here dealing with the ethic that governs the relationships between people. He asks, "Does it belong to the natural law that all things should be held in common?" Isidore is cited as supporting the common possession of all things, but the fundamental inheritance supporting the ideal of "all things in common" and thereby relegating private ownership (*proprium*) to the level of positive human law is from Augustine. Augustine writes in his commentary on John:

---

[27] For what follows see Hales, *Summa Theologica* (Quaracchi: Collegii S. Bonaventurae, 1948), IV, 362-64.

By right of which law does anyone possess whatever they do possess? Is it not by right of human law? Because by divine law the earth is the Lord's and its fullness (Ps 23.1); God made the poor and the rich from one and the same slime, and one and the same earth supports both rich and poor alike. All the same, it is by right of human law that one says, "This villa is mine, this house is mine, this slave is mine." Why? Because God allotted the human race these very laws enacted by the emperors and kings of the world.[28]

Note that Augustine perceives a real difference in terms of its impact on human relationships between God's ownership of all things and the positive human law which separates things into "mine" and "yours." Peace comes from following the path where all things belong to God and all are treated as neighbors with respect to the community of goods. Following the path of private ownership will lead to division. As we shall see, these citations from Isidore and Augustine orient how the Franciscan masters would interpret natural law in its relationship to private property.[29] Bonaventure states the ideal succinctly in the *Collations on the Six Days*: "If indeed man had not sinned, there would not have been a division of lands, but all would have been in common."[30] Scotus argues the same theme in his citation of both Gratian's *Decretum*

---

[28] Augustine, *Homilies on the Gospel of John* 1-40, *The Works of Saint Augustine*, trans. Edmund Hill, O.P., ed. Allan D. Fitzgerald, O.S.A., series editor Boniface Ramsey (New York: New City Press, 2009), 6.25, 143.

[29] For Bonaventure see *Commentary on the Sentences*, II.dXLIV, aII, QII, ad.4. in *Opera Omnia* (Quaracchi: Collegii S. Bonaventurae, 1885), 1009. Background for the whole tradition may be found in Joan Lockwood O'Donovan, "Christian Platonism and Non-proprietary Community," in Oliver O'Donovan & Joan Lockwood O'Donovan, *Bonds of Imperfection, Christian Politics, Past and Present* (Grand Rapids, MI: Wm. B. Eerdmans, 2004), 73-96.

[30] St. Bonaventure, *Collations on the Six Days*, *The Works of Saint Bonaventure*, trans. José de Vinck, 18.7 (Paterson, NJ: St. Anthony Guild Press, 1970), 270.

and Augustine: "By the law of nature, all things are common to all."[31]

It is important to recognize that when the Franciscans glossed "in common" they departed from the inherited monastic and ecclesial tradition and its interpretation of the early Christian community in Acts. The contrast went to the spiritual, economic and political heart of the Franciscan movement as identified with the "conversion to poverty."[32] In the monastic world, which was the dominant paradigm of an ecclesial religious life up to the time of Francis, a monk renounced private ownership but the community itself owned land and goods; it possessed juridical rights in the society. On a personal level the monk gave up his own will [voluntas propria] and adopted a common will [voluntas communis], putting on the "one mind and heart" of the community, the common good, the common life.[33] Francis, of course, renounced both his own will and the ownership of goods in private and in common. His ideal was enshrined in the Rule (Chapter VI) and incorporated into the law of the Church with Gregory IX's Quo elongati (1230). Bonaventure's Disputed Questions on Evangelical Perfection (1255) makes the explicit point that the Franciscan political economy is based on "the renunciation of all things, both in common and in private."[34] His great chapter nine of The Defense of the Mendicants (1269) explicitly defends the ideal of "most strict poverty" as

---

[31] Ordinatio IV, d 15, q2, cited in Allan B. Wolter, O.F.M., ed., John Duns Scotus' Political and Economic Philosophy (St. Bonaventure, NY: The Franciscan Institute, 2001), 29.

[32] For background see Giovanni Miccoli, Chiesa Gregoriana, Richerche Sulla Riforma de secolo XI (Firenze, 1966), 255-99; and "Chiesa, riforma, vangelo e povertà: un nodo nella storia religiosa del XII secolo," in Francesco d'Assisi, Realtà e memoria di un'esperienza Cristiana (Torino: Giulio Einaudi, 1991), 3-32.

[33] See Edith Scholl, O.C.S.O., "A Will and Two Ways: Voluntas Propria, Voluntas Communis," Cistercian Studies 30 (1995), 193-203.

[34] See Disputed Questions on Evangelical Perfection, WSB XIII, Introduction and Notes by Robert J. Karris, O.F.M., Translations and notes by Thomas Reist, O.F.M., Conv. and Robert J. Karris, O.F.M. (St. Bonaventure, NY: Franciscan Institute Publications, 2008), Q.II, a1 (54), and arguments in 2, 6, 18, 22, 24, 25, 27, 30. Hereafter cited as DQEP.

a way of life in the Church.[35] The testimony of Nicholas III in *Exiit qui seminat* (1279) reaffirmed the tradition.[36] Perhaps most significant of all was Olivi's commentary on the two passages in Acts (2:42-47, 4:32-35) which were used to defend the monastic way of life. In actuality, Olivi argued, the text taught:

> first, at that time there was a single and uniform community for the apostles and the other believers. Second that the community did not appropriate anything to its fellowship in common. Rather it was of such a nature that the entire community of men and women were in the state of innocence, and it was of such a nature as should exist among all people, if there were not the corruption and weakness of original and actual sin, and it was of such a nature as that where air and sun were common to all.[37]

In summary, the catch phrase *omnia esse communia* implies a host of values which God intended to guide human society from the beginning. First, the values are captured in the Franciscan catch phrase: voluntarily living "without anything of one's own." This does not mean that one lives as an indigent, without anything – involuntary poverty as a human condition is not a value – but that one takes a non-proprietary stance toward one's own things and directs the use of all things toward the love of God and neighbor, toward sharing with others and the building up of human

---

[35] *Defense of the Mendicants*, WSB, XV, Introduction and Notes by Robert J. Karris, O.F.M., Translation by José de Vinck and Robert J. Karris, O.F.M. (St. Bonaventure, NY: Franciscan Institute Publications, 2010), IX.3-4, 250-53.

[36] For texts see *Exiit qui seminat*, article 1, in Regis J. Armstrong, O.F.M. Cap., J.A. Wayne Hellmann, O.F.M. Conv., William J. Short, O.F.M., eds., *Francis of Assisi: Early Documents*, Volume 3, *The Prophet* (New York: New City Press, 2001), 737-64; Cf. *Ordinatio* IV, d15, q2, a4, ad 5 in Wolter, *John Duns Scotus, Political and Economic Philosophy*, (76).

[37] David Flood, ed., *Peter of John Olivi on the Acts of the Apostles* (St. Bonaventure, NY: The Franciscan Institute, 2001). I am grateful for the translation provided by Robert J. Karris, O.F.M. The text cited is from 11 of the commentary on AA 2:42-47.

community. Second, in living *sine proprio* people commit themselves toward the public performance of the rectitude of justice, the returning of all things to God, their proper "owner." "The earth and its fullness" (Psalm 34), since their ownership belongs to God, are continually bestowed as gifts. "Every good which we have is a gift and a task given by God."[38] A Franciscan political economy exists within this gift economy.[39] Thus, completely decentering ownership of any kind as the privileged foundation of human society, the Franciscan vision re-centers all relationships around responsibility to Another who continually gifts us and around responsibility for others with whom we are the recipients of a common gift, "the earth and its fullness."[40] We can only keep this reality of "gift" alive by continuously giving it away, circulating it amongst our fellow recipients. Thirdly, *omnia esse communia* necessitates the inclusion of the "elsewhere." It promotes the equal claim of all to some elemental goods of the earth so that human beings can lead a "common life as if they were equal, even co-equal in all things."[41] Lastly, *omnia esse communia* places an ethical demand on people that they create a "fraternal economy" or an economy that provides for each other, protects each other, creates meaning for each other.[42] Because the power which human beings have to create, to build, to establish relationships is also a gift, human activity in the world—material, biological, and spiritual—is to be used to return praise to God and to sustain self and neighbor as equal creatures of the same Creator. This is "work for everyone" as David Flood argues

[38] Bonaventure, *Commentary on the Sentences*, IV, d. XXXIV, Dub. VI (IV.764), originally cited in Cullen, "Property in the Writings of St. Bonaventure," 829.

[39] This is precisely the starting point for the reflections of Benedict XVI, *Caritas in veritate*, 34.

[40] With respect to the natural environment, see the parallel comments in Benedict XVI, *Caritas in veritate, Charity in Truth*, 48-51.

[41] Bonaventure, *Defense of the Mendicants*, IX:4, 252; Olivi, *Acts of the Apostles*, 2:42-47, 5.

[42] See David B. Couturier, *The Fraternal Economy*; Benedict XVI, *Caritas in veritate*, 34-42; The last phrases are taken from Marvin T. Brown, *Civilizing the Economy, A New Economics of Provision* (New York: Cambridge University Press, 2010), 3.

in his analysis of Francis's vision.[43] Embedded in this vision is a whole philosophy which values the best in the human created order in its technological advancements, intellectual growth, and socio-political aspirations and places these at the service of God and humankind.

This radical notion of "all things in common" is preeminently a theological and biblically humanistic vision founded on the reality of the Trinitarian life. At first glance, it appears to have something in common with the ideals of what could be termed modern "socialism," even "communism" (e.g., sharing, communitarianism). But confinement of the vision to this category of analysis does it a grave injustice. The vision also privileges the capacity of the individual human being to provide for self and others, thus highlighting some of the elements of the contemporary "capitalist economy" (individual initiative, responsibility, creativity, productivity). The human being as *imago Dei* is built to create, to make, to build, to imagine, to take initiatives, to decide, even to co-create a better world. Bonaventure's anthropology privileges the restoration of the human powers of intelligence, affection, and will. The vision therefore is neither socialist nor capitalist.

The key to the vision as we have seen in earlier chapters is the human being who takes a non-proprietary stance toward everything because everything is a gift which in justice must be given back to Another and to the neighbor. This fundamental reality of "gift" and the accompanying response of living "without anything of one's own" by "giving back" departs dramatically in its twin starting points from other traditions in the Church that adopt the more monastic and/ or Aristotelian views of property, dominion, and ownership. As numerous studies of "gift economies" indicate, this ethical stance privileges honor, disinterestedness, generosity, reciprocity, personal relationships, corporate solidarity, and hospitality.[44] While it will never be the common opinion that

---

[43] David Flood, O.F.M., *Work for Everyone, Francis of Assisi and the Ethic of Service* (Quezon City, Philippines: Inter-Franciscan Center, 1997).

[44] See, for example, Marcel Mauss, *The Gift, the Form and Reason for Exchange in Archaic Societies*, trans. W.D. Halls (New York: W.W. Norton,

will shape a national and globalized system of exchange based primarily on market principles, its focus on a natural economy of abundance provided by God and the duty to reciprocate by including the "elsewhere" can help initiate a "new trajectory of thinking."

## 2. Omnium una libertas. ("One freedom for all")

The Franciscan commentators on the *Sentences* also questioned whether slavery and the dominion of one person over another was "according to nature." Implied in this question was the issue of freedom. Alexander of Hales cited Isidore to the effect that according to nature *omnium una libertas*, there is one freedom for everyone. The major reference was again Augustine, Book 19 of the *City of God*: "God did not wish the rational being, made in his own image, to have dominion over any but irrational creatures, not man over man, but man over the beasts." And, "by nature, in the condition in which God created man, no man is the slave either of man or of sin."[45] Gregory provided another authority: "Nature has begotten all equal, but, the order of merits varying, secret appointment sets some above others." And Hales glosses: "Therefore, prelacy and subjection, existing by appointment, are not of natural law, and so servitude and dominion are not of natural law."[46]

For Hales, this classical tradition was simply too strong to ignore. Before the Fall, as God intended and created human nature, people were both free and equal. Slavery and the dominion which produced the subjection of one person

---

1990). Mary Douglass notes in her introduction how this thinking on the gift conflicted directly with a utilitarian viewpoint. See also Lewis Hyde, *The Gift, Imagination and the Erotic Life of Property* (New York: Vintage Books, 1983) which contrasts a "market economy" with a "gift economy."

[45] Hales, *ST* Part II, Inq. II, MIII, ch. 3, IV, 363-64. Cf. Augustine, *The City of God* XIX. 15, trans. Henry Bettenson (New York: Penguin Books, 1972), 874.

[46] Hales, *ST* Part II, Inq. II, MIII, ch. 3; Gregory the Great, *Morals on the Book of Job* XXI.15 (Oxford: John Henry Parker, 1845), 534. For background see J. N. Bezancon, "Égalité et pouvoir dans les Morales de Grégoire le Grand," *Recherches Augustiniennes* XXVII (1994), 97-129.

to another entered into the picture only as the result of sin. Only if one took "according to nature" or "by natural law" to apply to the human being's fallen state, could one argue that slavery and dominion-subjection were "natural."[47] Bonaventure agreed and added a typically vertical argument about God's sovereignty over all things: Man was originally made in God's image and inasmuch as he or she is in God's image, he or she is immediately made by God. Therefore, if only God is the greater one, then nothing according to nature is over men and women but God. There can be no dominion but God's according to this nature as God made it.[48] As Augustine had indicated, viewed from the vertical order of things, men and women were under God and above all other creatures; each was therefore equal in terms of what was above and what was below. Each was also equal as an image of God. Equality, freedom and relationality were concomitant marks of the image of God in human beings. From this Trinitarian perspective, freedom consisted not in autonomy but in ordered loving, the giving of oneself to another in a perfect act of charity. Social but not necessarily political by nature, men and women were meant to be turned toward the other. The ideal society was a fellowship of friends, free, equal, and loving:

> When a friend asks for a gift from his friend, he violates no law; neither the first friend by his asking nor the second by his giving, nor again the first by his accepting. But the law of charity and divine love involves a greater exchange than the law of society.[49]

---

[47] Hales, *ST* Part II, Inq. II, MIII, ch. 3.

[48] The arguments occur in Bonaventure, *Commentary on the Sentences*, II, d XLIV, aII, Q II, 1007-1008. For an exposition of Bonaventure's argument, his distinctions, and the importance of these as enabling a continuation of Augustine see R. A. Markus, "Two Conceptions of Political Authority: Augustine, *De Civitate Dei* XIX.14-15, and Some Thirteenth Century Interpretations," *Journal of Theological Studies* n.s. XVI (April 1965): 68-100.

[49] DQEP, QII,a2, d 36, 105.

In the reflections of the Franciscans, this created equality and freedom did not mean that everyone was the same – equality and sameness were not to be subsumed into each other. Bonaventure knew Augustine's axiom: "If all things were equal, all things would not exist."[50] One primary characteristic of the created order was its diversity and multiformity: "The love of charity rejoices in a multitude of good companions."[51] "Order" as Bonaventure understood it, following Augustine, "is the arrangement of things equal and unequal in a pattern which assigns to each its proper place."[52] Therefore, when one viewed the diversity of peoples in a horizontal way, even in the state which God instituted, some authority could exist. Remaining in the grade to which they were assigned as God intended, people could relate to each other in patterns of authority and obedience (e.g. husband/wife, father/son). This was a natural arrangement encouraged by differences. Clearly men and women could exercise authority over things and in some ways over each other. But in God's intention this exercise of authority did not imply exploitation or slavish subjection. Instead authority and obedience were reciprocally given in mutual exchange as willing, generous service to the other.

Preserving this reality of *omnium una libertas* as more natural to the human being than the subjection which arose after the "fall into the private" carries important implications for the Franciscan social project. It seeks to anticipate within the present social arrangements the "always more" of God's original intention. The equality, freedom, loving exchange, and authority instituted by God commissions the believer in God to exclude, as much as possible, from the

---

[50] DQEP, QI, resp. 15, 54; Q4, a1, d6, 211; cf. Augustine, *Miscellany of Eighty-Three Questions* XLI and LXXIV, in Raymond Canning, ed, *Responses to Miscellaneous Questions, The Works of St. Augustine I / 12* (Hyde Park, NY: New City Press, 2008): "Because if they were equal they would not all exist. For there would not be the many kinds of things out of which the universe is constructed, with creatures in the first place and in the second, and thence all the way to the last place. And that is what is meant by 'all'" (XLI).

[51] *Sentences*, II.d3, p1, a2, q1, 103.

[52] Augustine, *The City of God*, Bk. XIX.13, 870.

political, economic, and cultural spheres relational patterns which produce servile subjection, fear, slavery, exploitation, emotional manipulation, or coercive power. God-imaging relationships and their institutionalization, even those of authority/obedience, create a social order which is more compatible with the freedom and reciprocal dependence given to all. As Bonaventure notes, when asking the question whether there is order in the Church: "The one who is subject by love, walks in liberty of spirit; the one who is subject out of fear is in some measure a slave; and in the good and in the just there is subjection not out of fear but out of love, and such subjection does not prejudice freedom."[53] This is a tall order indeed in a world which can consider the subjection of one person to another, economically, culturally, politically, a "natural" state of things.[54]

Searching continuously for the elsewhere, living as if everything belongs to God and in the common possession of all, creating a society of friends who are equal and free and loving, willingly exchanging bonds of authority and obedience because of differences in the gifts that are given – in the Franciscan sources, these are the ideals of those who wish to regain a social paradise. Ultimately, this political economy which creatures were originally called to realize in justice is based on a collective imaging of God's relationality in a trinity of persons who share all things equally in a dance of communion or friendship. In a startling phrase for those enamored of other visions of the "common good," Scotus refers to the "common good" of all as God's very self:

> God, the common good of all, does not want to be the private or proper good of any person exclusively, nor

---

[53] *Sentences*, IV, d24, q21, d3 (615). For Scotus see Allan B. Wolter, O.F.M., *Duns Scotus on the Will and Morality* (Washington, DC: The Catholic University of America Press, 1986), 310-17, 458-63, 522-33. On Scotus's focus on freedom with respect to the problem of slavery see Antonie Vos, *The Philosophy of John Duns Scotus* (Edinburgh: Edinburgh University Press, 2006), 446-51.

[54] See the perceptive comments of Marvin T. Brown on Adam Smith's silence about an Atlantic economy which exploited human slavery in *Civilizing the Economy*, Part II.

would right reason have someone appropriate this common good.... For this is what perfect and orderly love of God means. And in so loving I love both myself and my neighbor by charity, by willing that both of us love God in himself.[55]

God is not the rival of human flourishing but the Creator who wishes the creatures to be fully realized as human beings in relationship.

### 3. The Turn toward the Private

This Franciscan vision has often been associated with an ideal utopianism in such a way that the realism embedded in its analysis of society, the political and economic relationships between people, has been lost. Yet, running throughout all the early sources is an acute awareness that the world is not the way God intended it to be. Something has happened to human beings which has severely affected their ability to mirror God's Trinitarian sharing. In the lexicon of medieval speech that "something" is communicated in the code term "Fall." Francis summarized the problem in one line: "Through our own fault we fell."[56] Living as he did at the time of the birth of a commercial economy, Francis glossed earlier interpretations of this root cause of human social unhappiness in the following way:

The Lord said to Adam: *Eat of every tree; you may not eat, however, of the tree of the knowledge of good and evil.*

He was able to eat of every tree of paradise, because he did not sin as long as he did not go against obedi-

---

[55] Scotus, *Ordinatio* III, d.28 (Vives, 15.378), as cited in Herbert Schneider, O.F.M., ed., *John Duns Scotus and the Question: Can I Love God Above All? A Treatise of John Duns Scotus in Four Languages* (Monchengladbach, 1999), 51-53, based on the Latin of *Deus, quia est bonum commune* ... Cf. Mary Beth Ingham, *The Harmony of Goodness, Mutuality and Moral Living According to John Duns Scotus,* revised second edition (St. Bonaventure, NY: Franciscan Institute Publications, 2012), 203.

[56] *Earlier Rule*, 22:2, *FA:ED* 1, 82.

ence. For that person eats of the tree of the knowledge of good who makes his will his own and, in this way, exalts himself over the good things the Lord says and does in him.[57]

The central problem, as Francis saw it, was not the goodness or seductive beauty of the world and human beings; nor was it the creative good which people accomplished through their hard work and ingenuity. Rather, the problem was that people moved outside of the intention and command of God through an interior action of the will which became manifest in their behaviors and patterns of relationships. The key phrase was "to make his will his own and exalt himself over the good things that the Lord says and does." This phrase described the human choice to claim ownership and dominion over that which came as a gift. Three key vices are here joined: disobedience, avarice, and pride, all of which touch the fundamental rules of relationality as described in God's Great Commandment. On a human level these vices cut against *omnia esse communia* and *omnium una libertas*. The tenses Francis used in his admonition are not past, but present; a biblical motif interprets contemporary social ills.[58]

In Francis's experience, the desire to appropriate for private use that which was common, or given to all by God, issued in social violence, division, exploitation, unnecessary and contentious stratification. Symbolized by "money" or "reward," this claiming as one's own what belonged to another caused blindness and twisted the human being's relationships to other people, to creation, work, and the goods of the earth.[59] All of this proceeded from the human heart or will: "From the heart of man come forth and flow evil thoughts, adulteries, fornications, murders, thefts, avarice,

---

[57] *Admonition* II, in *FA:ED* 1, 129.

[58] For "appropriation" and its relationship with a commercial economy of money and reward in the "world" see *Admonitions* 11, 18, 21, 28; *Earlier Rule* 9.9, 16.16, 17.13, 22.20, 22.25, all in *FA:ED* 1.

[59] For social background see Lester K. Little, "Pride Goes Before Avarice. Social Change and the Vices in Latin Christendom," *American Historical Review* 76 (February 1971): 16-49.

wantonness, deceit, lewdness, evil looks, false testimonies, blasphemy, foolishness." These inner vices took concrete form in the social disruption of the human world the way God intended it to be.[60]

With its focus on the will, on the interior drives of human affection, and on the conjunction of disobedience/pride/avarice, this existential diagnosis found a ready traditional grounding in the social thought of St. Augustine and it was so interpreted by the theological masters who followed Francis.[61] Perhaps clearest of all in his social commentary was St. Bonaventure in his *Disputed Questions on Evangelical Perfection*. Written in the mid-1250s this treatise set out to defend the Franciscan vision in the Church and society of the time. Underneath the polemic lay some simple questions: Are the current arrangements of ownership, property, power, exchange mechanisms, rents, taxes, fees, credits fully obedient to the will of God? Are the present patterns of relationality, authority/obedience in the Church completely adequate reflections of the Gospel? Bonaventure did not condemn the contemporary arrangements but argued for the insertion into them of a "most perfect way," the way of evangelical poverty, or, from the perspective of our analysis, a way that included the elsewhere and embodied God's original intention for the flourishing of human beings. The critical biblical text was 1 Tim 6:10: *radix omnium malorum est cupiditas*, "the root of all evils is cupidity."[62]

When speaking of the "order of love" which should guide human behavior, the scholastic master noted that "the

---

[60] *Earlier Rule* 22 is a commentary on Francis's anthropology with citations from Mark 7:21-22, Matt 15:19. Cf. Jan Hoeberichts, *Paradise Restored, The Social Ethics of Francis of Assisi, A Commentary on Francis' "Salutation of the Virtues"* (Quincy, IL: Franciscan Press, 2004).

[61] For Augustine see *The City of God*, XIV:11 (568-74), with its focus on the will, arrogance, and self-pleasing. For complete exposition see Robert Dodaro, *Christ and the Just Society in the Thought of Augustine* (Cambridge: Cambridge University Press, 2004), 58-70, especially where he notes the political implications of the fall.

[62] See for examples *DQEP* Q1, Conclusion, 71, 75-76.

creature that acts most contrary to this order is the individual person with his private good."[63]

> Again, there are two elements to sin, namely, inordinate desire and contempt of God.[64]
>
> God disposes and orders all things in his own times.... So in the last times he has introduced men who beg voluntarily and are poor in worldly things ... and this indeed was entirely appropriate, so that ... avarice [might be destroyed] ... avarice that reigns above all at the end of the world.[65]

Bonaventure cited Augustine:

> The poison of love is the hope of getting or holding onto temporal goods. The nourishment of love is the lessening of cupidity. The perfection of love is no cupidity. The sign of its progress is the lessening of fear. The sign of its perfection is no fear, for 'the root of all evils is cupidity,' and 'perfect love casts out fear.'[66]

Bonaventure clearly recognized the social vision at stake in the contemporary world:

> There are two cities, namely, God's and the devil's, Jerusalem and Babylon. They are opposed to one another both in themselves and in their foundations. Now, as Augustine states, the foundation of the city of Babylon is cupidity. Therefore the more a person moves away from cupidity, the more that person moves away from the devil's city.[67]

---

[63] *DQEP*, QI, argument for the negative 2, reply, 49.

[64] *DQEP*, Q1, argument for the affirmative 18, 35.

[65] *DQEP*, QII, a2, reply to negative 20, 133.

[66] *DQEP*, QII, a1, Conclusion, 71, citing *Eighty-three Different Questions* (#36) and 1 John 4:18. See Augustine, *Responses to Miscellaneous Questions*, 51-54 for the analysis of greed.

[67] *DQEP* QII, A1, affirmative 26, 64-65; see also Q 2, a1, conclusion, 70-71.

Scotus, reliant on Augustine but moving beyond Bonaventure in his modification of Anselm's understanding of the affections, later acknowledged his roots in a similar analysis when he considered the initial sin of Lucifer: "The first source from which the city of the devil stems, then, is inordinate friendship-love, whose root germinates until it yields contempt of God, in which malice reaches its peak. It is clear, then, that the initial disorder in an unqualified sense consists in that inordinate love that was simply first."[68] This initial inordinate desire did not spring from the affection for justice, which has been referred to in a previous chapter, but from an inordinate affection for the advantageous: "And a will that fails to follow the rule of justice will seek most of all what is most advantageous, and thus it will seek such first, for nothing else rules that unrighteous will but an inordinate, immoderate appetite for that greatest beneficial good, namely, perfect happiness."[69] For the subtle doctor, if the affection for justice did not moderate the affection for the advantageous, inordinate self-love would create a relational order destructive of the "order of love." If people were ruled by this initial disorder in the will between its two affections, the truth of human social and economic relationality would be infected with a virus; their heart, love, and affections would will to live primarily *ad tempus* (for immediate and earthly gain) and not primarily *ad Deum* (in accordance with God's will). Such was the world, not instituted by God, which people could create for themselves. It was a world oriented by a "turn towards the private good." It does not take a great leap to understand how this analysis of the early development of a market society even today carries relevance in a contemporary world shaped by the political and economic structures of globalization.

*Cupiditas*, inordinate self-love, exclusive "self-pleasing," the grasping for oneself that which belongs to another, the claiming for one's own dominion and power that which was

---

[68] Ord. II, dist. 6, q.2, as translated in Wolter, *Duns Scotus on the Will and Morality*, 296. It should be noted that Scotus also cites Augustine, *Eighty Three Questions*, # 30.

[69] Ord. II, dist. 6, q.2.

given as a gift, self-exaltation, pride, avarice, autonomous self-sufficiency, the turn toward the private — all of these vices produce a social situation excluding the elsewhere and destructive of *omnia esse communia* and *omnium una libertas*. The "Fall" carries political consequences which permeate the social structures which humans create. Such is the argument of the Franciscan masters. The analysis has special relevance in what one recent commentator describes is a contemporary "age of greed."[70] It should be noted that this approach focuses the discussion not on inherently evil structures nor on cultural determinisms beyond human control (an "abstract market," an "invisible hand," a "culture of poverty," a "culture of death," an "oppressive structure," a "dysfunctional system") but on the human beings who create the structures. This anthropological turn places human choice, intentionality, interior purification, freedom and self-mastery, as this book has argued, at the center of the moral analysis.

## III. THE DYNAMISM OF HUMAN MORAL LIFE IN POLITICS AND ECONOMICS

In their very realistic view of the human world the Franciscan masters note that the exercise of true human freedom in the present state of things is marked with the tension between the "turn towards the private" and the desire for something more – a human paradise which requires the exercise of self-control, self-restraint, the willingness to moderate the affection for possession by the affection for justice, obedience to the Great Commandment. The "retreat into the private" which all people share does not destroy the image of God in human beings. Francis describes the tension between the world of the gift and the world of self-aggrandizement in these terms: "let us all love the Lord God Who has given and gives to each one of us our whole body, our whole soul and

---

[70] Jeff Madrick, *Age of Greed, The Triumph of Finance and the Decline of America, 1970 to the Present* (New York: Alfred A. Knopf, 2011).

our whole life. Who has created, redeemed and will save us by His mercy alone, Who did and does everything good for us, miserable and wretched, rotten and foul, ungrateful and evil ones."[71] In the current order of things, as Bonaventure notes, the human being has in his or her self "something of deiformity by reason of its being made by God, something of defect by reason of its origin [from nothing], and something of deformity by reason of the vice to which it is subject."[72] And Scotus argues that the human being experiences not the destruction but the loss of harmony between the affection for what is advantageous and the affection for what is just.[73] These tensions, however they are described, are at the heart of a Franciscan social asceticism that struggles against any social theory which equates human flourishing with political influence, status, power, possessions, or an economic quest for self-interested gain.

Flowing from this view of the person, the realities of human life, its social energies and loves, its expressions in work and political and economic structures, bear the mark of a fundamentally good but partially disordered human condition. On an anthropological level the turn toward the private cuts through all of reality, making the historical engagement with the contingencies of history saturated with both moral possibility and moral incompleteness. Human life as it was created and is now experienced is thus to be both affirmed and purified, its positive reflection of God's Trinitarian life acknowledged, its deformed expressions and inordinate loves critiqued and reformed. The realization of *omnia esse communis* and *omnium una libertas* is always an eschatological project for the *viatores* (pilgrims) in their movement through time. The complete plentitude of how God intended things to be will occur only at the end of time and the advent of the Kingdom of God. In the meantime, people

---

[71] *Earlier Rule* 22:8, *FA:ED* 1, 84.

[72] *DQEP*, QI, reply to negative 5, 51; cf. Prologue to the *Second Book of Sentences,* 13, in *Writings on the Spiritual Life*, 354: "Humankind fell from rectitude such that rectitude was lost, but not the tendency to rectitude; lost the habit but not the appetite for rectitude."

[73] Ingham, *The Harmony of Goodness*, 64-68.

engage the world so as to move it toward greater perfection and greater consonance with God's will. The question before humans is always: How do I want to use my freedom?

Such an historically engaging approach of affirmation and purification suffuses Bonaventure's argument in the *Reduction of the Arts to Theology*. He divides moral philosophy into three subsections, "namely, ethical, economic, and political, the content of each being clearly indicated by its name."[74] "Great prudence is required to govern one's personal life [the ethical sphere of virtue]," he argues in the *Collations on the Seven Gifts of the Holy Spirit*.

> Even greater prudence is required to govern the life of the family [the economic sphere of the regulation of the household]. And the greatest prudence is required to govern the life of the city [the political sphere concerned with the welfare of the society].[75]

Natural law, freedom of the will, *synderesis*, conscience, the light to distinguish absolute from relative goods, the role of the moral virtues (prudence, justice, fortitude, temperance), all of these elements comprise the science of the moral life.[76] A similar approach of affirmation/purification, growth and discernment, structures the *Itinerarium Mentis in Deum* and Bonaventure's ascetical writings. An analogous dynamic is played out in a highly scholastic form in Scotus's discussion of the relationship between the two affections. The component parts of this moral "thought style" have been articulated in other chapters of this book. Selected examples from the

---

[74] Cf. *De Reductione Artium ad Theologiam*, *WSB* I, ed. Philotheus Boehner, O.F.M., and Sr. M. Frances Laughlin, S.M.I.C, a commentary with introduction by Sister Emma Thérèse Healy (St. Bonaventure, NY: The Franciscan Institute, 1955), 4, 27.

[75] *Collations on the Seven Gifts of the Holy Spirit*, IV:10, Introduction and Translation by Zachary Hayes, O.F.M., Notes by Robert J. Karris, O.F.M, *WSB* XIV (St. Bonaventure, NY: Franciscan Institute Publications, 2008), 90.

[76] St. Bonaventure, *The Reduction of the Arts to Theology*, with notes on moral philosophy, 88-99.

Franciscan sources will now indicate its application to the world of politics and economics.

## A. Political Authority and the Search for Justice and Peace

It has already been noted that for Bonaventure authority as the power to coerce others did not exist in the world that God first intended, but only in a world which had experienced a "turn towards the private." This coercive power carried a certain restriction on freedom; it was properly called *dominium* with its corresponding term *servitus*. With respect to political authority, the Franciscan master followed Augustine's *City of God* (XIX.14-15). Both argued that while in their created nature human beings were harmoniously social and shared all things in common, after the "Fall" into the private, private property arose and with it contention and strife. In this "fallen state" people needed not only the authority which was service but also a coercive authoritative power so that vice might be curtailed and human beings might live in relative peace.[77] The political world in its coerciveness was a consequence of the Fall. The function of law and the state was "to restrain violence and secure peace; its use should be impersonal and never vengeful, and limited to the minimum necessary."[78] For both Augustine and Bonaventure, while the state and the Church both possessed coercive power out of necessity, the order of charity was to be the primary referent and the ever pressing ideal for social engagement.[79]

---

[77] *Commentary on the Sentences* II, d XLIV, a 2, reply 4; *DQEP*, Q 4 a 1. For background on Augustine see Markus, "Two Conceptions of Political Authority"; "The Latin Fathers," in J. H. Burns, *The Cambridge History of Medieval Political Thought c. 350-c.1450* (New York: Cambridge University Press, 1988), 92-122.

[78] See E. M. Atkins and R. J. Dodaro, *Augustine, Political Writings* (Cambridge, Cambridge University Press, 2001, 2006), xviii.

[79] This issue of dominion and the origin of political authority clearly touches the question of the relationship between Church, state, and society, and the respective domains of each. While the state exists primarily

Perhaps the Franciscan master who best summarized this vision of the exercise of authority in a fallen world and its significance for an ethics of political engagement was Scotus.[80] He codified the inherited position even more strictly than Bonaventure:

> According to right reason men should have the use of things in such a way as, first, to contribute to a peaceful and decent life, and [second] to provide needed sustenance. But in the state of innocence, common use with no distinct ownership would have been more conducive to this than individual ownership, for no one would have taken what another needed, nor would the latter have had to wrest it by force from the other; rather each would have taken what first came to hand as needed for that person's use. In this way also a greater sufficiency for sustenance would have obtained than if one person's use of a thing were precluded because another had monopolized it.[81]

---

to limit the excesses of freedom as self-reference, the society, or in modern terms the public sphere, exists so that the positive resources of freedom may be exercised for others. It should be noted that Scotus wrote his reflections on political authority in the same period as the papalist Giles of Rome and his Dominican opponent John of Paris. The Augustinian option, which the Franciscans generally followed, could be made to argue against a total *societas Cristiana* and for a more pluralistic social arrangement where the maximum amount of peace is continually and prudentially negotiated. As with Francis of Assisi himself, there is a certain openness in this thinking to God's hidden presence in the domain of the "secular," the domain of the lay world, as differentiated from the domain of the "sacred," the domain of the Church. The distinction is not sacred/secular but sacred/ secular and profane. For Augustinian roots and contemporary reflections see Robert A. Markus, *Christianity and the Secular* (Notre Dame, IN: University of Notre Dame Press, 2006); Eric Gregory, *Politics and the Order of Love, An Augustinian Ethic of Democratic Citizenship* (Chicago, IL: University of Chicago Press, 2008).

[80] For context see Roberto Lambertini, *La Povertà pensatà: Evoluzione storica della definizione dell'identità minoretica da Bonaventura ad Occam* (Modena: Mucchi Editore, 2000), Chapter IV.

[81] John Duns Scotus, *Political and Economic Philosophy*, 29-35.

But with the "turn to the private" this law of nature was revoked for two reasons: "communality of all property would have militated against the peaceful life. For the evil and covetous person would have taken more than needed and, to do so, would also use violence against others who wished to use these common goods for their own needs." Scotus continues, "The original law would also have failed to ensure the necessary sustenance of mankind, for those stronger and more belligerent would have deprived the others of necessities." And so the right to private property arose not by a law of nature but by positive law, for while the original law was suppressed, it was not reversed. In other words, finding themselves confronted with "the turn to the private" people had to legislate "the first division of property," who possessed what and how much, so as to keep peace in a world which "militated against the peaceful life" by its tendencies towards violence and selfishness.[82]

Scotus then asks: In such a situation what would make the law which people choose to pass "just"? Two things were necessary: authority established "by common consent and election on the part of the community" and, on the part of the vested political authority (vested in one person or in the body politic), prudence. In his whole treatment of the political question, the origin of property was here related to the issue of power and power to the question of its origin in the polis. Scotus places human social life in the domain of political freedom. What type of society do people choose to create?

Three things should be noted in this argument of Scotus which was perhaps founded on the experience of English constitutional law.[83] First, the Franciscan master maintains through his distinction between "revocation" and "reversal" the vision of the original intention: *omnia esse communis*,

---

[82] John Duns Scotus, *Political and Economic Philosophy*.

[83] Philippe Yates, O.F.M., "The English Context of the Development of the Franciscan Constitutions and of the Franciscan Intellectual Tradition," in André Cirino O.F.M., Josef Raischl, S.F.O., eds., *A Pilgrimage through the Franciscan Intellectual Tradition* (Canterbury, England: Franciscan International Study Centre, 2008), 65-82. Scotus here moved beyond Bonaventure's more paternal view of authority.

*omnium una libertas.* The private possession of property and the coercive exercise of authority exist by way of concession and purposely serve the maintenance of social peace. Even if the original situation is not practicable in the present order of things, it remains the standard which should guide the actions of people as they approach issues of property and dominion. Each human being who belongs to God by his or her very existence makes an ethical demand for dignity, sustenance, and freedom. Scotus, although he does not condemn private property in his argument, shows himself very reluctant to make the right of private property a subsection of "natural right." His Franciscan move is more in line with Augustine and Bonaventure, and wary of Aristotle and Aquinas.[84] Since ownership is not a natural right, the question for the polis changes from adjudicating "what is mine" and "what is yours" to "how do I keep peace and also use for myself and others what has been given to me?" The pilgrim/*viator* is one who lives in the tension between these questions. This opens up social reality to the much more radical and eschatological demand of a God-intended political economy.

Second, the laws governing the ownership of property and its equitable distribution are not fixed either by tradition or by an abstract and impersonal force, such as the market or the invisible hand. Instead, they are placed under the freedom of public authority (whether vested in one person or in the body politic) who is charged to make positive law, and this in turn

---

[84] See for example, R.W. Dyson, ed., *Aquinas, Political Writings* (Cambridge: Cambridge University Press, 2002, 2008), sections 1 and 5. Comparing the approaches of Bonaventure, Aquinas, and Scotus on the issues of authority, slavery, and property would take this chapter too far afield, and the difference may be more one of "tendencies" than dichotomies. But historical tendencies have their own laws and expressions, shaping public life differently in slightly different directions. See for examples, the argument over Aquinas's interpretation of slavery in Joseph E. Capizzi, "The Children of God: Natural Slavery in the Thought of Aquinas and Vitoria," *Theological Studies* 63 (March 2002): 31-52; and the discussion of dominion in Christopher A. Franks, *He Became Poor, the Poverty of Christ and Aquinas' Economic Teachings* (Grand Rapids, MI: William B. Eerdmans, 2009), 56-66. A good overview of the complexity is found in Janet Coleman, "Property and Poverty," in J.H. Burns, *The Cambridge History of Medieval Political Thought*, 607-48.

is subject to the rule of justice and the need for peace. Yet, the demands of positive law and the question of justice in a contingent world consistently change depending on social mutation and the new appearance of an "elsewhere." Positive law is a response to concrete circumstances. Prevailing political and economic arrangements are always under the control of human freedom and always subordinate to an ethical end.

Third, public authority in this historical field needs to be governed by prudence, "a dynamic activity of rationality within the concrete dimension of human life."[85] Here, the moral reasoning so well explained in a previous chapter comes into play:

> Prudential judgment, the excellence of moral reasoning, belongs to one who knows what to do, not merely because he knows the theoretical rules and deduces from them, but on the basis of years of training and experience (rehearsals) informed by rational reflection. Moral rehearsals, like musical rehearsals, involve ongoing and continual practice.

Political engagement and the division of goods in the Franciscan tradition involves continual moral judgments of a prudential nature, assessing each historical situation in its uniqueness, interrogating it as to its relationship with the Great Commandment, searching for the horizon of the "elsewhere," and making judgments in such a way that the maximum amount of justice and peace which the situation will bear is attempted. In other terms, the proper exercise of authority is directed toward the flourishing of persons and demands a continual rereading, hermeneutic, or "contuition" of the book of creation, the book of experience, and the book of God's revelation. Freedom and moral choice are placed at the very center of political life. The justice of the situation will depend on the intensiveness and extensiveness of the prudence which is exercised.

---

[85] Ingham, *Harmony of Goodness*, 165.

## B. Making Gospel Decisions in the Economic Life

The development of an ethic for commercial life also runs through the sources of the Franciscan masters. Alexander of Hales was one of the first to address this in his *Summa* when he asked the question "whether business (banking) transactions could be licit?"[86] He cited John Chrysostom to the effect that merchants could not please God and marshaled several biblical texts and interpretations which had been used in the tradition to argue for illicitness. Money changers did not belong in the temple. In the context of an expanding market economy, in an attempt to engage the changing historical landscape, the Franciscan master sought to limit this inherited "thought style." Augustine, he noted, had made a distinction, arguing that at times exchanges, buying something low and selling it higher, could be licit. Negotiation itself did not make someone evil, but rather his or her unfairness and lying. It was a question of relationality. Aristotle had also argued for the importance of commercial life in addressing the mutual needs of people. Merchants, Alexander concluded, could be like honest craftsmen provided they were not motivated by greed, did not conduct their affairs falsely, or conspire to take over a whole marketplace so as to sell goods at higher prices. People needed to conduct their business so that they might provide for needs, contribute to public utility, or out of piety be merciful to the poor. The working principle was simple: Commercial transactions were under the freedom of the person; they became disordered when conducted by someone whose final intention was profit, and who without labor or care avariciously sought to acquire through negotiation superfluities without end or measure.[87] Clearly, commerce was fraught with dangers, but as a human creative activity its morality depended on motivations,

---

[86] Alexander of Hales, *ST*, IV, Pars II, Inq. III, Sec. II, Q. II, Titulus III, c1, *Utrum negotiari sit licitum*, 721-24.

[87] Alexander of Hales, *ST*, 724.

ultimate purpose, times, places, circumstances, and the employment of means (e.g., lying or truthful presentation).

Bonaventure, following Hales, argued similarly: Commercial activity was a civil work by which society satisfied its needs; a merchant could remain in his trade as long as he abandoned deception.[88] When commenting on the seventh commandment, the teacher noted that if something was not done out of avarice, then it was not stealing. At stake in any exchange were the qualities which governed social relationships. "There are different kinds of stealing," he commented, "since stealing is the taking of things belonging to another against the owner's will." This could be done by "pure deceit, by violence, or by fraud."

> If the taking of things belonging to another is done by fraud, this can involve an agreement in one of three ways. It can be done with an agreement that is fraudulent, sinful or sacrilegious. The first way happens in business and can be done in one of three ways: in weight, or in number, or in measure. Merchants rarely escape committing this sin. If it is done by a sinful agreement it is called usury, in which that which is sold is public, namely time. If it is done by a sacrilegious agreement, in which things belonging to God are sold, it is called simony.[89]

Although Peter John Olivi and John Duns Scotus developed their insights in a more sophisticated and precise fashion and applied them to the commercial problems of their own times, the same "thought style" or stance as their predecessors marked their economic thought. They developed an economic vision which both emerged from a God-centered commitment to living "without anything of one's own" and also engaged the eschatological project of making God's

---

[88] St. Bonaventure, *Commentary on Sentences*, IV, d 16, a1, dub. XV, 402.

[89] *Collations on the Ten Commandments*, VI.18, *WSB* VI, Introduction and translation by Paul J. Spaeth (St. Bonaventure, NY: The Franciscan Institute, 1995), 91.

desire for human happiness more evident. Pilgrims needed to take up the cross of their own history so as to move it toward God's intentionality. Olivi may be taken as a prime example. His treatises on contracts and theory of the just price asked significantly new questions. He emphasized an economic ethic adapted to an imperfect world but one which still critiqued patterns of exchange based on self-interest, compulsion, and unnecessary accumulation. He affirmed patterns involving the mutual free consent of peoples and an analytic approach which rigorously distinguished between what was necessary for life and what was superfluous, a distinction to be adapted to each person or group's position in society. Philosophically, he developed the tradition's reflections on the nature of the will by making it a reflexive power which operated on the self. Freedom here became self-mastery and self-restraint, the ability economically to be free of compulsion, personal or societal, and to choose to turn the world of things toward public usefulness. This proper exercise of freedom made human society possible.[90] It also placed the exercise of freedom and discretion or prudence at the center of a multitude of social situations.

In all of this argumentation there is the same pattern of affirmation and purification which has already been noted. Economic activity, inasmuch as it is conducted by human beings, contains elements of goodness; there is no social classification, such as that of being a merchant, which lies outside the possibility of God's action. To engage in the affairs of the world is to have the possibility of living *ad Deum*. The Franciscan political and economic vision emerges from this ethical commitment to address emerging patterns of social change and zones of economic progress in human relations. This is a significant hermeneutical starting point

---

[90] For Olivi see Sylvain Piron, "Perfection Évangelique et Moralité Civile"; Mary Beth Ingham, "Self-mastery and Rational Freedom: Duns Scotus' Contribution to the Usus Pauper Debate," *Franciscan Studies* 66 (2008): 337-68; Todeschini, *Franciscan Wealth*, 92-103. For some ecclesiological implications see Frank Lane, "Freedom and Authority: The Law, Peter Olivi, and the Second Vatican Council," *Franciscan Studies* 62 (2004): 155-76.

in the public sphere, as it is in other areas. Yet, in this world the way it is, these patterns of exchange are mixed with human desires which are not completely ordered to charity. Something, great or small, needs to be purified; the possibility of breaking communion through commercial manipulation always remains. In this fashion, the ethic which must be applied is one which emphasizes as its primary criterion four elements:

1. the intentionality and freedom of the subject in his or her social relationality;
2. the ultimate purpose of the action;
3. the choice to use one's creative powers for sustenance, usefulness, or piety (economic terms for love of self, love of neighbor and the consideration of the else-where); and
4. the constant use of the power to discriminate and to judge social practice in all of its variations in the light of a higher standard of charity.

Is it too much to see that behind this approach lies, on the one hand, the initial insight contained in the code term "poverty": "The earth is the Lord's and the fullness thereof," *omnia esse communia, omnium una libertas*; and, on the other hand, the willingness, in a world which has "turned to the private" in its patterns of dominion and ownership, to affirm the good and try to direct it toward the better through the use of freedom? What the Franciscan masters attempted is twofold: to inject into the political choices which join our national and global societies a vision of human solidarity; and to inject into the economic patterns of social relationships the surplus value of a gratuitous God.[91]

---

[91] Cf. for parallel but much more philosophical comments Orlando To-disco, "L'être comme don et la valeur-lien: La practique économique fran-ciscaine du solidarisme," in Luca Parisoli, ed., *Pauvreté et Capitalisme, Comment les pauvres franciscaines ont justifié le capitalisme et le capital-isme a préféré la Modernité* (Palermo: Officina di Studi Medievali, 2008), 213.

## IV. CONCLUSION: THE MEDICINE OF PUBLIC VIRTUE

The Franciscan stance of how the "surplus value of a gratuitous God" enters the public sphere requires a certain approach to virtuous living and decision making. We have already discussed the question of prudence and discriminating judgment suited to circumstances throughout this book. We have also seen that "generosity in action" is another name for "poverty." The human pilgrim is challenged in the present circumstances of the world to justly return to God what belongs to God alone: "The earth is the Lord's and the fullness thereof." In many respects the tradition provides an alternate vision which resonates with some of the best contemporary thinking on the interface between politics, economics, and human sustainability. As we conclude this short introduction to a complex and living tradition, the following points seem most pertinent.

(1) By placing the reality of "gift" at the center of its social project, the Franciscan moral stance privileges relationality, freedom, and communion between brothers and sisters. While valuing the individual, the exercise of the will, and self-love, this vision directly critiques political and economic arrangements founded on human autonomy, choice without limit, and actions based on private self-interest. The Franciscan view that the human being is made from and for communion with others is in tense conflict with political systems of dominance/subjection. It engages but also directly critiques free market thinking as the dominant paradigm for human flourishing.[92] The Franciscan tradition when placed over against but living within modern preconceptions of "utility" and "power"

---

[92] See for a contemporary analysis of the development and dominance of free market thinking Jeff Madrick, *Age of Greed, The Triumph of Finance and the Decline of America, 1970 to the Present*; Daniel T. Rodgers, *Age of Fracture* (Cambridge, MA: Harvard University Press, 2011).

has an affirmative prophetic edge.[93] The vision in its contemporary application entails what the Economics Commissioner for the Sustainable Development Commission in England has called "changing the social logic."[94]

(2) This tradition in its concrete acceptance of historical change has a certain "cutting edge" which forces continual reassessment of the world of the "elsewhere" and the prudential choice as to how best to realize God's original intentions for human flourishing in any given situation and with any given person or groups of persons. As a result, the dynamism of the tradition stresses free social engagement with a contemporary reality such as globalization. It refuses a retreat into idealism, determinism, or nostalgia. Benedict XVI in *Caritas in veritate* captures the heart of the challenge in these words: "The truth of globalization as a process and its fundamental ethical criterion are given by the unity of the human family and its development towards what is good. Hence a sustained commitment is needed so as to promote a person-based and community-oriented cultural process of worldwide integration that is open to transcendence."[95]

---

[93] For an analogous approach from a different tradition see John Hughes, *The End of Work, Theological Critiques of Capitalism* (Oxford: Blackwell Publishing, 2007).

[94] See Tim Jackson, *Prosperity without Growth, Economics for a Finite Planet* (London: Earthscan, 2009), a sophisticated analysis that one reviewer referred to as containing "an almost Franciscan vision of an alternative economic system that would respect ecological limits, halt consumerism and roll back inequality." See Paul Bodenham, "Virtue out of necessity," *The Tablet* (October 8, 2011): 8-9.

[95] *Caritas in veritate, Charity in Truth*, 42. It is too early to assess the overall interpretation of the recent encyclical *Caritas in veritate*. Perhaps, as some have argued, in contrast to what is presented here, it lacks a structural critique. Still, the encyclical opens the path toward the viewpoints expressed in Franciscan poverty. See for critical comments Bernard Laurent, "*Caritas in veritate* as A Social Encyclical: A Modest Challenge to Economic, Social, and Political Institutions," *Theological Studies* 71 (2010): 515-44.

(3) The tradition is both realistic and eschatological in that it takes seriously the "turn towards the private" and works to ameliorate it. In the present situation, the coercive use of political power ("regulation") is often necessary to curtail greed and prevent strife – the Augustinian political notion of the limited and limiting state. The tradition recognizes the necessity of coercive power. But it always holds out a greater hope for a public presence shaped by the free commitment to participate in the world of gift. Properly exemplified in people and institutions this cure for the "turn towards the private" appeals to the deepest drive of the heart, the affections, and the mind for free allegiance to a just society of persons-in-communion. Such a stance brings to the forefront an ethical methodology of rhetorical persuasion, intellectual clarification, institutional witness, personal influence, example, and solidarity.

(4) In this vision of penitential humanism the surplus value of the Gospel leads not to the rejection of institutions but the proclamation that the path to human flourishing lies through the creation of viable communal alternatives. On the one hand this requires both the use of contemporary technological tools and also political engagement for the inclusion of the elsewhere. On the other hand it requires at various levels the institutional embodiment of an "economy of communion."[96] The tradition engages well with contemporary theologies, networks, and practices of peacemaking, be they Church-based or secular.[97] This socialization and institutionalization of gratuity and solidarity implies personal conversion through

---

[96] See the various examples given in Lugino Bruni, ed., *The Economy of Communon*, passim.

[97] Cf. Robert J. Schreiter, R. Scott Appleby, Gerard F. Powers, eds., *Peacebuilding, Catholic Theology, Ethics, and Praxis* (Maryknoll, NY: Orbis Books, 2010).

the reception of grace and ascetical practices of self-restraint, self-giving, organization with others, and identification with the poor. The vision is not "otherworldly."

(5) It should be noted that because the human being is a *viator*, a just penitent experiencing the consequences of the "fall into the private," living in the world of the gift in whatever degree it is practiced is a lifelong project. There is no expectation that this Franciscan vision will become dominant in society. Yet its entrance into the national and international public sphere provides an important corrective and perspective to the contemporary discussions. Historically, the stance embodies a "prick of conscience" which disrupts the ordinary pathways of exchange. Perseverance and patience in a methodology of presence and a growth in virtue become key elements in an historical journey always incomplete and contingent.

(6) Lastly, the experience itself of engagement in political and economic life argues for a deep connection between moral practice, participation in the Church, spirituality, and, most importantly, the Incarnation-redemption-glorification accomplished in Christ and brought to full beatitude only at the end of time.[98] Without the underpinnings of faith and hope in Christ, the vision cannot sustain itself. It is not accidental that one of the great Dominican historians of moral theology, Servais Pinckaers, notes the significant contribution of Bonaventure to the theology of hope, that theological virtue that touches the affections and gives strength to the will. For the master of Franciscan theology, hope is marked primarily by

---

[98] The role of the following of Christ in the acquisition of the virtues as remedies for vice is well illustrated in Richard S. Martignetti, *Saint Bonaventure's Tree of Life, Theology of the Mystical Journey* (Roma: Frati Editori di Quaracchi, 2004). For significant background to the vision see Dodaro, *Christ and the Just Society in the Thought of St. Augustine*.

its confidence in a God who is completely generous. Now no longer tied to merit or success, hope becomes a completely gratuitous gift of God, the anchor of life. Hope provides sustenance for all the other virtues.[99] Hope energizes power over the long haul of reform. "Is the promise of love so great that it justifies the gift of myself?" Benedict XVI asks in his encyclical on hope.[100] The answer for the believer is "yes." For the Franciscan moral vision the social project that touches all of the relationships between human beings and the created order is accomplished both now and in the future through the grace of a faithful and generous God. Such is a Trinitarian-centered, eschatologically driven, penitential humanism in service to a more just political economy.

---

[99] See *Commentary on Sentences*, III, d XXVI, a 1, q 1, concl., 556. Cf. Pinckaers, "La nature vertueuse de l'espérance," *Revue Thomiste*, LVIII (Octobre-Décembre 1958): 405-42; Jean-Pierre Rézette, O.F.M., "L'esperance, Vertu du Pauvre selon S. Bonaventure," in Bruno Giordani, ed., *La speranza* II (Roma: Ed. Antonianum, 1984), 357-80.

[100] *On Christian Hope, Spe Salvi* (Vatican City: Libreria Editrice Vaticana, 2007), 39.

# Concluding Comments

Since the beginnings of the Franciscan Intellectual Tradition in the thirteenth century, morality has been an essential component of the Franciscan vision. This volume has explored the Franciscan moral vision by attending to eleven characteristics of that vision, described in the Introduction:

Characteristic One: The Franciscan moral vision affirms that on the human level there is a mirroring of the free and self-giving exchange of Father, Son, and Holy Spirit that calls people to live in free and self-giving relationships of mutuality.

Characteristic Two: The Franciscan moral vision emphasizes a dynamic realization of creative and loving freedom in response to God's love.

Characteristic Three: The Franciscan moral vision recognizes each person as an image of God. Since each person reflects the creativity of God in an individualized way, each person must be treated with profound respect.

Characteristic Four: The Franciscan moral vision is Christological in its emphasis on the Exemplarity of Christ and upon the Incarnation, Redemption and Consummation of all things in Christ. It is thus profoundly Christian and Catholic, but at the same time it is universal and inclusive of all creation.

Characteristic Five: The Franciscan moral vision takes into account the issues of time, history, and human contingency. Human growth means development and conversion. Human solutions are not perfect but are perfectible.

Characteristic Six: At the same time, the Franciscan moral vision accepts an Augustinian vision of the person that recognizes human limitations, including the real limitations of human reason and philosophy, and the reality of sin.

Characteristic Seven: The Franciscan moral vision is a holistic vision that involves a spiritual discernment by the whole person – intellectual, affective, and volitional. It acknowledges the importance of the community in such discernment.

Characteristic Eight: The Franciscan moral vision is an aesthetic vision, recognizing that the moral life is one of beauty, reflecting the beauty of God.

Characteristic Nine: The Franciscan moral vision is more properly understood as a wisdom tradition rather than a scientifically organized system of analytic thought.

Characteristic Ten: The Franciscan moral vision incorporates within it a tension that arises out of respect for both sides of several polarities – the institutional and the charismatic, the universal and the particular, the past and the future, the act and the person. It acknowledges that this tension is part of living as a pilgrim in this world.

Characteristic Eleven: The Franciscan moral vision embodies a distinct social vision that intersects the personal with the political, the individual with the communal, the singular life of virtue with the anticipation of the Reign of God for all.

Having employed these characteristics to explore both the spirituality of St. Francis and St. Clare and the theological reflection upon this spirituality by the important theologians of the Franciscan intellectual tradition such as St. Bonaventure and Blessed John Duns Scotus – and having engaged some contemporary ethical questions by using this tradition, we may now further specify how this tradition may be appropriated by Franciscans today and come to the following conclusions:

(1) **The Franciscan moral vision forms the basis for a contemporary moral theology in which spirituality is an essential component.** Moral theology and ethics focus on human behavior. For Franciscans, an ethical life must also be a "spiritual life," – a life in which one's spirituality is fundamental. Christian ethics is not simply casuistry, but it is based on a life which expresses a deep spirituality. In the history of Christian ethics, Franciscan moral theology has stressed this role of spirituality in a major way.

(2) **The Franciscan moral vision forms the basis for a moral theology that is fundamentally shaped and colored by a theology of our relational, triune God.** In the Franciscan tradition, God is described as diffusive goodness, love, and infinite freedom. It is this theology of God which cradles Franciscan moral theology and which shapes moral theology so that it reflects the diffusive goodness, love and infinite freedom of God. Since God is infinitely free, Franciscan moral theology places no limits on God's goodness and love. The arms of God not only reach out to the poor and needy, but also to the sinner and the morally weak.

(3) **The Franciscan moral vision leads to a Gospel-centered and Christologically grounded moral theology.** Francis of Assisi had a very clear goal for the life of a Franciscan, namely to observe the holy Gospel of our Lord, Jesus Christ. Franciscan moral theology continually asks the question: how does an ethical or moral law reflect the gospel? Franciscan moral theology continually attempts to evaluate morality through the example of Jesus as it is presented in the Gospels.

(4) **The Franciscan moral vision provides for a moral theology that exhibits a profound respect for the individual person.** The Franciscan tradition, and especially the theology of Blessed John Duns Scotus, maintains God did not create abstract human beings but rather particular individuals. Franciscan moral theology thus strives to honor the individuality of each human person. It honors the conscience of every woman and man, since God has "loved" each individual into existence.

(5) **Moral theology inspired by the Franciscan moral vision focuses on the beautiful and the good.** Franciscan moral theology begins with the good and beautiful and within this larger context of the beauty of creation understands sin and distortion. This appreciation of the beautiful goes beyond human life, for it takes into account the totality of creation. God created all things good. Today, when we are discovering more about the created world and its interconnection, Franciscan moral theologians tend to see the beauty of nature first and only then its distortions.

(6) **The Franciscan moral vision has made significant contributions to the understanding of political and economic life.** Franciscan moral theology is not simply a personalized or individualized theology. Rather, it is keenly aware of the political and economic situations in which real people live. Political and economic life is part of human circumstances, but both politics and economics should reflect the goodness and love of God as well as reflect the gospel values that Jesus lived.

Finally, what was said at the conclusion of the Introduction to this volume needs to be repeated at its conclusion: Francis of Assisi was a man critical of his time. He raised a prophetic voice against those who abused the poor and most vulnerable and provided the basis for a vision of life that, while profoundly Catholic, also acknowledges the unity and relationality of all people, and indeed of all creation, in anticipation of the Reign of God for all. The Franciscan moral vision, in fidelity to its founder, continues to raise a prophetic voice in our own age. The reality of such a vision, however, comes ultimately not from words on a page but rather from the example of the lives that are inspired by this Franciscan moral vision.

Thomas A. Nairn, O.F.M.

# Glossary

*Affectio commodi*. The "affection for possession/happiness." Originally from Anselm, this represents the natural disposition toward self-protection and perfection in every living being. In the will, this is the disposition whereby the will is drawn to love goods that bring pleasure and enjoyment to the self. It is a self-directed disposition that is perfected by hope.

*Affectio iustitiae*. The "affection for justice." Originally from Anselm, this represents the highest moral disposition in the will. It is that disposition whereby the will is drawn to love the good because of its intrinsic value (see *bonum utile*), and not because of any personal gain. For Scotus, this affection constitutes the will's native freedom or innate liberty; it was not lost after the Fall. This disposition is perfected by charity.

*Bonum est diffusivum sui*. A term from Neo-Platonic philosophy incorporated into the theology of the Victorine School in the Middle Ages. The term is translated as "goodness is diffusive of itself." The meaning is that goodness cannot be contained within itself but always seeks to offer itself to others.

*Bonum honestum*. Literally, "goods of value." It refers to those goods of intrinsic worth.

*Bonum utile*. Literally, "goods of use." It refers to those goods whose worth is derived from their use.

**Causality, free**. The order of free causality refers to the action of the cause that is rational, or capable of self-movement and self-restraint. The will alone belongs to the order of free causality.

**Causality, necessary or natural**. The order of necessary causality refers to the action of those causes that are determined to produce an effect, unless prevented or hindered by someone or something external to them. The intellect belongs to the order of necessary causality.

**Concupiscence**. A desire or movement of the affective appetite toward something capable of giving pleasure. Bonaventure associates concupiscence with sin, understanding it as an inordinate desire that seeks pleasure as an end in itself.

**Contingency**. The order of contingency refers to those beings that can exist but do not need to exist. In the case of an actually existing being or state of affairs, contingency refers to the fact that it might not have existed or not in this particular way.

**Contuition**. An indirect knowledge of God in His effects. It is an intuitive knowledge of God whereby God is perceived in the created world without the aid of exterior senses, a sense of the presence of God together with the consciousness of created being.

**Decorum**. The attribute of appearing fitting or seemly; what is appropriate to a being or an action.

***Deiformitas***. The term, which can be translated as "conformity to God," comes from Bonaventure's understanding of the destiny of the human. We are to be so transformed by grace that we indeed reflect some of the glory of God.

**Divine Command Morality**. The type of moral theory that relies solely on revelation (divine command) to ground moral propositions.

*Firmitas*. The term comes from Scotus's philosophy and can be translated as steadfastness or fidelity. The characteristic of the divine will where freedom and necessity coincide. See Quodlibet 16. When referring to humans, it connotes that someone who is so captivated by the good will simply not consider other alternatives but will remain faithful or steadfast in his or her pursuit of that good.

*Fontalis plenitudo*. This term from Bonaventure's theology is translated as fountain fullness. The term suggests the richness and overflowing nature of the love of God first internally within the Trinity and then externally to all of creation.

**Free will**. The will's capacity as an active potency to determine itself in opposite ways.

**Freedom**. The order of causality that includes and explains the will's ability to control and determine itself as well as the ability of the will to choose rectitude for its own sake (the perfection of the affection for justice). In Scotist thought, freedom explains why the will is independent from causal factors external to itself (its indetermination) and why it possesses the capacity for self-direction (its self-determination). Freedom also refers to the fullness of perfection in divine creative activity. In God, freedom and necessity coincide.

*Habitus*. A predisposition toward a way of acting. Either a virtue or a vice would be considered a habitus, but so would any predisposition for certain ways of acting.

*Haecceitas*. From *haec* (literally this). It is the individuating principle of each being, the ultimate reality of the being.

**Illumination**. Bonaventure used his theory of illumination to explain how contingent human beings can come to know truth, by means of the superior light given by God.

**Imputability.** When an act lies in the power of an agent, the act is imputable to the agent. The person can be considered morally responsible for the action, deserving praise or blame.

**Intellect.** One of the soul's powers, the intellect is that by which the human person knows and understands reality. According to Scotus, the intellect operates according to the order of natural or necessary causality.

**Irrational potency.** A power that is incapable of self-restraint or self-determination. Scotus claims that the intellect is an irrational potency.

**Moral illumination.** Bonaventure's explanation regarding how mutable and contingent humans understand the universal element in the natural law dictated by conscience, by means of a superior light given by God.

**Natural law.** For Bonaventure, the first principles of moral truth or the primary dictates of human nature. Natural law governs human conduct in relation to both God and neighbor. It is the law written on the human heart (see Rom 2:15). It is expressed in the two precepts of natural law: Do unto others as you would have them do unto you, and do not do unto others what you would not have them do unto you.

**Order of execution**. The sequence of events that flow in a purposeful manner from a rational will. It is the reverse of the order of intention, since the goal is the last in the order of execution.

**Order of intention**. The purpose for action. That for which one acts (the goal) is the first in the order of intention, since everything done to reach that goal is done because of the goal.

**Practical reason**. The capacity for identifying the good that ought to be done. It is contrasted with the speculative reason, which provides the universal, necessary principles of logic.

**Rational potency.** A power that acts with reason. For Scotus, this is the will.

**Self-evident principle**. A proposition whose truth is evident or obvious from its terms. It is also called an analytic proposition. Self-evident principles serve as foundations for arguments or, in this case, for moral reasoning

***Sine proprio***. Literally, "without anything of one's own." The Latin term is used in the Franciscan Rule to connote the highest form of poverty. The emphasis in the Franciscan tradition is on the renunciation of ownership or the possession of things for one's own benefit. To live "sine proprio" is not to live without anything (indigence) but rather to live within a world in which everything and everyone is recognized as a "gift" which can be kept only by sharing it with others.

***Synderesis***. The "spark of conscience." For Bonaventure, it is the fundamental desire to be good and to do the good.

**Utilitarian moral theory**. Proposed by J.S. Mill, utilitarian moral reasoning involves generating the "greatest good for the greatest number." Morally good acts are those whose outcome is good for the greatest number of people. Moral reasoning involves calculating the production of good results from a given action.

**Will.** A power of the soul, that by which the person desires and chooses the good. For Scotus, the will alone is the rational potency, since it is capable of self-restraint and self-movement.

# BIBLIOGRAPHY

## 1. OFFICIAL CHURCH SOURCES

*Constitutiones, Decreta, Declarationes*: *Sacrosanctum Oecumenicum Concilium Vaticanum II*, Cura et Studio Secretariae Generalis Concilii Oecumenici Vaticani II. Rome: Typis Polyglottis Vaticanis, 1966.

Denzinger, Henricus and A. Schönmetzer. *Enchiridion Symbolorum, definitionum et declarationum de rebus fidei et morum*. Freiburg: Herder, 1965

Paul VI. *Populorum progressio*. Vatican City: Libreria Editrice Vaticana, 1967.

_____. *Humanae vitae*. Vatican City: Libreria Editrice Vaticana, 1968.

_____. *Octogesima adveniens*. Vatican City: Libreria Editrice Vaticana, 1971.

_____. *Evangelii nuntiandi*. Vatican City: Libreria Editrice Vaticana, 1975.

John Paul II. *Laborem exercens*. Vatican City: Libreria Editrice Vaticana, 1981.

_____. *Salvifici doloris*. Vatican City: Libreria Editrice Vaticana, 1984.

_____. *Sollicitudo rei socialis*. Vatican City: Libreria Editrice Vaticana, 1987.

_____. *Mulieris dignitatem*. Vatican City: Libreria Editrice Vaticana, 1988.

_____. *Redemptoris missio.*Vatican City: Libreria Editrice Vaticana, 1990.

_____ *Centesimus annus*. Vatican City: Libreria Editrice Vaticana, 1991.

_____. *Evangelium vitae*. Vatican City: Libreria Editrice Vaticana, 1995.

Benedict XVI. *Deus caritas est*. Vatican City: Libreria Editrice Vaticana, 2006.

_____. *Spe salvi*. Vatican City: Libreria Editrice Vaticana, 2007.

_____. *Caritas in veritate*. Vatican City: Libreria Editrice Vaticana, 2009.

Pontifical Council for Justice and Peace, *Towards Reforming the International Financial and Monetary Systems in the Context of Global Public Authority*. 2011.

Sacred Congregation for the Doctrine of the Faith. *Declaration on Sexual Ethics*. 1975.

_____. *Declaration on Euthanasia*. 1980.

United States Conference of Catholic Bishops. *Economic Justice for All: A Pastoral Letter on Catholic Social Teaching and the U.S. Economy*. Washington, DC. 1986.

_____. *A Decade After "Economic Justice for All": Continuing Principles, Changing Contexts, New Challenges*. Washington, DC, 1997.

_____. *Ethical and Religious Directives for Catholic Health Care Services*. Washington, DC, 2001.

_____. *Consciences for Faithful Citizenship*. Washington, DC, 2007.

_____. *Human Costs and Moral Challenges of a Broken Economy*. Washington, DC, 2011.


## 2. FRANCISCAN SOURCES

Alexander of Hales. *Summa Theologica*. Quaracchi: Collegium S. Bonaventurae, 1924-1928.

Bonaventure. *Opera Omnia*, Quaracchi: Collegium S. Bonaventurae, 1882-1902.

_____. *St. Bonaventure's On the Reduction of the Arts to Theology*. *WSB* I. Translation with Introduction and Commentary by Zachary Hayes. St. Bonaventure, NY: Franciscan Institute, 1996.

_____. *Itinerarium Mentis in Deum*. *WSB* II. Latin text from the Quaracchi Edition, New English Translation by Zachary Hayes. Introduction and Commentary by Philotheus Boehner. St. Bonaventure, NY: Franciscan Institute Publications, 2002.

_____. *Commentary on Ecclesiastes*. *WSB* VII. Translation and Notes by Campion Murray and Robert J. Karris. Introduction by Robert J. Karris. St. Bonaventure, NY: Franciscan Institute Publications, 2005.

_____. *Collations on the Ten Commandments*. *WSB* VI. Introduction and Translation by Paul J. Spaeth. St. Bonaventure, NY: Franciscan Institute, 1996.

_____. *Disputed Questions on the Mystery of the Trinity*. *WSB* III. Introduction and Translation by Zachary Hayes. St. Bonaventure, NY: Franciscan Institute, 2000.

_____. *Writings on the Spiritual Life*. Introductions and Notes by F. Edward Coughlin. *WSB* X. St. Bonaventure, NY: Franciscan Institute Publications, 2006.

_____. *Commentary on the Gospel of St. Luke, Chapters 1-8, 9-16, 17-24*. *WSB* VIII/I-III. With an Introduction, Translation and Notes by Robert J. Karris. St. Bonaventure, NY: Franciscan Institute Publications, 2001-2004.

_____. *Breviloquium*. Introduction, Translation and Notes by Dominic V. Monti. *WSB* IX. St. Bonaventure, NY: Franciscan Institute Publications, 2005.

_____. *Disputed Questions on Evangelical Perfection*. Introduction and Notes by Robert J. Karris. Translation by Thomas Reist and Robert J. Karris. *WSB* XIII. St. Bonaventure, NY: Franciscan Institute Publications, 2008.

_____. *Defense of the Mendicants*. *WSB* XV; Introduction and Notes by Robert J. Karris. Translation by José de Vinck. St. Bonaventure, NY: Franciscan Institute Publications, 2010.

_____. *Collations on the Seven Gifts of the Holy Spirit*. *WSB* XIV. Introduction and Translation by Zachary Hayes. Notes by Robert J. Karris. St. Bonaventure, NY: Franciscan Institute Publications, 2008.

_____. *Collations on the Six Days.* Works of Bonaventure V. Translated by José de Vinck. Paterson, NJ: St. Anthony Guild Press, 1970.

John Duns Scotus. *Opera Omnia*, Civitas Vaticana, Typis Polyglottis Vaticanis, 1950 – 2011.

_____. *Ordinatio.* In *Opera Omnia*, Civitas Vaticana, vv. 5 to 9.

_____. *Quodlibetal Questions.* English translation by Alluntis, Felix and Allan Wolter, *God and Creatures: the Quodlibetal Questions.* Princeton, NJ: Princeton University Press, 1975.

_____. *Quaestiones super Libros Metaphysicorum Aristotelis.* Gen. ed. Girard Etzkorn., vv. 1-4. St. Bonaventure, NY. Franciscan Institute Publications, 1997.

_____. *Reportatio Parisiensis* I. Eng. trans. *The Examined Report of the Paris Lecture* I. Eng. trans. Oleg Bychkov. St. Bonaventure, NY. Franciscan Institute Publications, 2008.

_____. *Reportatio Parisiensis* III, d. 7, q. 4, 5, Opera Omnia, t. 23. Paris: Apud Ludovicum Vivès, Bibliopolam Editorem, 1894.

_____. *Lectura.* In *Opera Omnia,* Civitas Vaticana, v. 17.

Peter John Olivi. *Quaestiones de perfectione evangelica, n. 9. An usus pauper includatur in consilio seu in voto paupertatis evangelicae, ita quod sit de eius substantia et integritate.* MS Rome. Vat. Borgh. 357.

_____. *Peter of John Olivi on the Acts of the Apostles.* David Flood, ed. St. Bonaventure, NY: Franciscan Institute Publications, 2001.

## 3. SELECT GENERAL BIBLIOGRAPHY

Adams, Marilyn McCord. "Duns Scotus on the Will as Rational Power." In *Via Scoti. Methodologica ad mentem Joannis Duns Scoti*. Volume II. Ed. Leonardo Sileo. Rome: Antonianum, 1995. 839-54.

Alaimo, Bernardo. "Attualità della dottrina scotistica della carità." In *De doctrina Ioannis Duns Scoti*, Volume III. Rome: Scotus Commission,1968. 599-615.

Alliney, Guido. "L'acrasia secondo Duns Scoto: autonomia della volontà o disordine della passione?" In *Giovanni Duns Scoto: Studi e ricerche nel VII Centenario della sua morte*. Volume I. Ed. Martín Carbajo Núñez, Rome: Antonianum, 2008. 429-49.

Ambrose. *De Officiis*, edited with a translation and commentary by Ivor J. Davidson. Oxford University Press, 2001.

Anselm of Canterbury. *The Major Works of Anselm of Canterbury*. Ed. Brian Davies and G. R. Evans. Oxford: Oxford University Press, 2008.

_____. *On the Duties of Clerics*. NPNF1, v. 10. Grand Rapids: Eerdmans, 1955.

Arafat, Imam Bashar Mohammad. "Islam and Christianity: Two Faiths and One God." In *Islam and Franciscanism: A Dialogue*, 25-42. Ed. Margaret Carney. St. Bonaventure, NY: Franciscan Institute Publications, 2000.

Aristotle. "Nicomachean Ethics." In *The Basic Works of Aristotle*. Ed. Richard McKeon. New York: Modern Library, 1941. 935-1112.

_____. *Aristotle's Eudemian Ethics*. Ed. M. J. Woods. Oxford: Clarendon Press, 1982.

Armstrong, Regis, Wayne Hellmann and William Short. *Francis of Assisi: Early Documents.* Vol. I, *The Saint*; vol. II, *The Founder*; vol. III, *The Prophet.* New York: New City Press, 1999-2001.

Armstrong, Regis. *Clare of Assisi, the Lady: Early Documents.* New York: New City Press, 2006.

Astel, Ann W. *Eating Beauty, the Eucharist and the Spiritual Arts of the Middle Ages.* Ithaca, NY: Cornell University Press, 2006.

Atkins, E. M. and R. J. Dodaro. *Augustine, Political Writings.* Cambridge: Cambridge University Press, 2001.

Augustine of Hippo. *Basic Writing of St. Augustine.* Ed. Whitney J. Oates. New York: Random House, 1948.

_____. "Homilies on the Gospel of John 1-40." Translated by Edmund Hill. WSA I/12. Hyde Park, NY: New City Press, 2009.

_____. *Responses to Miscellaneous Questions,* Introduction, translation and notes by Boniface Ramsey. WSA I/12. Hyde Park, NY: New City Press, 2008.

Aulén, Gustav. *Christus Victor.* New York: Macmillan, 1969.

Baldanza, Giuseppe. "Attualità della dottrina di San Bonaventura sul matrimonio." In *San Bonaventura Maestro di vita francescana e di sapienza Cristiana.* Volume III. Ed. A. Pompei. Rome: Pontificia Facoltà Teologica "San Bonaventura," 1976. 303-15.

Bartlett, Anthony W. *Cross Purposes: The Violent Grammar of Christian Atonement.* Harrisburg, PA: Trinity Press International, 2001.

Basetti Sani, Giulio, *L'Islam nel piano della salvezza*. San Domenico di Fiesole: Edizioni Cultura della Pace, 1992.

Becker, Marie-Francis, Jean-François Godet, and Thaddée Matura, ed. *Claire d'Assise, Écrits, Introduction, texte latin, traducion, notes et index*. Sources Chrétiennes 325. Paris: Cerf, 1985.

_____. *Chiara d'Assisi: Scritti: Introduzione, Testo latino, Traduction, Notes e Index*. Paris: Cerf, 1985.

Bergson, Henri. *Two Sources of Morality and Religion*. Notre Dame, IN: Notre Dame University Press, 1994.

Berti, Enrico. "Parmenides." In *A Guide To Greek Thought*. Ed. Jacques Brunschwig and Geoffrey E. R. Lloyd. London: Belknap Press, 2000. 138-49.

Bettoni, Efrem. *Duns Scotus: Basic Principles of his Philosophy*. Washington, DC: Catholic University of America Press. 1961.

Bezancon, J. N. "Égalité et pouvoir dans les Morales de Grégoire le Grand." In *Recherches Augustiniennes* 27 (1994): 97-129.

Blastic, Michael. "Franciscan Spirituality." In *The New Dictionary of Catholic Spirituality*. Ed. Michael Downey. Collegeville: Liturgical Press, 1993. 408-18.

Boler, John. "The Moral Psychology of Duns Scotus: Some Preliminary Questions." *Franciscan Studies* 50 (1990): 31-56.

_____. "Transcending the Natural: Duns Scotus on the Two Affections of the Will." *American Catholic Philosophical Quarterly* 67 (1993): 109-26.

Bonansea, B. M. *Man and His Approach to God in John Duns Scotus*. Lanham, MD: University Press of America, 1983.

Borak, Adriano. "Le beatitudini come espressione della maturità della vita cristiana." In *San Bonaventura maestro di vita Francescana e di sapienza Cristiana*. Volume III. Ed. A. Pompei. Rome: Pontificia Facoltà Teologica "San Bonaventura," 1976. 281-92.

Boulnois, Olivier. "Si Dieu n'existait pas, faudrait-il l'inventer? Situation métaphysique de l'éthique scotiste." *Philosophie* 61 (1999): 50-74.

Bourdeau, Alain and Silvain Piron, eds. *Pierre de Jean Olivi (1248-1298). Pensée Scolastique, Dissidence Spirituelle et Sociéte*. Paris: J. Vrin, 1999.

Brady, Ignatius. *Francis & Clare. The Complete Works*. New York: Paulist, 1982.

Brennan, Karen, F. Feng, L. Hall, and S. Patrina. In B. David, ed., "On the Complexity of Technology and the Technology of Complexity." *Proceedings of the Fourth Complexity Science and Educational Research Conference*. Vancouver, BC, Canada. 2007. 47-73.

Bretzke, James. *A Morally Complex World: Engaging Contemporary Moral Theology*. Collegeville: Liturgical Press, 2004.

Brown, Marvin T. *Civilizing the Economy: A New Economics of Provision*. New York: Cambridge University Press, 2010.

Bruni, Luigino, "Toward an Economic Rationality 'Capable of Communion.'" In *The Economy of Communion, Toward a*

*Multi-Dimensional Economic Culture*. Ed. Bruno Luigi-no. Hyde Park, NY: New City Press, 2002. 41-67.

Burnaby, John. *Amor Dei. A Study of the Religion of St. Augustine*. Eugene, OR: Wipf & Stock, 2007.

Burnham, Louisa A. *So Great A Light, So Great A Smoke. The Beguin Heretics of Languedoc*. Ithaca, NY: Cornell University Press, 2008.

Burr, David. "Bonaventure, Olivi and Franciscan Christology." *Collectanea Francescana*, 53 (1983): 23-40.

_____. *Olivi and Franciscan Poverty: The Origins of the Usus Pauper Controversy*. Philadelphia: University of Pennsylvania Press, 1989.

_____. "Poverty: A Cause for Unity or Division?" In *Poverty and Prosperity: Franciscans and the Use of Money*. Washington Theological Union Symposium Papers, 2009. St. Bonaventure, NY: Franciscan Institute Publications, 2009. 65-80.

Burt, Donald X. *Friendship & Society. An Introduction to Augustine's Practical Philosophy*. Grand Rapids: Eerdmans, 1999.

Calisi, Maria. *Trinitarian Perspectives in the Franciscan Theological Tradition*. St. Bonaventure, NY. Franciscan Institute Publications, 2008.

Callahan, Daniel. *The Troubled Dream of Life: In Search of a Peaceful Death*. Washington, DC: Georgetown University Press, 2006.

Callahan, Sydney. *In Good Conscience*. New York: Harper-Collins, 1991.

Capitani, Ovidio. *Figure e motive del francescanesimo medieval*. Bologna: Pàtron, 2000.

_____. "Verso una nuova antropologia e una nuova religiosità." In *La Conversione alla povertà nell'Italia dei Secoli XII-XIV*. Ed. Enrico Menestò. Spoleto: Centro italiano di studi sull-alto Medioevo, 1991. 447-71.

Capizzi, Joseph E. "The Children of God: Natural Slavery in the Thought of Aquinas and Vitoria." *Theological Studies* 63 (2002): 31-52.

Carney, Margaret. *The First Franciscan Woman*. Quincy, IL: Franciscan Press, 1993.

Carpenter, Charles. *Theology as the Road to Holiness in St. Bonaventure*. Mahwah, NY: Paulist, 1999.

Casagrande, Giovanna. *Religiosità penitenziale e città al tempo dei communi*. Rome: Instituto Storico dei Cappucchini, 1995.

Casamenti, Silvestro. *Etica e persona Duns Scoto e suggestione nel moderno*. Bologna: Edizioni Franciscane Bologna, 1994.

Châtillon, Jean. "Le primat de la vertu de charité dans la théologie de Saint Bonaventure." In *San Bonaventura maestro di vita Francescana e di sapienza Cristiana*. Volume III. Ed. A. Pompei. Rome: Pontificia Facolta' Teologica "San Bonaventura," 1976. 217-38.

Chenu, M.-D. *L'éveil de la conscience dans la civilisation médiévale*. Montréal: Inst. d'études médiévales, 1969.

Chinnici, Joseph. *When Values Collide: The Catholic Church, Sexual Abuse, and the Challenge of Leadership*. Maryknoll, NY: Orbis, 2010.

_____. "Penitential Humanism: Rereading the Sources to Develop a Franciscan Urban Spirituality." In *Franciscans in Urban Ministry*. Ed. Ken Himes. St. Bonaventure, NY: Franciscan Institute Publications, 2002. 109-28.

_____. *Living Stones: The History and Structure of Catholic Spiritual Life in America*. Maryknoll, NY: Orbis, 1996, 2nd ed.

_____. "Deciphering Religious Practice: Material Culture as Social Code in the Nineteenth Century." *U.S. Catholic Historian* 19 (2001): 1-19.

Coleman, Janet. "Property and Poverty." In J. H. Burns, *The Cambridge History of Medieval Political Thought c. 350-c. 1450*. Cambridge: Cambridge University Press, 1988. 607-48.

Coleman, John A. and William F. Ryan, eds. *Globalization and Catholic Social Thought: Present Crisis, Future Hope*. Maryknoll, NY: Orbis, 2005.

Congar, Yves. "L'Église et Cité de Dieu chez quelques auteurs cisterciens a l'époque des Croisades, en particulier dans le De Peregrinante civitate Dei d'Henri D'Albano." In *Melanges offerts à Etienne Gilson*. Toronto: Pontifical Institute of Mediaeval Studies/Paris: J. Vrin, 1959. 173-202; Yves Congar, *Etudes d'ecclésiologie medieval*. London: Variorum Reprints, 1983. N. VIII.

Conn, Walter. *Christian Conversion: A Developmental Interpretation of Autonomy and Surrender*. New York: Paulist, 1986.

Courtier, David. *The Fraternal Economy. A Pastoral Psychology of Franciscan Economics*. South Bend, IN: Cloverdale Books, 2007.

Cousins, Ewert H. *Bonaventure and the Coincidence of Opposites: The Theology of Bonaventure*. Chicago, IL: Franciscan Herald Press, 1978.

Crosby, Michael. "Francis of Assisi's Strategic Insight about Power in a World of Greed and Lust: A Model [of Asceticism] for Every Age." In *Greed, Lust, and Power: Franciscan Strategies for Building a More Just World*. Franciscan Symposium at the Washington Theological Union. St. Bonaventure, NY: Franciscan Institute Publications, 2011. 23-44.

Crowe, Michael Bertram. *Changing Profile of the Natural Law*. Leiden: Kluwer Law International, 1978.

Cullen, Bernard, "Property in the Writings of St. Bonaventure." In *L'Homme et Son Univers au Moyen Agê*. Ed. Christian Wenin, Volume II. Louvain-la-Neuve: Éditions de L'Institut Supérieur de Philosophie, 1986. 827-34.

Cullen, Christopher M. *Bonaventure*. New York: Oxford University Press, 2006.

Curran, Charles, ed. *Moral Theology. Challenges for the Future. Essays in Honor of Richard A. McCormick*. New York: Paulist, 1990.

Cusato, Michael F. "The Early Franciscans and the Use of Money." In *Poverty and Prosperity: Franciscans and the Use of Money*. Washington Theological Union Symposium Papers, 2009. St. Bonaventure, NY: Franciscan Institute Publications, 2009. 13-38

Cushing, Vincent. "A Franciscan Economy." In *Greed, Lust, and Power: Franciscan Strategies for Building a More Just World*. Franciscan Symposium at the Washington

Theological Union. St. Bonaventure, NY: Franciscan Institute Publications, 2011. 59-66.

Damiata, Mariano. "Duns Scoto davanti a G. d'Ockham." In *Via Scoti. Methodologica ad mentem Joannis Duns Scoti.* Volume II. Ed. Leonardo Sileo. Rome: Antonianum, 1995. 873-925.

DeBenedictis, Matthew. *The Social Thought of Saint Bonaventure. A Study in Social Philosophy.* New Edition. Westport, CT: Greenwood Press, 1972.

Dalarun, Jacques. *Francis of Assisi and the Feminine.* St. Bonaventure, NY: Franciscan Institute Publications, 2006.

Delhaye, Philippe. "Les conditions générales de l'agir chrétien selon Saint Bonaventure." In *San Bonaventura maestro di vita francescana e di sapienza Cristiana.* Volume III. Ed. A. Pompei. Rome: Pontificia Facoltà Teologica "San Bonaventura," 1976. 183-215.

Delio, Ilia. "Religious Pluralism and the Coincidence of Opposites." *Theological Studies* 70 (2009): 822-44.

_____. "Theology, Metaphysics and the Centrality of Christ." *Theological Studies* 68 (2007): 254-73.

_____. *Simply Bonaventure: An Introduction to His Life, Thought, and Writings.* Hyde Park, NY: New City Press, 2001.

Dennis, Marie. "The Cry of the Poor: Are We Listening?" In *Poverty and Prosperity: Franciscans and the Use of Money.* Washington Theological Union Symposium Papers, 2009. St. Bonaventure, NY: Franciscan Institute Publications, 2009. 1-12.

Dillistone, F. W. *The Christian Understanding of Atonement*. London: Westminster, 1968.

Di Mattia, Giuseppe. "L'antico' e il 'novo' sull'essenza e sui fini del matrimonio canonico," *San Bonaventura maestro di vita Francescana e di sapienza Cristiana*. Volume III. Ed. A. Pompei. Rome: Pontificia Facoltà Teologica "San Bonaventura," 1976. 317-34.

Dodaro, Robert. *Christ and the Just Society in the Thought of Augustine*. Cambridge: Cambridge University Press, 2004.

D'Onofri, Tobia. "San Bonaventura nella concezione etica dantesca." In *San Bonaventura maestro di vita Francescana e di sapienza Cristiana*. Volume III. Ed. A. Pompei Rome: Pontificia Facoltà Teologica "San Bonaventura," 1976. 351-57.

Dotto, Gianni. "'Conversio' e 'communicatio': un 'engagement' comunitario fondato sulla 'caritas'." In *San Bonaventura maestro di vita francescana e di sapienza Cristiana*. Volume III. Ed. A. Pompei. Rome: Pontificia Facoltà Teologica "San Bonaventura," 1976. 239-44.

Douglas, Mary. *How Institutions Think*. Syracuse, NY: Syracuse University Press, 1986.

Dumont, S. "The Necessary Connection of Moral Virtue to Prudence According to J. Duns Scotus." *Recherches théologie ancienne et médiavale* 55 (1988): 184-206.

Dyson, R. W. *Aquinas: Political Writings*. Cambridge: Cambridge University Press, 2008.

Elsässer, Antonellus. *Christus der Lehrer des Sittlichen: Die christologischen Grundlagen für die Erkenntnis des*

*Sittlichen nach der Lehre Bonaventuras.* Paderborn: Schöningh, 1968.

Epictetus, *The Discourses and Manual, Together with Fragments of His Writings.* Oxford: Clarendon Press, 1916.

Esser, Cajetan. *Opuscula Sancti Patris Francisci Assiensis.* Grottaferrata: Collegium S. Bonaventurae Ad Claras Aquas, 1978.

\_\_\_\_\_. *Repair My House.* Ed. Luc Mély. Chicago, IL: Franciscan Herald Press, 1963.

Etzkorn, Girard, ed. *Essays Honoring Allan B. Wolter.* St. Bonaventure, NY: Franciscan Institute, 1985.

Fehlner, Peter D. *The Role of Charity in the Ecclesiology of St. Bonaventure.* Rome: Editrice "Miscellanea Francescana," 1965.

Felder, Hilarin. *The Knight-Errant of Assisi.* Milwaukee, WI: Bruce Publishing Company, 1948.

Ferguson, Niall, et al. *The Shock of the Global: The 1970s in Perspective.* Cambridge, MA: Harvard University Press, 2010.

Flood, David. *Work for Every One. Francis of Assisi and the Ethic of Service.* Quezon City, Philippines: CCFMC Office for Asia/Oceania, 1997.

\_\_\_\_\_. *Poverty in the Middle Ages.* Werl: Dietrich-Coelde, 1975.

Fortini, Arnaldo. *Nova vita di S. Francesco.* Assisi: Porziuncula, 1959. 4 volumes.

Frank, William A. and Allan B. Wolter. *Duns Scotus, Metaphysician*. West Lafayette, IN: Purdue University Press, 1995.

Frank, William. "Duns Scotus' Concept of Willing Freely: What Divine Freedom Beyond Choice Teaches Us." *Franciscan Studies* 43 (1982): 68-89.

Franks, Christopher A. *He Became Poor: The Poverty of Christ and Aquinas's Economic Teachings*. Grand Rapids: Eerdmans, 2009.

Freppert, Lucan. *The Basis of Morality according to William Ockham*. Chicago, IL: Franciscan Herald Press, 1988.

Freyer, Johannes. *Homo Viator: Der Mensch im Lichte der Heilsgeschichte*. Kevelaer: Butzon & Bercker, 2001.

Fuchs, Josef. "A Harmonization of the Conciliar Statements on Christian Moral Theology." In *Vatican II Assessment and Perspectives: Twenty-five Years After (1962-1987)*. Volume Two. Ed. René Latourelle. New York/Mahwah: Paulist, 1989. 479-500.

Gestori, Gervasio: "La legge naturale in San Bonaventura e il suo influsso su Duns Scoto." In *San Bonaventura maestro di vita francescana e di sapienza Cristiana*. Volume III. Ed. A. Pompei. Rome: Pontificia Facoltà Teologica, 1976. 245-55.

Gilson, Étienne. *The Philosophy of St. Bonaventure*. New York: Sheed and Ward. 1938.

_____. *Jean Duns Scot: Introduction a ses positions fondamentales*. Paris: J. Vrin, 1952.

Girard, René. *I See Satan Fall Like Lightning*. Maryknoll, NY: Orbis, 2001.

Gregory the Great. *Morals on the Book of Job*. Oxford: John Henry Parker, 1844-50, three volumes. Anonymous translator.

Gregory, Eric. *Politics and the Order of Love. An Augustinian Ethic of Democratic Citizenship*. Chicago, IL: University of Chicago Press, 2008.

Grisez, Germain. "The Duty and Right to Follow One's Judgment of Conscience," *Linacre Quarterly* 56/1 (February 1989): 13-23.

Guimet, Fernand. "Conformité à la droite raison et possibilité surnaturelle de la charité." In *De Doctrina Ioannis Duns Scoti*, Volume III. Rome: Scotus Commission, 1968. 539-97.

Habig, Marion. *St. Francis: Omnibus of Sources*. Chicago, IL: Franciscan Herald Press, 1964.

Hayes, Zachary. "Bonaventure: Mystery of the Triune God." In *The History of Franciscan Theology*. Ed. Kenan B. Osborne. St. Bonaventure, NY: Franciscan Institute, 2007.

_____. *The Hidden Center. Spirituality and Speculative Christology in Bonaventure*. St. Bonaventure, NY: Franciscan Institute, 1992.

_____. *Bonaventure: Mystical Writings*. New York: Crossroad, 1999.

_____. "Christ, Word of God and Exemplar of Humanity." *The Cord* 46 (1996): 3-17.

Heinz, Hanspeter. *Trinitarische Begegnungen bei Bonaventura*. Münster: Aschendorff, 1985.

Hellmann, Wayne. "Gospel: Life or Observance: Observations on a Language Shift in the Early Documents." *Franciscan Studies* 64 (2006): 281-92.

Hoeberichts, Jan. *Paradise Restored. The Social Ethics of Francis of Assisi, A Commentary on Francis' "Salutation of the Virtues."* Quincy, IL: Franciscan Press, 2004.

Hone, Mary Frances, General Editor, *Towards the Discovery of Clare of Assisi*. Volume II, *Clare Discovers the Love of God in the Church*. Ed. Regis Armstrong and Pacelli Millane. St. Bonaventure, NY: Franciscan Institute Publications, 1992.

Hughes, John. *The End of Work: Theological Critiques of Capitalism*. Cambridge, MA: Harvard University Press, 2007.

Hunt, Anne. *Trinity: Nexus of the Mysteries of Christian Faith*. Maryknoll, NY: Orbis, 2006.

Iammarrrone, Giovanni. "The Timeliness and Limitations of the Christology of John Duns Scotus for the Development of a Contemporary Theology of Christ." *Greyfriars Review* 7 (1993): 229-48.

Ingham, Mary Beth. "Self-mastery and Rational Freedom: Duns Scotus's Contribution to the Usus Pauper Debate," *Franciscan Studies* 66 (2008): 337-69.

_____. "Scotus's Franciscan Identity and Ethics: Self-Mastery and the Rational Will." In *Duns Scotus, Philosopher*. Proceedings of "The Quadruple Congress" on John Duns Scotus Part 1. Ed. Mary Beth Ingham and Oleg Bychkov. *Archa Verbi, Subsidia* 3. St. Bonaventure, NY: Franciscan Institute Publications/Münster: Aschendorf, 2010. 139-55.

_____. *Rejoicing in the Works of the Lord: Beauty in the Franciscan Tradition*. St. Bonaventure, NY. Franciscan Institute Publications, 2009.

_____. *La Sagesse Morale: Le Stoïcism au Moyen Age*. Paris: Cerf, 2007.

_____. *Scotus for Dunces: An Introduction to His Life, Thought, and Writings*. St. Bonaventure, NY: Franciscan Institute Publications, 2003.

_____. *The Harmony of Goodness: Mutuality and Moral Living According to John Duns Scotus*. Revised, Second Edition. St. Bonaventure, NY: Franciscan Institute Publications, 2012.

_____. "Duns Scotus' Moral Reasoning and the Artistic Paradigm." In *Via Scoti: Methodologica ad mentem Joannis Duns Scoti*. Volume II. Ed. Leonardo Sileo. Rome: Antonianum, 1995. 825-38.

_____. "Ea Quae Sunt ad Finem: Reflections on Virtue as Means to Moral Excellence in Scotist Thought," *Franciscan Studies* 50 (1990): 177-95.

_____. *Ethics and Freedom: An Historical-Critical Investigation of Scotist Ethical Theory*. Lanham, Maryland: University of America Press, 1989.

Ingham, Mary Beth and Mechthild Dreyer, *The Philosophical Vision of John Duns Scotus*. Washington, DC: Catholic University of America Press, 2004.

Jackson, Tim. *Prosperity without Growth: Economics for a Finite Planet*. London: Earthscan, 2009.

Jeusset, Jean Gwenolé. *Dieu est Courtoisie: François d'Assise, son Ordre et l'Islam*. Nantes: n. p., 1985.

Johnson, Timothy. *The Soul in Ascent. Bonaventure on Poverty, Prayer, and Union with God*. Quincy, IL: Franciscan Press, 2000; rep. St. Bonaventure, NY: Franciscan Institute Publications, 2012.

Karris, Robert J. *The Admonitions of St. Francis: Sources and Meanings*. St. Bonaventure, NY: Franciscan Institute, 1999.

Keane, Kevin. "Why Creation? Bonaventure and Thomas Aquinas on God as Creative Good." *Downside Review* 97 (1975): 100-21.

Kelly, J. N. D. *Early Christian Doctrines*. London: Continuum, 2004, 5th ed.

Kopas, Jane. "Is It Possible to Live Franciscan Poverty Today?" In *Poverty and Prosperity: Franciscans and the Use of Money*. Washington Theological Union Symposium Papers, 2009. St. Bonaventure, NY: Franciscan Institute Publications, 2009. 81-100.

LaCugna, Catherine. *God for Us*. New York: HarperCollins, 1993.

Lambertini, Roberto. *La povertà pensata: Evoluzione storica della definizione dell'identità minoretica da Bonaventura ad Occam*. Modena: Mucchi, 2000.

Lambertini, Roberto and Andrea Tabarroni. *Dopo Francesco: L'Eredità Difficile*. Turin: Abele, 1989.

Lane, Frank. "Freedom and Authority: The Law, Peter Olivi, and the Second Vatican Council." *Franciscan Studies* 62 (2004): 155-76.

Langholm, Odd. *Economics in the Medieval Schools. Wealth, Exchange, Value, Money and Usury according to the Parish Theological Tradition 1200-1350*. Leiden: Brill, 1992.

Langston, Douglas C. *Conscience and Other Virtues*. University Park, PA: University of Pennsylvania Press, 2001.

Leclerc, Eloi. *The Canticle of Creatures: Symbols of Union*. Chicago, IL: Franciscan Herald Press, 1977.

Leclercq, Jean. *The Love of Learning and the Desire for God. A Study of Monastic Culture*. New York: Fordham University Press, 1961.

LeGoff, Jacques. *Francis of Assisi*. London: Routledge, 1999.

LeGoff, Jacques. "Merchant's Time and Church's Time in the Middle Ages." In *Time Work and Culture in the Middle Ages*. Chicago, IL: University of Chicago Press, 1980. 29-42.

Lindbeck, George. *The Nature of Doctrine: Religion and Theology in a Postliberal Age*. Louisville: Westminster John Knox, 1984.

Little, Lester K. *Religious Poverty and the Profit Economy in Medieval Europe*. Ithaca, NY: Cornell University Press, 1983.

_____. "Pride Goes Before Avarice. Social Change and the Vices in Latin Christendom." In *American Historical Review* 76 (1971): 16-49.

Lonergan, Bernard. "The Transition from a Classicist Worldview to Historical Mindedness." In *A Second Collection by Bernard J. F. Lonergan*. Ed. William F.J. Ryan and Bernard J. Tyrrell. Philadelphia: Westminster, 1974. 1-9.

Lottin, Odon. *Psychologie et morale aux XII et XIII siècles.* Gembloux: Duculot. 1957 – 1960. Six volumes.

MacIntyre, Alisdair. *Whose Justice? Which Rationality?* Notre Dame, IN: Notre Dame University Press, 1988.

Madrick, Jeff. *Age of Greed: The Triumph of Finance and the Decline of America, 1970 to the Present.* New York: Knopf, 2011.

Maguire, Daniel and A. Nicholas Fargnoli. *On Moral Grounds: The Art / Science of Ethics.* New York: Crossroad, 1991.

Manning, Rita. *Speaking from the Heart. Feminist Perspectives on Ethics.* Lanham, Maryland: Rowan and Littlefield, 1992.

Manselli, Raoul. "Evangelisme et mythe dans la foi cathare." *Heresis* 5 (1985): 9-17.

Markus, R. A. "The Latin Fathers." In *The Cambridge History of Medieval Political Thought c. 350- c. 1450.* Ed. Burns, J. H. Cambridge: Cambridge University Press, 1988. 92-122.

_____. *Christianity and the Secular.* Notre Dame, IN: University of Notre Dame Press, 2006.

_____. *Saeculum. History and Society in the Theology of St. Augustine.* Cambridge: Cambridge University Press, 1970.

_____. "Two Conceptions of Political Authority: Augustine, De Civitate Dei XIX. 14-15, and Some Thirteenth Century Interpretations." *Journal of Theological Studies* 16 (1965): 68-100.

Martignetti, Richard S. *Saint Bonaventure's Tree of Life, Theology of the Mystical Journey*. Grottaferrata: Frati Editori di Quaracchi, 2004.

Matanić, Atanasio. "'Beatitudo est in unione': La felicità dell'uomo all luce del magistero bonaventuriano." In *San Bonaventura maestro di vita Francescana e di sapienza Cristiana*, Volume III. Ed. A. Pompei. Rome: Pontificia Facoltà Teologica "San Bonaventura," 1976. 269-80.

Matanić, Atanasio. "Dottrina di Giovanni Duns Scoto sulla connessione delle virtù morali (con special riguardo alla povertà)." In *De doctrina Ioannis Duns Scoti*, Volume. III. Rome: Scotus Commission,1968. 617-30.

Mathieu, Luc. "Était-il nécessaire que le Christ mourût sur la croix? Réflexion sur la liberté absolue de Dieu et la liberté de Jésus-homme, d'après Jean Duns Scots (Op. ox. III, dist. 20, quaest. unic.)." In *Duns Scot à Paris, 1302-2002: Actes du colloque de Paris*, 2-4 septembre 2002. Ed. Olivier Boulnois et al. Turnhout: Brepols, 2004. 581-91.

Matura, Thadeo. "La vision teológica de San Francisco de Asís y su relación con la teología ortodoxa," *Selecciones de Francescanismo* 25 (1996): 367-75.

Mauss, Marcel. *The Gift: The Form and Reason for Exchange in Archaic Societies*. New York: W.W. Norton, 1990.

McCarthy, Donald, ed. *Moral Theology Today: Certitudes and Doubts*. St. Louis, MO: The Pope John Center, 1984.

McCormick, Patrick T. "A Right to Beauty. A Fair Share of Milk and Honey for the Poor." *Theological Studies* 71 (2010): 702-20.

McMichael, Steven. "Sharing the Wealth of Poverty: Franciscan Friars at the End of the Middle Ages." In *Poverty and*

*Prosperity: Franciscans and the Use of Money*. Washington Theological Union Symposium Papers, 2009. St. Bonaventure, NY: Franciscan Institute Publications, 2009. 39-64.

Merino, José Antonio and Francisco Martinez Fresneda, ed. *Manual de Teología franciscana*. Madrid: Biblioteca de Autores Cristianos, 2003.

Merlo, Grado Giovanni. I*n the Name of St. Francis: History of the Friars Minor and Franciscanism until the Early Sixteenth Century*. Saint Bonaventure, NY: Franciscan Institute Publications, 2009.

_____. *Contro gli eretici*. Bologna: Mulino, 1996.

_____. "La conversione alla povertà nell'Italia del secoli XII-XIV." In *La Conversione alla Povertà nell' Italia dei Secoli XII-XIV*. Ed. Enrico Menestó. Spoleto: Centro italiano di studi sull-alto Medioevo, 1991. 3-32.

Messerich, Valerius. "The Awareness of Causal Initiative and Existential Responsibility in the Thought of Duns Scotus." In *De doctrina Ioannis Duns Scoti*, Volume II. Rome: Scotus Commission, 1968. 629-44.

Miccoli, Giovanni. *Francesco d'Assis. Realità e memoria di un'esperienza Cristiana*. Turin: Enaudi, 1991.

_____. *Chiesa gregoriana: Richerche sulla riforma del secolo XI*. Rome: Herder, 1999.

Miller, Vincent J. "Where Is the Church? Globalization and Catholicity." *Theological Studies* 69 (2008): 412-32.

Min, Anselm. *Paths to the Triune God*. Notre Dame, IN: University of Notre Dame Press, 2005.

Mollat, Michael. *The Poor in the Middle Ages. An Essay in Social History*. New Haven, CT: Yale University Press, 1986.

Monastère de Nantes. *À la découverte de Claire d'Assise*. Nantes, n.d.

Moses, Paul. *The Saint and the Sultan*. New York: Doubleday, 2009.

Mueller, Joan. *Clare's Letters to Agnes: Text and Sources*. St. Bonaventure, NY. Franciscan Institute Publications, 2001.

Munir, Fared. "Islam and Franciscanism: Prophet Mohammad of Arabia in the Spirituality of Mission." In *Islam and Franciscanism: A Dialogue*. Ed. Margaret Carney. St. Bonaventure, NY: Franciscan Institute Publications, 2000. 25-42.

Murray, Alexander. "Piety and Impiety in Thirteenth-Century Italy." In *Popular Belief and Practice*. Ed. G.J. Cumin and Derek Baker. Cambridge: Cambridge University Press, 1972.

Nairn, Thomas, *The Seamless Garment: Writings on the Consistent Ethic of Life*. Maryknoll, NY: Orbis, 2008.

_____. *The Consistent Ethic of Life: Assessing its Reception and Relevance*. Maryknoll, NY: Orbis, 2008.

_____. "Reclaiming our Moral Tradition." In *Health Progress* 78 n. 6 (November/December 1997): 36-39.

Nangle, Joseph. "Greed, Lust and Power: Franciscan Strategies for Building a More Just World: Three Disturbing Hypotheses." *Greed, Lust, and Power: Franciscan Strategies for Building a More Just World*. Franciscan Symposium at the Washington Theological Union. St. Bonaventure, NY: Franciscan Institute Publications, 2011. 15-22.

Nelson, Janet L. "Society, Theodicy and the Origins of Heresy: Towards a Reassessment of the Medieval Evidence." In *Schism, Heresy and Religious Protest*. Ed. Derek Baker. Cambridge: Cambridge University Press, 1972. 65-77.

Nothwehr, Dawn M. *The Franciscan View of the Human Person: Some Central Elements*. St. Bonaventure, NY: Franciscan Institute Publications, 2005.

Nothwehr, Dawn M., ed. *Franciscan Theology of the Environment: An Introductory Reader*. Cincinnati: St. Anthony Messenger Press, 2002.

O'Connell, Timothy. *Principles for a Catholic Morality*. Revised edition. New York: Harper and Row, 1990.

O'Donovan, Joan Lockwood. "Christian Platonism and Nonproprietary Christian Politics, Past and Present." In Oliver O'Donovan and Joan Lockwood O'Donovan, *Bonds of Imperfection: Christian Politics, Past and Present*. Grand Rapids: Eerdmans, 2004. 73-96.

Ormerod, Neil. *Creation, Grace and Redemption*. Maryknoll, NY: Orbis, 2007.

Osborne, Kenan. "The Trinity in Bonaventure." In *The Cambridge Companion to the Trinity*, ed. Peter Phan. Cambridge: Cambridge University Press, 2011.

_____. *A Theology of the Church for the Third Millennium. A Franciscan Approach*. Leiden: Brill, 2009.

_____. "A Scotistic Foundation for Christian Spirituality." *Franciscan Studies* 64 (2006): 363-405.

_____. *The Franciscan Intellectual Tradition*. St. Bonaventure, NY: Franciscan Institute Publications, 2003.

Parada Navas, José Luis and Francisco Martinez Fresneda. *Introducción a la Teología y Moral Franciscana*, Murcia: Espigas y Azucenas, 2002.

Parada Navas, José Luis. "Teología moral y política." In *Manual de Teología Franciscana*, Ed. José Antonio Merino and Francisco Martinez Fresneda. Madrid: Biblioteca de Autores Christianos, 2003. 415-72.

Parisoli, Luca, ed. *Pauvreté et Capitalisme. Comment les pauvres franciscaines ont justifié le capitalisme et le capitalism a préféré la Modernité*. Palermo: Officina di Studi Medievali, 2008.

Peirce, Charles Sanders. "A Guess at the Riddle." In *Collected Papers of Charles Sanders Peirce*, Two Volumes in One. Ed. Charles Hartshorne and Paul Weiss. Cambridge, MA: Belknap Press, 1960. Volume I, Book III, ch. 3, 181-226.

Pellegrin, Pierre. "Aristotle." In *A Guide to Greek Thought*. Ed. Jacques Brunschwig and Geoffrey E. R. Lloyd. Cambridge, MA: Belknap Press, 2003. 32-53.

Pellegrini, Luigi. "L'ordine francescano e la società cittadina en epoca bonaventuriana. Un analisi del Determinationes questionum super Regulam Fratrum Minorum." *Laurentianum* 15 (1974): 154-200.

Peter, Karl. *Die Lehre von der Schönheit nach Bonaventura*. Werl: Dietrich-Coelde, 1964.

Peter Lombard. *Sententiae in IV Libris Distinctae*. Grottaferrata [Rome]: Collegium Sancti Bonaventurae ad Claras Aquas, v. 1, 1971 – v. 2, 1981.

Pinckaers, Servais. "La nature vertueuse de l'espérance," *Revue Thomiste* 58 (1958): 405-42.

_____. *The Sources of Christian Ethics*. Washington, DC: Catholic University of America Press, 1995.

Pini, Georgio. *Categories and Logic in Duns Scotus: An Interpretation of Aristotle's Categories in the Late Thirteenth Century*. Leiden: Brill, 2002.

Piron, Sylvain. "Perfection évangelique et moralité civile: Pierre de Jean Olivi et l'étique économique franciscaine.'" In *Ideologia del Credito fra Tre e Quattrocento: Dall' Astesano ad Agnelo da Chivasso*. Ed. Barbara Molina and Giulia Scarcia. Asti: Centro Studi sui Lombardi e sul credito nel Medioevo, 2001. 103-43.

Pizzo, G. "La giustizia nella dottrina della volontà di G. Duns Scoto," *Revue Philosophique Neoscholastique* 81 (1989): 3-26.

Pompei, Alfonso. "Teologia della storia della salvezza in Bonaventura." In Alfonso Pompei, *San Bonaventura da Bagnoregio: Il pensare francescano*. Rome: Miscellanea Francescana, 1993. 335-47.

Pomplum, Trent. "Notes on Scotist Aesthetics in Light of Gilbert Narcisse's Les Raisons de Dieu," *Franciscan Studies* 66 (2008): 247-68.

Popper, Karl. *The Open Society and Its Enemies*. Princeton: Princeton University Press, 1962.

Porter, Jean. *Natural and Divine Law: Reclaiming the Tradition for Christian Ethics*. Grand Rapids: Eerdmans, 1999.

Prentice, R. "The Contingent Element Governing the Natural Law on the Last Seven Precepts of the Decalogue according to Duns Scotus." *Antonianum* 42 (1967): 259-92.

Pryds, Darleen. "The Scandal of Equality: Franciscans and Women in the Thirteenth and Fourteenth Centuries and Today." In *Greed, Lust, and Power: Franciscan Strategies for Building a More Just World*. Franciscan Symposium at the Washington Theological Union. St. Bonaventure, NY: Franciscan Institute Publications, 2011. 45-58.

Quill, Timothy. "Death and Dignity: A Case of Individualized Decision Making." *New England Journal of Medicine* 324 (March 7, 1991): 691-94.

Quinn, John F. "St. Bonavenure's Fundamental Conception of Natural Law." In *S. Bonaventura 1274-1974*. Vol. III. Ed. Jacques Guy Bougerol. Grottaferrata: Collegium S. Bonaventura, 1973. 571-98.

Radding, Charles. "Evolution of Medieval Mentalities: A Cognitive-Structural Approach," *American Historical Review* 83 (1978): 577-97.

Rahner, Karl. "On the Question of a Formal Existential Ethics," *Theological Investigations*. Volume II. New York: Seabury, 1964. 217-34.

Ratzinger, Joseph. *The Theology of History in St. Bonaventure*. Chicago, IL. Franciscan Herald Press, 1971.

Rézette, Jean-Pierre. "L'esperance, vertu du pauvre selon S. Bonaventure." In *La speranza 2: Studi biblico-teologici e apporti del pensiero francescano*. Ed. Bruno Giordani. Brescia: La Scuola/Rome: Antonianum, 1984. 357-80.

Richard of St. Victor. *Richard of St Victor: Selections*. English translation by Grover Zinn, New York: Paulist, 1979.

_____. *The Twelve Patriarchs, The Mystical Ark, Book Three of Trinity*. English translation by Grover Zinn. New York: Paulist, 1979.

Ricon, Antonio. "I testamenti come atti di religiosità pauperistica." In *La Conversione alla Povertà nell Italia dei Secoli XII-XIV*. Ed. Enrico Menestò. Spoleto: Centro italiano di studi Sull-Alto Medioevo, 1991. 391-414.

Rodgers, Daniel T. *Age of Fracture*. Cambridge, MA: Harvard University Press, 2011.

Rorem, Paul. *Hugh of Saint Victor*. Oxford: Oxford University Press, 2009.

Rosales, Eduardo. "La visión escotista y la teología moral." In *De doctrina Ioannis Duns Scoti*, Volume III. Rome: Scotus Commission, 1968. 511-23.

Rusconi, Roberto. "I franciscani e la confessione nel secolo XIII," Francescanesimo e vita religiosa del laici nel '200." Atti del viii convegno della società internazionale di studi francescani, Assisi, 1980. Assisi: Società internazionale di studi francescani, 1981. 251-309.

Saggau, Elise, ed. *Franciscans and Health Care: What is the Future?* St. Bonaventure, NY: Franciscan Institute Publications, 2001.

Sala, G. "Il valore obligatorio dell coscienza nei Pimi scotastici." *Studi Francescani* 54 (1957): 174-98.

Sala, G. "Il concetto di sinderesi in S. Bonaventura." *Studi Francescani* 54 (1957): 3-11.

Scapin, Pietro. "Il significato fondamentale de la libertà divina secondo Giovanni Duns Scoto." In *De doctrina Ioannis*

*Duns Scoti*. Volume II. Rome: Scotus Commission, 1968. 519-66.

Scarry, Elaine. *On Beauty and Being Just*. Princeton: Princeton University Press, 1999.

Schillebeeckx, Eduard. *Jesus: An Experiment in Christology*. New York: Crossroad, 1981.

Schmaus, Michael. "Trinität bis zum Ausgang der Scholastik," *Handbuch der Dogmengeschichte*, Volume II/Ib. Freiburg im Br.: Herder, 1985.

Scholl, Edith. "A Will and Two Ways: Voluntas Propria, Voluntas Communis," *Cistercian Studies* 30 (1995): 193-203.

Schreiter, Robert J., R. Scott Appleby, Gerard F. Powers, eds. *Peacebuilding, Catholic Theology, Ethics, and Praxis*. Maryknoll, NY: Orbis, 2010.

Schwager, Raymund. *Jesus in the Drama of Salvation: Toward a Biblical Doctrine of Redemption*. New York: Crossroad, 1999.

Seneca. *Ad Lucillium Epistulae Morales*. English trans. by Richard M. Gummere, 3 vols. Internet Archive.

Shannon, Thomas and James J. Walter. *Contemporary Issues in Bioethics: A Catholic Perspective*. New York: Sheed and Ward. 2005.

Shannon, Thomas with Nicholas Kockernack. *The New Genetic Medicine*. New York: Sheed and Ward. 2003.

Shannon, Thomas with James DiGiacomo. *An Introduction to Bioethics*. 4th edition. New York: Paulist, 2009.

Shannon, Thomas and David O'Brien. *Catholic Social Thought: The Documentary Heritage*. Maryknoll, NY: Orbis, 2010.

Shannon, Thomas. "The Roman Catholic Magisterium and Genetic Research: An Overview and Evaluation." In *Design and Destiny: Jewish and Christian Perspectives on Human Germline Modification*. Ed. Ron Cole-Turner. Cambridge, MA: MIT Press, 2008. 51-71.

_____. *The Ethical Theory of John Duns Scotus*. Quincy, IL: Franciscan Press, 1995.

_____. "The Existential Modality of the Person According to Gabriel Marcel." *Insight: Quarterly Review of Religion and Mental Health*. 4 (1965): 35-44.

Sherman, Susan. "Feminist and Medical Ethics: Two Different Approaches to Contextual Ethics," In *Feminist Perspectives in Medical Ethics*. Ed. Helen B. Holmes and Laura M. Purdy. Bloomington, IN: Indiana University Press, 1992. 17-31.

Sileo, Leonardo, Ed., *Via Scoti: Methodologica ad mentem Joannis Duns Scoti*. Atti del Congresso Scotistico Internazionale,1993. Rome: Scotus Commission, 1995.

Smith, Christian. *Lost in Transition: the Dark Side of Emerging Adulthood*. New York: Oxford University Press, 2011.

Solaguren, Celestino. "Contingencia y creación en la filosofía Duns Escoto," *De doctrina Ioannis Duns Scoti*, Volume II. Rome: Scotus Commission, 1968. 297-348.

Spargo, E. J. *The Category of the Aesthetic in the Philosophy of St. Bonaventure*. St. Bonaventure, New York: Franciscan Institute, 1953.

Squarise, Cristoforo. "Attualità della dottrina bonaventuri-ana sulla coscienza," *San Bonaventura maestro di vita francescana e di sapienza Cristiana*. Vol. III. Ed. A. Pompei. Rome: Pontificia Facoltá Teologica "San Bonaventura," 1976. 293-302.

Stout, Jeffrey. *Ethics After Babel: The Languages of Morals and Their Discontents*. Boston, MA: Beacon Press, 1988.

Thompson, Augustine. *Cities of God. The Religion of the Italian Communes, 1125-1325*. University Park, PA: Pennsylvania State University Press, 2005.

Todeschini, Giacomo. *Franciscan Wealth, From Voluntary Poverty to Market Society*. St. Bonaventure, NY: Franciscan Institute Publications, 2009.

Todisco, Orlando. "Ética y Economía," *Manual de Filosofía Franciscana*. Madrid: BAC, 2004, 249-324.

Todisco, Orlando. "L'etica francescana e la soggesttività moderna," *Miscellanea Francescana*, 102 (2002): 84-142.

Todisco, Orlando. "L'être comme don et la valeur-lien: La practique économique franciscaine du solidarisme." In *Pauvreté et Capitalisme: Comment les pauvres franciscaines ont justifié le capitalism et le capitalism a préféré la Modernité*. Ed. Luca Parisoli. Palermo: Officina di studi Medievali, 2008. 175-214.

Todisco, Orlando. "L'attualità del volontarismo intellectualista di G. Duns Scoto," *Miscellanea Francescana* 69 (1969): 28-61.

Torgal, Januario Mendes Ferreira. "O Problema do mal a luz da concepçao antropologica de São Bonaventura." In *S. Bonaventura, 1274-1974*. Volume IV. Ed. Jacques Guy

Bougerol. Grottaferrata [Roma]: Collegium S. Bonaventura, 1974. 523-32.

Tracy, David. *The Analogical Imagination: Christian Theology and the Culture of Pluralism*. New York: Crossroad, 1981.

Vauchez, André. "L'Utopie franciscaine dan l'église medieval," *Lumiere et Vie*, 33 (April-June, 1984): 39-47.

Veuthey, Leo. *S. Bonaventurae Philosophia Christiana*. Rome: Officium Libri Catholici, 1943.

Vos Jaczn, Anton et al. *John Duns Scotus. Contingency and Freedom*. Lectura I, d. 39. Dordrecht: Kluwer, 1994.

Vos, Jaczn Anton. *The Philosophy of John Duns Scotus*. Edinburgh: Edinburgh University Press, 2006.

Wachter, Maurice de. *Le Péché actuel selon Saint Bonaventure*. Paris: Éditions franciscaines, 1967.

Walter, James J. "What does Horizon Analysis Bring to the Consistent Ethic of Life?" In *The Consistent Ethic of Life: Assessing its Reception and Relevance*. Ed. Thomas A. Nairn. Maryknoll, NY: Orbis, 2008. 3-15.

Weinstein, Idit Dobbs. "Jewish Philosophy." In *The Cambridge Companion to Medieval Philosophy*. Ed. A. S. McGrade. Cambridge: Cambridge University Press, 2003. 122-46.

Wiederkehr, Dieter. *Belief in Redemption: Explorations in Doctrine from the New Testament to Today*. Louisville: Westminster/John Knox, 1979.

_____. "Entwurf einer systematischen Christologie," *Mysterium Salutis*, Volume III. Einsiedeln: Herder, 1970. 477-648.

Wippel, John F. *The Metaphysical Thought of Thomas Aquinas*. Washington, DC: Catholic University of America Press, 2000.

Wolter, Allan. *John Duns Scotus. Political and Economic Philosophy*. St. Bonaventure, NY: Franciscan Institute Publications, 2001.

_____. "Scotus' Eschatology: Some Reflections," *That Others May Know and Love. Essays in Honor of Zachary Hayes, OFM: Franciscan, Educator, Scholar*. Ed. Michael J. Cusato and F. Edward Coughlin. St. Bonaventure, NY: Franciscan Institute, 1997. 305-48.

_____. "Native Freedom of the Will as a Key to the Ethics of Scotus." In Allan B. Wolter, O.F.M., *The Philosophical Theology of John Duns Scotus*. Ed. Marilyn McCord Adams. Ithaca, NY: Cornell University Press, 1990. 148-62.

_____. *Duns Scotus on the Will and Morality*. Washington, DC: Catholic University of America Press, 1986.

Wolter, Allan, ed. and Eng. trans. *John Duns Scotus: A Treatise on God as First Principle*. Chicago, IL: Franciscan Herald Press, 1966. Revised edition, 1983.

Yates, Philippe. "The English Context of the Development of the Franciscan Constitutions and of the Franciscan Intellectual Tradition." In *A Pilgrimage through the Franciscan Intellectual Tradition*. Ed. Andre Cirino and Josef Raischl. Canterbury: Franciscan International Study Centre, 2008. 65-82.

Zavaloni, Roberto. "Personal Freedom and Scotus' Voluntarism." In *De doctrina Ioannis Duns Scoti*. Volume II. Rome: Scotus Commission, 1968. 613-27.

Zečević, Seraphinus. "Problema actuum moraliter indifferentium." In *De doctrina Ioannis Duns Scoti*, Volume III. Rome: Scotus Commission, 1968. 525-38.

# Authors' Biographies

**Joseph P. Chinnici, O.F.M.**, is a Franciscan Friar and a Professor at Graduate Theological Union, Berkeley. An Oxford-educated historian, Joe is a widely-respected scholar, teacher and speaker in the history of American Catholicism and the development of Franciscan theology and spirituality. His ground-breaking work *Living Stones: The History and Structure of Catholic Spiritual Life in the United States* (second edition 1996) has been followed by numerous articles in *U.S. Catholic Historian*, the co-edited *Prayer and Practice in the American Catholic Community*, and significant studies on the history of prayer and on the reception of Vatican II in the United States. He published *Church, Society, and Change, 1965-1996*, a history of the post-conciliar period in American Catholicism. His most recent work, *When Values Collide: The Catholic Church, Sexual Abuse, and the Challenges of Leadership*, was published in 2010. In addition to his current faculty duties, Joe is Chairman of the Commission for the Retrieval of the Franciscan Intellectual Tradition (CFIT) and editor of the Franciscan Heritage Series.

**Mary Beth Ingham, C.S.J.**, is Professor of Philosophical Theology at the Franciscan School of Theology, Graduate Theological Union, Berkeley. She earned her Ph.D. from Universite de Fribourg, Switzerland. Her specialties include the History of Medieval Philosophy, Franciscan tradition, John Duns Scotus, Stoicism and its influence on Medieval Philosophy, and Franciscan spiritual tradition and its influence on Scotus and others. Ingham has authored several texts on

Scotus including the best-selling, *Scotus for Dunces – an Introduction to the Subtle Doctor* and the recently re-released *The Harmony of Goodness: Mutuality and Moral Living According to John Duns Scotus*. She is also the author of *Rejoicing in the Works of the Lord: Beauty in the Franciscan Tradition*.

**THOMAS A. NAIRN, O.F.M.**, is a senior director of Ethics at the Catholic Health Association, USA. Prior to this appointment, he served as the Erica and Harry John Family Professor of Catholic Ethics at Catholic Theological Union and Director of its Health Care Mission Leadership Program. He holds a Ph.D. from the University of Chicago Divinity School. He has taught at many schools in the United States as well as in Melbourne, Australia; Harare, Zimbabwe; and Singapore. He has lectured or given workshops in the United States, Australia, Great Britain, Ireland, Japan, Kenya, Papua New Guinea, Singapore, South Africa, Trinidad, and Zimbabwe.

**KENAN B. OSBORNE, O.F.M.**, is a member of the Order of Friars Minor, Province of St. Barbara, California, and Professor Emeritus of Systematic Theology at the Franciscan School of Theology, Berkeley. He is an internationally recognized theologian who specializes in sacramental theology, Christology, ecclesiology and the multicultural dimensions of Christian theology. He earned a B.A. at San Luis Rey College, a B.Th. at Old Mission Theological seminary, a Licentiate in Sacred Theology at The Catholic University of America and a Doctorate in Theology at Ludwig-Maxmilian Universität. He has published the following books with Franciscan Institute: *The History of Franciscan Theology* (2007) and *The Franciscan Intellectual Tradition: Tracing Its Origins and Identifying Its Central Components* (2003).

**THOMAS A. SHANNON** is Professor Emeritus, Religion and Social Ethics at Worcester Polytechnic Institute. Shannon specializes in the areas of social justice and bioethics. His interest in social justice surrounds the topics of conscientious objection and the social encyclical tradition within Roman

Catholicism. He has also focused on the moral standing of developments in the field of genetic engineering. Author of several books, Shannon has focused his attention on care-based reasoning and genetic engineering. Included in his works are: *The Context of Casuistry; Genetic Engineering: A Documentary History; Made in Whose Image? Genetic Engineering and Christian Ethics; American Catholic Social Teaching and A Call to Fidelity. On The Moral Theology of Charles Curran.*

He earned his Master's Degree in Sacred Theology from Boston University School of Technology and a Ph.D. from the Division of Theological and Religious Studies in 1973. Shannon holds two Bachelor's degrees, a Bachelor of Sacred Theology from St. Joseph Seminary, Teutopolis, IL and a Bachelor of Arts from Quincy University.

# Index of Terms

## A

*affectio commodi* 110, 144, 147, 152, 181, 203
*affectio justitiae* 110, 144-47, 152, 181, 203

## B

*bonum est diffusivum sui* 53, 130
*bonum honestum* 126
book of creation 32-33, 46, 48, 72, 256
book of one's internal life 32-33
book of the Gospels 32

## C

conscience 12, 18, 26, 91, 127, 161-69, 171-76, 180-92, 222, 227,
    251, 264, 270, 276-77, 289
contingency 10, 16, 79, 97, 151, 174, 180, 267, 274
contuition 222, 256

## D

*decorum* 96
Divine Command Theory 97

## F

*firmitas* 140-43, 160, 162
*fontalis plenitudo* 61, 131
freedom 14, 16, 18, 23, 41, 56-58, 60, 65-67, 69, 70-72, 80, 82, 87,
    91, 100, 103, 110-11, 121, 125-27, 129, 134, 136, 140-42, 144,
    146-47, 161, 165, 190, 198-203, 206, 208, 211, 216, 219, 223-
    24, 240-43, 249-52, 254-57, 259, 260-61, 267, 269, 273, 275
free will 62, 71, 72, 79, 80, 87, 140, 147, 150

# Index of Names